The 'Imagined Sound' of Australian Literature and Music

The 'Imagined Sound' of Australian Literature and Music

Joseph Cummins

ANTHEM PRESS

Anthem Press
An imprint of Wimbledon Publishing Company
www.anthempress.com

This edition first published in UK and USA 2021
by ANTHEM PRESS
75–76 Blackfriars Road, London SE1 8HA, UK
or PO Box 9779, London SW19 7ZG, UK
and
244 Madison Ave #116, New York, NY 10016, USA

First published in the UK and USA by Anthem Press in 2019

Copyright © Joseph Cummins 2021

The author asserts the moral right to be identified as the author of this work.

All rights reserved. Without limiting the rights under copyright reserved above,
no part of this publication may be reproduced, stored or introduced into
a retrieval system, or transmitted, in any form or by any means
(electronic, mechanical, photocopying, recording or otherwise),
without the prior written permission of both the copyright
owner and the above publisher of this book.

British Library Cataloguing-in-Publication Data
A catalogue record for this book is available from the British Library.

Library of Congress Control Number: 2020952976

ISBN-13: 978-1-78527-972-0 (Pbk)
ISBN-10: 1-78527-972-6 (Pbk)

This title is also available as an e-book.

CONTENTS

Foreword   vii
Acknowledgements   xi

Introduction: *Imagined Sound*   1

Part One Listening to the Continent

1 Reimagining 'The Centre': Francis Webb's 'Eyre All Alone' and David Lumsdaine's *Aria for Edward John Eyre*   17

2 Midnight Oil: Sounding Australian Rock around the Bicentenary   45

3 Sound and Silence: Listening and Relation in the Novels of Alex Miller   65

Part Two Listening to Islands and Archipelagos

4 An Archipelago of Convicts and Outsiders: The Songs of the Drones and Gareth Liddiard   85

5 Echoes between Van Diemen's Land and Tasmania: The Space of the Island in Richard Flanagan's *Death of a River Guide* and Carmel Bird's *Cape Grimm*   99

6 A Sonic Passage between Islands: *Mutiny Music* by Baecastuff   115

Part Three Listening to the Continental Archipelago

7 Noisy Songlines in the Top End   139

Coda   161

Notes   167
Works Cited   169
Index   181

FOREWORD

Hearing is the first of our senses to be activated, and the last to be extinguished. Of all our sensory conduits to the world, being heard is the most powerful evidence of life. As Shakespeare dramatized in *Hamlet*, the dead may be seen, smelled, tasted and touched, but they cannot be heard; after death, 'the rest is silence'. In the public sphere, two senses above all are felt to be both competent and appropriate in the exchange of complex meanings: sight and hearing. Yet while they might be traversing the same material terrain, the two are such dissimilar vehicles that they disclose and create very different political spaces.

Vision is the faculty most closely implicated in scientific discourse, and approved forms of knowledge are invariably visual metaphors: vision, perspective, revelation, imagination, enlightenment. These describe forms of knowledge whose objective is to exercise control over the universe. In the (spurious) mind–body split, science elevates the activities of the former over the latter, and vision is the sense most closely associated with the analytical mind. Vision is an instrument of regulation, power (the controlling gaze, the panopticon). It is a distancing faculty, with high powers of analytical separation and is thus associated with the axiom that 'knowledge is power', the foundations of the Enlightenment paradigm. This historical association has given vision great authority.

But sound is a very different mediator. It floods the social space so that all its occupants hear much the same thing, share the experience in a way that looking cannot do. We cannot see ourselves or the community of which we are memebers *in toto*, but we can hear ourselves, immersed in a collective identity. Sound also penetrates the body – the voice in the ear is extraordinarily intense and intimate. In many ways, then, our understanding of our social being is mediated more fully and intensely acoustically than visually. Sound can also instantly modify the nature and the horizon of identity. We shout, we whisper, we snarl or vocally caress. This is why sound is such a powerful and flexible tool of social negotiation. And while we 'stand back to get a better look', our voices are channels of propinquity, ways of drawing us nearer to each other.

It is these distinctive attributes of sonic negotiation which have made sound the oldest way of defining territory and identity. From war cries of the ancients, the trumpets that brought down the walls of Jericho, to church bells, village clock chimes, political and sports stadium chants, we define our space through sound. Sound defines collective identity among all communities. The community in this case is defined in terms of nation: the Australian soundscape and some of what R. Murray Schafer, in his benchmark study *The Tuning of the World*, called its 'keynote sounds', sonic markers of place. In the essays collected here, Joseph Cummins has explored the way in which sound is interwoven with various attempts to articulate Australian identity. Using as his platform the idea of 'imagined sound', he explores

> the imaginative and spatio-temporal relations created by sound within literature and music [...] It is *imagined* sound because it is created by descriptive language, by ideas, even by imagines, not just the physical vibration of heard sound [...] In contrast to thinking about sight, attending to sound lets me consider how space and time are remapped and reconfigured by what we *hear*.

In the following studies it is primarily the soundscape as mediated through artistic representations of place and space, an approach that lifts the study well above simplistic sonic postcards, to disclose the complex ambiguities in the relationship between sonic and visual space, and the national imaginary. The work thus overlaps with a form of 'literary criticism', the analysis of why literature 'works'. But it is distinguished by its recognition of the link between sound and language, a link that was largely elided as poetry increasingly became a medium of print, a process that turned critics into eyes rather that ears, that turned Shakespeare from a master of the stage and a sound engineer, into a 'literary genius', from the mid-seventeenth century, the era in which print became the primary authoritative medium of information. That shift from aural to visual authority was crystallized in Samuel Johnson's decision for his *Dictionary* that the English vocabulary should be confined exclusively to words that had appeared in print. It was a development that laid down the foundations of a critical tradition in which even scholars of popular music often feel that an analysis of the subject equates to a discussion of lyrics, without reference to the crucial role played by music – sound – in the formation of meaning and affect.

This collection of essays moves us further towards, or back to, a recognition of the role of sound in the definition and projection of national identity, a role which, as these studies disclose, is far more complex than simplistic celebrations of, for example, 'national' musics. These case studies in the way sound functions in the articulation of place and space reveal the complexities, contradictions and fissures in the bland generalizations that have framed so many representations of Australian identity.

Bruce Johnson
Leura, NSW, June 2019

ACKNOWLEDGEMENTS

This book is underpinned by a sort of *refusal* to stop thinking and writing about music and literature together. Such a project would not have been possible without the support of Elizabeth McMahon and John Napier at the University of New South Wales (UNSW). Their encouragement, knowledge, advice and cross-disciplinary enthusiasm was vital. Alister Spence, Phil Slater and Helen Groth were also mentors to me during my time at UNSW. A particular thank you to Al and Phil, from whom I learnt so much.

Various chapters of this book were road-tested at conferences held by the Association for the Study of Australian Literature (ASAL), the Australasian Association for Literature, the Australia/New Zealand and UK/Ireland branches of the International Association for the Study of Popular Music, the Centre for Modernist Studies in Australia and the American Comparative Literature Association. A particular thank you to everyone at ASAL, the most supportive scholarly community I can imagine. Tej P. S. Sood and Abi Pandey at Anthem Press were integral to the transformation of my manuscript into a book.

Thanks to my parents Anthony and Mary-Anne, my brother and sisters, Serge Stanley, Dirk Kruithof, On the Stoop, Lines of Flight, the Splinter Orchestra and the NOWnow, Matt Syres. Thanks also to Paul Jones and Jimena Acevedo at Ian Barker Gardens, and to the music staff at International Grammar School, Sydney.

A very special thank you to Ashley Barnwell, for all your encouragement, inspiration, support and love. You are my partner in crime, always willing to discuss, deconstruct, and argue.

As a young child my grandmother Colleen read me Roald Dahl's *Boy* and *Going Solo*, igniting my interest in history and writing. As I got older, and to the present day, she is always ready to discuss books, history and politics. For sparking my love of these topics, and for her encouragement, example of open mindedness and discussion, and genuine interest in my work, *Imagined Sound* is dedicated to Nan Colleen.

Early versions of parts of this book were previously published as 'An Archipelago of Convicts and Outsiders: The Songs of The Drones and Gareth Liddiard' in *Southerly* 72.3 (2013), 'Listening to Alex Miller's Soundscapes' in *Journal of the Association for the Study of Australian Literature* 13.2 (2013), 'Echoes between Van Diemen's Land and Tasmania: Sound and the Space of the Island in Richard Flanagan's Death of a River Guide and Carmel Bird's Cape Grimm' in the *Journal of Commonwealth Literature*, 49.2 (2014) and 'Mutiny Music: A Sonic Passage between Islands' in *Perfect Beat* 16.1/2 (2015). The International Australian Studies Association generously helped me with their early career researcher publishing subsidy scheme. The Dead Heart' (pp. 58–59) and 'Beds Are Burning' (p. 63) have been granted by Sony/ATV Music Publishing.

The Dead Heart (P. Garrett/P. Gifford/R. Hirst)/J. Moginie/ M. Rotsey)
© 1987 Sprint Music
For Australia and New Zealand: Sony/ATV Music Publishing Australia Pty Limited
(ABN 93 080 392 230) Locked Bag 7300, Darlinghurst NSW 1300. Australia
International copyright secured. All rights reserved. Used by permission

Beds Are Burning (R. Hirst/J. Moginie/P. Garrett)
© 1987 Sprint Music
For Australia and New Zealand: Sony/ATV Music Publishing Australia Pty Limited
(ABN 93 080 392 230) Locked Bag 7300, Darlinghurst NSW 1300. Australia
International copyright secured. All rights reserved. Used by permission

Introduction

IMAGINED SOUND

While reading the classics of Australian fiction as a student I was also training in music. During that time – immersed in Alexis Wright's *Carpentaria*, Joseph Furphy's *Such Is Life* and Alex Miller's *Journey to the Stone Country* – one of the formative ensembles I played in was the Splinter Orchestra. Comprised of anywhere between three and upwards of 30 players, in Splinter there was an emphasis on being able to *hear* each other, and we frequently experimented with our instruments to produce unusual sounds. Splinter often performed in the open air, surrounded by the unique resonances of natural or man-made landscapes. One of my most memorable outside performances with the group was at Crater Cove, on Sydney Harbour; another took place in an abandoned air-raid bunker, on Cockatoo Island. During the three years I was a regular member of this unique ensemble, Splinter taught me, above all, to listen. Listening is one of the most vital features of life, integral to all forms of communication – face-to-face conversation, television, radio, sport, and of course, music. Listening captures an unrepeatable experience of a time, a place, a community. It connects us to the past and grounds us in the present. It needs to be practiced and is always open to improvement. It can be a challenge to the visual realm, an ethical imperative, a mode of resistance. It was in this context, exploring the worlds of both literature and music, that my practices of reading and listening converged into the approach that underpins this book.

Imagined Sound listens to the landscapes and histories of Australian post-World War II literature and music. In the seven chapters that follow, I will examine a range of novels, poems, songs, song suites, film clips and art music compositions using a method I term 'imagined sound'. Through a return to various times in the past, these works – which encompass a diverse array of narratives – offer a remapping of Australian landscapes and histories. In *Imagined Sound* I trace the explorer's journey through the desert centre, imagined in Francis Webb poetic sequence 'Eyre All Alone' (1961), David Lumsdaine's electro-acoustic composition *Aria for Edward John Eyre* (1972) and Midnight Oil's rock music. The convict and outsider songs of the Drones and Gareth Liddiard (2006 and 2010), the complex postcolonial novels of Alex Miller, and the island soundings in the novels of Richard Flanagan and Carmel Bird or the jazz of Baecastuff's *Mutiny Music* (2006–present) all move away from the centre, and Alexis Wright's novel *Carpentaria* (2006) stages the destruction and rebirth of the continental top-end.

These works resonate within and reform key moments of the post-war era and depict Indigenous and non-Indigenous experiences of a range of Australian 'geoimaginaries' – the bundle of both real and imaginary ideas relating to geographic spaces such as the centre, the bush, the coast, the island and the archipelago. Listening to imagined sound generates a unique cartography of the artistic, historical and political harmonics of these works. It also creates a productive dialogue between their distinct mediums. This book is an experiment in method: imagined sound is an investigative and analytical machine for engaging with literary and musical texts. The soundings of postcolonial spatiotemporal difference produced by this *listening* deepen our understanding of the complexity of fundamental national landscapes and histories. It maps the development of pivotal geoimaginaries that accompanied the historical terrain of the post-war period.

But what is *imagined sound*? The concept describes the imaginative and spatiotemporal relations created by sound within literature and music. It is *imagined* sound because it is created by descriptive language, by ideas, even by images, not just the physical vibration of heard sound. The concept emerges from a throwaway phrase made by Benedict Anderson in his study of nationalism, *Imagined Communities* (1983). Discussing the role of song in the formation of the nation and the 'unisonance' produced by the singing of un-official national anthems like 'the Marseillaise, Waltzing Matilda, and Indonesian Raya' (145), Anderson says, 'Nothing connects us all but imagined sound' (145). For Anderson, imagined sound operates in two ways: it organizes and interpolates the listener into the nation, and it bypasses the problem of both space and time, enabling listeners from across a vast space to, simultaneously, become one (6). Imagined sound is a conceptual subset of Anderson's analysis of the nature of the national community, which 'is *imagined* because the members of even the smallest nation will never know most of their fellow-members, meet them, or even hear them, yet in the minds of each lives the image of their communion' (6). My use of imagined sound follows Anderson's emphasis on the importance of the imagination in the formation of landscapes, and of communities. In contrast to thinking about sight, attending to sound lets me consider how space and time are remapped and reconfigured by what we *hear*.

The genesis of this listening method began with my habit of reading novels with close attention to any description of sound. Building on sonically acute scholarship by Paul Carter, Josh Kun, Jean-Luc Nancy, Gilles Deleuze and Felix Guattari, and R. Murray Schafer, this attention developed to encompass listening to and reading literature and music side by side, with an ear attuned to how authors and composers working in the period between mid-century and the present represent Australian landscapes and histories. The pairing is inspired, in equal parts, by the close reading of texts common to literary studies and the score analysis familiar to musicology. Refocusing these scholarly approaches via listening and sound bridges the chasm between two mediums and fields of inquiry that feature as many conceptual similarities as they do material, methodological and generic differences. Listening to imagined sound creates fluid dialogue between mediums and genres that remains alert to the unique ways Australian landscapes and histories are represented.

How does imagined sound work? What is imagined sound in music, a medium built from 'real' physical sound? How does listening to imagined sound differ from the way we might already listen to music? And how does one 'listen' to novels or poems? The imagination is imperative. Listening to the imagined sound of a folk song means listening to how the lyrics create connections between different spaces and times in the past and the present. Listening to the imagined sound of the jazz suite *Mutiny Music* means thinking about where song forms, instruments, sampled voices and even musical traditions come from, and what histories and landscapes they evoke. Listening to the imagined sound of rock music means viewing performances, album art and film clips and thinking about how these visual texts interlock with the lyrics and structures of songs. This mode of listening, perhaps counter-intuitively, can silence the aspects of the medium that distinguish it from literature, but the strength of imagined sound lies with its uniquely close scrutiny of the production and interconnection of space-time, a common element of both mediums. Listening in this way also underscores the imaginative and interpretative labour in the act of listening to a medium built from a bundle of abstract physical sounds, images and linguistic signs. By foregrounding the *imagining* of space and time through sound, listening to the imagined sound of music also amplifies the relationship between real geographic locations and their representation as imagined spaces, as geoimaginaries. Mirroring the formal and material variety of the music assembled here, my engagement with each composition is sensitive to textual, historical, sociological and technological distinction. The music by David Lumsdaine, Midnight Oil, the Drones, Gareth Liddiard and Baecastuff is a continuum of imagined (musical) sound, stretching across histories, from the seventeenth century to the present, and between islands, archipelagos and the Australian continent.

Listening to a silent medium, literature, relies just as heavily on the imagination. Manifesting sound via the written word, the poets and novelist we encounter in the coming chapters describe a symphonic range of sounds, from bird song to the rumble of heavy machinery or the all-encompassing noise of a storm. In literature the sonic is only limited by the skill and imagination of the writer. Listening to imagined sound in novels means reading and imagining intricate combinations of sounds and the relationships between people and landscapes these sounds create. Similar to narrative perspective, the 'listening perspective' of written works adds another layer of complexity to imagined sound – who hears these sounds, and what do they mean to various listeners? All styles of music are described, from Indigenous song to American hip-hop to wild electric guitar-driven pub rock to celestial choirs of angels singing hymns of destruction – listening to the imagined sound of this literary music means registering the symbolism of a genre, the meaning of a lyric or the intertextual resonance of a musical reference. Imagined sound in literature can structure the experience of being in landscapes, drive the recollection of memories and dreams, and prompt the uncovering of secret histories. At the same time, and often in concert with non-sonic descriptions, imagined sound opens a fertile ground for revealing the internal state of a character – from paranoia and fear to ecstatic joy to feelings of guilt. Like in music, in literary works imagined sound enables places, histories and ideas to resonate together.

Imagined Sound draws together a polyphonous field of inquiry that encompasses literary studies, musicology, Australian history, cultural studies and sound studies. Paul Carter's *The Road to Botany Bay* (1987) and Roslyn Haynes's *Seeking the Centre* (1998) are the foundational – but silent – historico-literary investigations of the Australian landscape. More sound-sensitive is Carter's *The Sound in Between: Voice, Space, Performance* (1992) and Jane Belfrage's 'The Great Australian Silence', both of which inform my listening to both frontier and contemporary soundscapes. Setting the stage for my analysis of key landscapes and histories in art music, rock, folk and contemporary jazz genres is Australian-focused musicology including John Connell and Chris Gibson's *Sound Tracks* (2003), Fiona Richards's edited collection *The Soundscapes of Australia: Music, Place and Spirituality* (2007), Joy Damousi and Desley Deacon's edited collection *Talking and Listening in the Age of Modernity* (2007) and Shane Homan and Tony Mitchell's collection of essays *Sounds of Then, Sounds of Now: Popular Music in Australia* (2008). Lacking the narrative attention, dual-medium focus and geoimaginary specificity of the present study, such musicology is nevertheless essential to *Imagined Sound* because it opens the way for thinking through the connection between musics, histories and landscapes.

Just as significant to my analysis of postcolonial Australian literature and music is the field of sound studies. Following R. Murray Schafer's essential *The Soundscape: The Tuning of the World* (1977), my sound studies touchstones include Jacques Attali's diagnosis of the prophetic role of music in *Noise: The Political Economy of Music* (1977), scholarship that examines the voice, such Roland Barthes's essay 'The Grain of the Voice' (1977) and Steven Connor's *Dumbstruck*

(2000), Martin Jay's *Downcast Eyes* (1993), a history of 'ocularcentricism', the dominance of vision over other senses, and Jonathan Sterne's analysis of sound technology and modernity in *The Audible Past* (2003). Summing up the historical turn towards sound, Sterne suggests that just as 'there was an Enlightenment, so too was there an "ensoniment" […] a series of conjunctures among ideas, institutions, and practices [that] rendered the world audible in new ways and valorized new constructs of hearing and listening' (2). More recently, David Toop's *Sinister Resonance: The Mediumship of the Listener* (2010) investigates a mode of listening to visual art (as well as a broader cultural inquiry) that takes up a similar imperative to my concept of imagined sound.

Sound Concepts

Two theorizations of sound and space – the soundscape and the refrain – drive my method of imagined sound. These concepts provide detailed and productive accounts of how sound structures space and connects people to each other and their environment. The soundscape, first theorized by Schafer, is the overarching conceptual sonic framework of this book. I draw on Barry Truax's definition of the soundscape: 'An environment of sound (sonic environment) with emphasis on the way it is perceived and understood by the individual, or by society. It thus depends on the relationship between the individual and any such environment' (1978, 126). Truax's focus on relation through sound – between the listener, or a society of listeners, and the surrounding sounds of a space – is the basis of the soundscape as a tool of critical close listening. Emphasizing the relationship between listener, sound and landscape, soundscapes take a number of manifestations: they can comprise multiple elements, such as sounds from nature and of industry, as we hear in Alex Miller's novels, or they can be dominated by one sound, such as the noise of the storm in Alexis Wright's *Carpentaria*. Different types of characters and different registers of sound and silence create complex connections between the histories and landscape. The soundscape enables me to tease out the immersive coexistence of the listener or reader and the environment and to examine characters and the ways they relate to each other through sound.

Offering a rhythm-attuned theorization of how sound creates space, Gilles Deleuze and Felix Guattari's concept 'the refrain', what they call 'a prism, a crystal of space-time' (1987, 385), complements and extends the soundscape. Explicated at length in *A Thousand Plateaus*, the refrain is a repeating melody or rhythm that captures and organizes territory. The rhythmic and territorial nature of the refrain makes it useful for approaching soundscapes that feature reoccurring patterns or structures. There are three stages or types of refrain: the first – 'A child in the dark, gripped with fear, comforts himself by singing under his breath' (343) – describes the creation of a 'centre in the heart of chaos' (343). The second stage – which does not feature prominently in my use of the refrain in *Imagined Sound* – is the formation of a home space. 'Sonorous or vocal components are very important: a wall of sound, or at least a wall with some sonic bricks in it' (343). The final stage is the 'line of flight' (225) – in Deleuze and Guattari's language 'a deterritorialisation' (191) – the emergence from controlled and defined space: 'One launches forth, hazards an improvisation [...] One ventures from home on the thread of a tune' (344). Elizabeth Grosz describes the refrain as 'rhythmic, melodious patterns, small chants, ditties, that shape the vibrations of milieus into the harmonics of territories, the organization of a wall or barrier' (2008, 54). While the refrain is extremely productive in close reading situations for both literature and music, it is also useful for thinking about the production of space on a large scale, or the movement out of or reformation of a structure like a continent or a nation.

The soundscape and the refrain are augmented by several additional concepts that respond to the particular formal or thematic configurations of imagined sound in literature or music. Jean-Luc Nancy's detailed and idiosyncratic concept of listening and 'the referral' accounts for the meeting of characters from distinct cultural and historical backgrounds in Alex Miller's novelistic soundscapes. While the referral opens the same basic relation between listener and environment as the soundscape, Nancy's almost utopian sense of community through relation, or 'being with', which underpins all of his thinking, resonates with the connections we see in Miller. Bypassing the tonal or textural character of a sound (or silence), Nancy's conceptualization of sonic relation – like Truax's soundscape and Deleuze and Guattari's refrain – is abstract, without historical context. While these sound concepts are malleable in their application, the utility of a theorization of sound that takes spatio-temporal specifics into account is great. Like the soundscape or Nancy's referral, Paul Carter's 'sound in between' describes the relation between sound and space, but Carter's concept is unique through its alignment with a precise time and place – the Australian frontier or first contact between Indigenous people and European settlers. This event is explicitly performed in novels by Richard Flanagan and Carmel Bird, and I deploy the 'sound in between' in consort with the refrain to investigate the use of song structures in the soundscapes of these works. The contested nature of this frontier space means that its soundscape is frequently one dominated by violence that, when it manifests in the present, takes the form of a haunting. The registration and conceptualization of the historico-sonic texture of Australian experience and expression in Carter's 'sound in between' is important because it follows the same impulse as *Imagined Sound* and at the same time helps tether the theorizations of sound used here to the Australian contexts of the literature and music.

Other resonant conceptualizations offer accounts of different types or tonalities of imagined sound. Silence is an inverted type of approach to the space and connection created by sound, and I draw ideas about silence from a range of scholarly fields including art theory and philosophy. Redefining sound and presence, silence underscores the resonances between histories, space and people, relations played out in Miller's novels in Chapter Three. Noise, like silence, moves beyond the basic relation between people and landscapes created by the soundscape. A resonance that can disrupt and destroy just as readily as it can redefine and reconstruct, theorizations of noise emerge from art theory, technology studies and philosophy. Functioning in a similarly reconstructive mode is the abject, one of the key concepts of Julia Kristeva's *The Powers of Horror* (1982). Operating in the songs of the Drones and Gareth Liddiard in Chapter Four, the abject provides a realization of imagined sound in song lyrics that allows me to trace the movements of a mode of figurative language and to map disparate times and locations.

Rethinking language as imagined sound through the abject also foregrounds the medium of these works, and a number of sound concepts amplify the unique aspects of imagined sound in literature or music. The complex production of space facilitated by the speech samples used in *Mutiny Music*, discussed in Chapter Six, is illuminated by Steven Connor's theory of voice. Examining the formation of 'vocalic space', Conner helps me track the movement of voice-as-sound across complex Pacific archipelagic voyages into the past. The function of sound in mapping and aligning space is also foregrounded by the songline, an Indigenous practice combining storytelling, singing, dance and art at the centre of Wright's *Carpentaria*. The geography opened by the songline is one that departs from Western notions of both linear time and the topographic and synoptic ordering of space, instead charting a landscape, and a narrative, reliant on memory and performative retelling.

Listening to the Island Continent

This harmony of sound concepts plots two geoimaginaries, the continental interior and the island and archipelago, configurations of space that have their origins in the tradition of Australia's self-conception as an 'island continent'. Based on myths of the antipodes (Dunmore 1987; Johnston and Anderson 2005; Ryan 1996; McMahon 2010; Joseph 2010), for Elizabeth McMahon the 'island continent' 'comprehends the two major topographies of land [...] in a reversal of scale, for islands are meant to be small and continents large' (2016, 3). The two spatial formations are constantly in a state of interrelation and tension, but in an effort to elicit the maximum critical leverage out of my discussion of the continental interior and the island and archipelago, I will group the seven chapters into three parts. Part one, 'Listening to the Continent', includes Chapters One to Three, and Part two, 'Listening to Islands and Archipelagos', includes Chapters Four to Six. Part three, 'Listening to the Continental Archipelago', reconfigures continental and national territories into the archipelagic. Assembling the chapters along these parameters highlights how the different concerns and medium of each writer/composer reify or subvert the defining characteristics of the continent or the island and archipelago. This grouping of chapters provides opportunities to examine the intersection of these landscapes within the historical debates of the post-war era and creates unique dialogues between the two mediums. How is the continent imagined in the Modernist poetry of Webb, the electro-acoustic composition of Lumsdaine or the rock music of Midnight Oil? How is the haunted island in the novels by Flanagan and Bird unique from the islands depicted in *Mutiny Music*?

Weaving together the dynamics of Australian colonial and postcolonial history, a return to the past energizes each work assembled here. In a broad sense this makes all the works part of the genre of historical fiction. The landscapes each return to are varied: some journey with European explorers in search of the centre, others look to colonial frontiers with escaped convicts or witness violent meetings of settlers and Indigenous Australians, others move wholly away from the mainland of Australia, into the islands and archipelagos that redefine the borders of the continent. Central to the movement of the return is both a critique of the past and an examination of the present time of production. From a publishing or recording perspective, the earliest work I discuss – Webb series of poems 'Eyre All Alone'– was published in 1962, while the most recent – Baecastuff's *Mutiny Music* – has been performed since 2006, with a studio recording released in 2016. While all of the literature and music emerge from the post-war period, the distances covered in the return from the present to the past vary. For example, *Mutiny Music* sounds the space between the present and the 1790s, Webb and Lumsdaine move between the 1960s or 1970s and the 1840s, Richard Flanagan writes from the 1990s back to the 1820s, Wright novelistic songline *Carpentaria* reaches from creation to the present.

The 64-year period of this time of production encompasses two seismic shifts in the geoimaginary self-awareness and reinvention of Australia. First, the years following World War II were characterized by a concerted 'search for the centre' (Haynes 1998). Key creative figures – Sidney Nolan in *Central Australia* (1950), Patrick White in *Voss* (1957) and Peter Sculthorpe in the *Sun Music* series (begun in 1965) – 're-discovered' and celebrated (or fetishized) the desert centre as the spiritual and aesthetic locus of authenticity for the nation. It is also important to recognize that this artistic flowering was accompanied by a range of other forces, such as the efforts of state and federal governments to exploit the economic and tourist potential of the centre (Robin 2007). Following White's novelistic vision of the harrowing psychospiritual journey of Voss the *ur*-European explorer, one important strand of the search for the centre restages the journeys of the explorers: the poetry and music by Francis Webb and David Lumsdaine I discuss in Chapter One take up this imperative. Returning to the 1840s from their positions in the 1960s and 1970s respectively, Webb and Lumsdaine's poetic and musical visions (or nightmares) of the search for the centre articulate a combination of European and North American Modernist formal experimentation and inner exploration with their own unique and personal artistic concepts.

Unfolding in the 1990s, the second pivotal shift marked in *Imagined Sound* is the post-*Mabo* period. At the head of this decade was the *Mabo* decision in 1992, the court ruling that recognized Indigenous land rights and the falsity of *terra nullius* – land that is unoccupied or unworked – and while the term was not used in the eighteenth and nineteenth centuries, 'the contemporary use of the idea *terra nullius* is consistent with a tradition in which natural law was used to oppose colonisation' (Fitzmaurice 2007, 1). The works in Chapters Three to Seven are all post-*Mabo* in their publication or recording. A critical facet of the post-*Mabo* period was 'The History Wars', the ideological battle fought over recognition or denial of colonial violence and the genocide of Aboriginal people by European settlers. Bain Attwood argues that 'The History Wars' debates are concerned with contesting 'the public memory of nations […] the ways in which the national past is remembered, commemorated and celebrated. In short these are debates about national identity' (2005, 1). Centered on contemporary events such as the *Mabo* ruling, the *Bringing Them Home* report of 1997, the *Wik* land rights court decision in 1996, and the subsequent acknowledgement of the Stolen Generations by the Rudd Government apology in 2006, the debate was at its most intense during conservative Prime Minister John Howard's leadership (1996–2007). If the History Wars are 'about national identity', as Attwood contends, then imagined sound registers the haunting reverberations of this debate within continental, island and archipelagic soundscapes and refrains.

My way forward into the histories and landscapes of *Imagined Sound* is explicated in the direct comparative discussion between musical and literary mediums that takes place in Chapter One. Setting out the method for the next six chapters, Chapter One is like a microcosm for the book as a whole: from Chapter Two onwards I move back and forth between music and literature. The oscillating structure highlights my through-running concerns with how imagined sound offers a number of approaches to similar histories or landscapes, which in turn amplifies both work-specific and medium-related nuances in the representation of the geoimaginaries of the continent and the island/archipelago. The differences between this literature and music is productive for understanding the many tonalities of Australian landscape and history via imagined sound, but the shifts of medium engineer conceptual continuity. This diverse range of material also underscores the importance of these geoimaginaries to multidisciplinary artistic production in that timeframe.

Moving between the literary and the musical also uncovers a seldom encountered comparative territory between works. For example, the transition between the nationalist/Modernist vision of the centre and the return to that space with popular rock music elicits a distinctive conversation on the power of the centre and its ongoing importance to debates about place, as well as illuminating both positive developments and stagnant repetitions more recently. Listening to soundscapes and song structures as they arise in the convict songs of the Drones and Gareth Liddiard, the Tasmanian novels of Richard Flanagan and Carmel Bird or Baecastuff's jazz suite amplifies the geoimaginary harmonics of islands and archipelagoes. Placing these mediums into critical proximity also reveals new historical or conceptual contexts for engaging with a work, such as when I deploy Kristeva's theory of the abject to the songs by the Drones and Gareth Liddiard. The use of critical theory and the placement of the songs into an archipelagic chain magnifies their relevance to wider concerns with Australian mythic space. Such a discussion also casts light on the resonance of this music to both the post-war and post-*Mabo* periods.

In Chapter One, 'Reimagining the Centre', I listen to the series of poems 'Eyre All Alone' (1962) by Webb, and the electro-acoustic composition *Aria for Edward John Eyre* (1973) by Lumsdaine. Webb and Lumsdaine both reconfigure Edward John Eyre's journey from Adelaide to Albany in 1840–41 to create unique reimaginings of this search: Webb's series of poems is aligned along transcendent and spiritual lines, while Lumsdaine's composition emphasizes the alienation and terror of the desert journey. As the title of the chapter suggests, both works reimagine the centre: Webb's Eyre finds solace on the continental border, while Lumsdaine's explorer experiences fragmentation and disorientation. Like the real Eyre, Webb and Lumsdaine's explorer fails to find the true mythic or geographic centre. My analysis is positioned within a number of interconnected discourses: the history of desert representation emerging from Western Judeo-Christian traditions of the wilderness and the transcendent visionary, contemporary Modernist concerns with interiority and musical aesthetics. From a specifically Australian perspective, Judith Wright's characterization of the relationship between settler societies and the landscape 'as the outer equivalent of an inner reality' (1965, xi) is the contextual and conceptual linchpin of the chapter. The various configurations of this tension in Webb and Lumsdaine's are addressed through the rhythmic repetitions of Deleuze and Guattari's refrain, a listening device that unpacks the imagined sound of Webb's space of religious exultation on the beach in 'To The Gulls' and Lumsdaine's space of despair at the climax of *Aria for Edward John Eyre*.

Fifteen years after *Aria* and twenty-five years after 'Eyre All Alone', Midnight Oil's rock music restages the journey in search of the centre. Midnight Oil, particularly their work on both sides of the 1988 Bicentenary, mark a pivotal transition into the 1990s, a decade of immense change for the non-Indigenous relationship with Australian history and space. Chapter Two, 'Midnight Oil: Sounding Australian Rock around the Bicentenary', listens to three pivotal moments from Midnight Oil's career as the band attempted to remap the space of the centre previously imagined by Webb and Lumsdaine. I track Midnight Oil's journey from the fringe of the continent and their beginnings in Oz rock, through their 1986 Blackfella/Whitefella tour of Central Australia, the *Diesel and Dust* (1987) album and 'The Dead Heart' film clip. I conclude with the Sydney 2000 Olympic games closing ceremony performance of 'Beds Are Burning', a powerful statement recognizing Australia's First Peoples made to national and international audiences. Despite moving beyond the European explorer and creating public awareness of Indigenous Australian history and environmental conservation, I argue that Midnight Oil nevertheless repeat many of the fetishistic tropes first made concrete in the Australian Modernist quest. This partial failure to resist the influence of the post-war era belies Midnight Oil's position on the eve of the 1990s, specifically the outpouring of nationalistic pride surrounding the 1988 Bicentenary. Engaging with multiple types of musical artefact (tour, film clip, song lyrics, album covers and performance), my critical close listening approach is informed by the sociology of music and cultural studies. Shifting from the Modernist poetry and the avant-garde art music discussed in Chapter One, I again make use of the refrain to map Midnight Oil's 'line of flight' trajectory out of earlier conceptions of the centre.

Chapter Three, 'Sound and Silence', continues the exploration of continental interiority of the first two chapters. Instead of Webb, Lumsdaine and Midnight Oil's search for the geographic centre, Alex Miller's move into the continent, placed in the midst of the post-*Mabo* era, meditates on the experience of an outsider as he or she comes to know a new landscape. My critical close listening to soundscapes from across Miller's *oeuvre* reveals the intricate relations opened by sound and silence. Engaging with Nancy's conception of listening and 'the referral' as well as several theorization of silence, I argue that Miller's use of sound and silence enables him to depict his characters and surroundings and intensify shared experience, despite vast continental and historical distance. Miller's postcolonial vision, while at times utopian, moves towards a future of reconciliation, and his evocation of Australian landscapes, particularly those of Central Queensland, for the most part avoids the fetishization that characterizes both the post-war Modernists' and Midnight Oil's later efforts. Shifting from the broad symbolic strokes and imagery of the popular rock music multimedia of Midnight Oil, Miller's delicate portraits of Indigenous and non-Indigenous relationships are defined by complex layerings of landscape, history and character interiority. I track the development of Miller's use of imagined sound from some of his earlier novels – *The Tivington Nott* (1989) and *The Sitters* (1995) – through to his two Central Queensland novels *Journey to the Stone Country* (2002) and *Landscape of Farewell* (2007), ending with *Autumn Laing* (2011).

Launching away from the continent and out into a global constellation of islands and archipelagos, Part Two begins with 'An Archipelago of Convicts and Outsiders', a close listening to three songs by rock band the Drones and folk artist Liddiard. Accounting for the presence of the abject in the lyrics of 'Words from the Executioner to Alexander Pierce' and 'Sixteen Straws' by the Drones, and 'The Radicalisation of D' by Liddiard, I argue that the songs reinscribe the site of the convict myth of the continent by placing it within a global carceral archipelago. Chapter Four traces the formation of a key site of national mythology – the convict era – within a web of more recent spatio-temporalities, including just before the September 11 attacks in the United States, the contemporary performance site of the songs and more distant locations and histories from across the globe. The abject lyrical imagery used in the songs sets up the relationship between convicts, a contemporary outsider in Liddiard's 'The Radicalisation of D', and the Australian landscape. This soundscape of imagined sound amplifies the rejected status of these outsider figures, while also reconfiguring the convict myth – part of the bedrock of white Australian continental identity – within a global archipelago. Returning to the field of popular culture and the musical medium in this chapter, the relevance of these songs by the Drones and Liddiard to a popular youth audience recalls Midnight Oil, but I diverge from the approach taken in Chapter Two by augmenting the close analysis of lyrics and musico-historical context with Kristeva's theory of the abject. This reflects both the lyrical sophistication of these songs and the differences in geoimaginary, period of composition (2006–10), and the historical period to which they return.

Moving back into the novelistic medium, Chapter Five, 'Echoes between Van Diemen's Land and Tasmania', continues to map the territory between the 1820s and the present. Here the move away from the continent initiated by the Drones and Liddiard is transferred onto the space of the island. The sense of visceral return at the heart of the previous chapter also lingers on, as does the form of imagined sound that conveys the shift into the past. This chapter focuses on two novels that stage the haunting of the present by the colonial past and uncover the forgotten or suppressed soundscapes of the Australian island geoimaginary. Flanagan's *Death of a River Guide* (1994) and Bird's *Cape Grimm* (2004), both Tasmanian novels by Tasmanian authors, explore themes of extinction, genealogy and haunting by presenting historical fictions that oscillate between the present and the colonial past, a time defined by violent confrontations between settlers and Indigenous people. Taking into account their explicit dialogue with 'The History Wars', the traditions of Australian Gothic sound, and the discourse of islands, I argue that a continuum of sound is central to the movement of uncovering and recognizing the past. Critically listening to two soundscapes from each novel, one located in the suppressed colonial past and a second located in the present, I map the shared coordinates of these soundscapes using the refrain and the sound in between to gauge resonances between the past and the present. Rhythmic echoes, song structures and ghostly screams haunt the spatio-temporal continuums opened by both the novels. The medium of these two island geoimaginaries focalizes the passage of time through characters, a perspective that endow both novels with strikingly personal and genealogical overtones. The spatio-sonorous organization of these soundscapes also strikes a chord with the chapters on either side, both of which adopt structured formations of sound – songs – to create island and archipelagic territory.

Floating beyond the haunted soundscapes of the island of Tasmania/Van Diemen's Land, Chapter Six, 'A Sonic Passage between Islands', sails far out into the Pacific in search of two islands, Pitcairn and Norfolk. In *Mutiny Music* (2016) – a suite of 12 compositions composed and performed by Sydney-based jazz ensemble Baecastuff – the continental dominance of Australia is passed over in favour of archipelagic relations between islands. *Mutiny Music* is a contemporary retelling of the mythic foundations of Pitcairn and Norfolk, two island communities with historical ties to Australia dating back to the convict era. Using a combination of musical materials – original compositions in the unique style of Baecastuff, musical symbolism, hymns and speech sample pieces – the work sounds a wide sonic net. I argue that the imaginative cartography created by this diversity of sound sources, and the contextual, historical, technological and sonic complexity of some of the sounds, amplify the dynamics of interconnection that are key to the geoimaginary of the archipelago. Through close listenings to three of the twelve compositions, I investigate how the various musical elements create a series of connections between the narrative of *Mutiny Music* (the eighteenth century), the diverse spaces the story actually emerges from (the eighteenth to twentieth centuries) and the space of the performance and recording (the present). On the surface *Mutiny Music* is wholly committed to retelling a mythic story, but powerful currents drag the islands of Pitcairn and Norfolk towards a range of locations, including the British Isles, the United States and Sydney.

Following the voyage out into the Pacific heralded by *Mutiny Music*, I return to the mainland with the contemporary songline and noisy reformation of Alexis Wright's *Carpentaria* (2006), a novel whose massive synoptic and sonic energies are directed towards the destruction and rebirth of the continent. Chapter Seven, 'Noisy Songlines', listens to *Carpentaria*'s evocation of both colonial and Indigenous noises, charting the cyclical weather patterns and movements of heroic characters across a terrain as much colonial continent as postcolonial archipelago. At the core of my listening to *Carpentaria* is the songline, a culturally refined Indigenous Australian sound and space concept that extends the sound/environment/listener relation of the soundscape. I argue that in addition to several pivotal scenes that gesture towards songlines, the novel as a whole performs a songline that realigns the confines of the continent and the Top End of Australia along renewed spatio-temporal coordinates. The resonance of noise, associated with both interruption and reconstruction, augments the mapping of the songline. Imagined sound is recast in *Carpentaria* as imagined noise. The timeless movements of the Ancestral Serpent and the awesome power of the storm – the novel's two creative/destructive bookends – epitomize Wright's noisy reimagining of the Australian continent. And while Wright's anger at colonial violence and injustice is an important part of the harmony of *Carpentaria*, the novel does offer hope for future dialogue through intergenerational forgiveness and knowledge transmission. *Carpentaria*'s cyclic timescale echoes my return to the continental mainland in this final chapter. After pursuing the diverse musical relations through sound in *Mutiny Music* – spatially the largest of the works in *Imagined Sound* – the virtuosic soundscapes and epic space-time continuum of *Carpentaria* could only be realized in the novel form.

Part One

LISTENING TO THE CONTINENT

Chapter One

REIMAGINING 'THE CENTRE': FRANCIS WEBB'S 'EYRE ALL ALONE' AND DAVID LUMSDAINE'S *ARIA FOR EDWARD JOHN EYRE*

For Francis Webb and David Lumsdaine, along with many other visual artists, writers and composers, the years after World War II were an intense period of engagement in the mythopoeic practice of 'seeking the centre' (Haynes 1998). Presenting the explorer's journey in search of the mythical inland sea, Webb, Lumsdaine and their cohort helped to define, but also problematize, the non-Indigenous relationship to Australian space in the post-war period. Moving away from the bush – the geoimaginary validated by earlier generations attempting to define the space of the nation – the centre was a *tabula rasa*, capable of supporting both the search for an Australian spatiality and contemporary Modernist concerns with interiority, both spiritual and continental.

Although Webb's 'Eyre All Alone' (1961) and Lumsdaine's *Aria for Edward John Eyre* (1972) are clear evocations of the Modernist monad – the titles of both works indicate shadings of Romantic heroic individualism – Webb and Lumsdaine follow the facticity of the historical events in not allowing Edward John Eyre (1815–1901) to locate a geographic centre or the mythical inland sea. In Webb's poetic series and Lumsdaine's composition the failed moment of transcendence central to modernism is doubled, resonating with the explorer's failure to locate the fabled centre. Despite being based on the same figure and journey, Webb and Lumsdaine's representations of the search for the centre are singular, a reflection of the originality of their wider artistic missions. At the same time the supposed 'blankness' of the Australian desert, an important aspect of the relevance and appeal of the desert as a mythopoeic spatiality for those working in the post-war period, masks the erasure of Indigenous people.

Webb's 'Eyre All Alone', built from a refrain of transcendence at the seaside, replaces the centre, moving it to the continental border. Intensifying focus on interiority and paranoia while immobilizing forward momentum, Lumsdaine's *Aria* fragments the centre, creating a fissure within the figure of Eyre. Webb aligns the site where Eyre came closest to the geographic centre with the structural centre of his poetic sequence. This narrative re-ordering is also a feature of *Aria*, serving to emphasize the transcendence or horror of the centre, rather than its centrality. The episode with Hag Torrens is a radical departure from the historical sequence of events: the fiasco at Lake Torrens in fact occurred around 8 July 1840, almost nine months prior to the death of Baxter, Eyre's expedition overseer, on 29 April 1841. The death of Baxter is a pivotal event for both works, signaling Eyre's isolation in the face of significant indigenous presence throughout the historical journey.

Despite their different registers and evocations of imagined sound, both works show how the imperative to rewrite mythic stories was not a mission to reify the glory of the centre and rehearse the heroics of European exploration and quest. Instead, these two works reposition the supposed treasures of the continental interior, and the interiority of the self, while meditating on the existential crisis or mystical epiphany of the individual in relation to an Australian desert landscape. My discussion of Webb's poem shows how Eyre is learning to listen. In *Aria*, the fragmentation of Eyre's consciousness ensnares him in the labyrinth of his own mind, disabling him from experiencing anything other than the presence of his own isolation.

Listening to the soundscapes and refrains in 'Eyre All Alone' and *Aria*, we hear distinct landscapes that align with the different artistic and conceptual aims of Webb and Lumsdaine. In 'Eyre All Alone' the soundscape works like an echo chamber, simultaneously projecting Eyre's consciousness onto the exterior landscape. At the same time, sound permeates Eyre, filtering back into his thoughts and feelings. In *Aria* the psychic distress of Eyre's confrontation with the landscape is internalized and fractured, a process signaled both by Lumsdaine's treatment of Eyre's diaries and his use of the two narrators and soprano. In this way the soundscape of *Aria* functions differently from 'Eyre All Alone', with Lumsdaine's composition operating as a soundscape of the centre that very literally works against the relation between interior and exterior. Lumsdaine's soundscape becomes a purely internal labyrinth of the mind.

The structuring of imagined sound via the refrain is apparent in both Webb and Lumsdaine's imaginings of Eyre's journey, and although my deployment of the concept in 'Eyre All Alone' and *Aria* is different, repetition is central to both works. Webb's refrains are rooted in the foundations of Modernist poetics and they give a rhythmic gravity to the key moments of the poem. Mapping Eyre's experience of disorientation in the desert, for Lumsdaine the refrain takes on a lyrical character. As Deleuze and Guattari proclaim, 'One ventures from home on the thread of a tune' (344): while the 'tune' and the 'home' of Webb's and Lumsdaine's works are different, both 'venture' through their journey on the 'thread' of sound and repetition. My analysis of Webb's 'Eyre All Alone' focuses on how the poetic series performs between the wilderness and prophet images of the desert. With its fracturing of Eyre's interiority, *Aria* is tightly focused on the existential terror culminating at Baxter's death, and therefore, to continue the mapping metaphor, the cartography of that work is smaller in scale but finer in detail in comparison to 'Eyre All Alone'.

Behind the poetic and musical historiography of Eyre created by Webb and Lumsdaine sits the historical Eyre. As we know from the *Journals of Expeditions of Discovery into Central Australia, and Overland from Adelaide to King George's Sound, in the Years 1840–1*, published in 1845, Eyre attempted, and failed, to navigate a South to North crossing of the continent in 1840–1. After much hardship he did manage to explore the land between Streaky Bay and Albany, a journey East to West. This was a time when the geographic centre of Australia was still a mystery. Popular belief had it that there was an inland sea or lake: the explorer Charles Sturt even dragged boats with him on his 1844 journey. Paul Carter suggests that the curiosity about the centre had 'political and economic, as well as geographical, overtones' citing the pastoral interests of the South Australian government and squatters as key motivations behind Eyre's expedition (1988, 87). Born in Bedfordshire, Eyre arrived in Australia as a teenager and initially worked as a farmer, later in life becoming the governor of the Colony of Jamaica, where he oversaw the violent suppression of the Morant Bay rebellion in 1865. Eyre's *Journals* were one of several explorer accounts that inspired Australian creative artists working in the post-war period. Carter calls Eyre's *Journals* one of the classics of the 'romantic genre of travel writing' (88), and alongside journals by Leichhardt, Cook, Mitchell, Giles, Warburton and Grey, it cements the white masculinist character of this tradition, a convention upheld by Webb and Lumsdaine.

But what was it about Eyre's *Journals* that made them so important to the post-war mythopoeic movement? Patrick White – whose novel *Voss* (1957) is perhaps the most well-known and influential work to deal with the spiritual and mythic implications of the fatal trek of the explorer into the desert – commented that reading Eyre's *Journals* was a major impetus behind his return to Australia, and an important inspiration for his novel. Heavily based on Leichhardt's disappearance, Voss's experience of isolation is a clear echo of Eyre's travails. Positioned as a hinge between the first and second volumes of his *Journals* – 'a more dramatic ending to the first act could hardly have been devised' (Carter 1988, 90) – the extreme trauma of Baxter's death and the sustained focus on Eyre's existential isolation struck a chord with Webb, and later Lumsdaine, although there is no evidence to suggest Lumsdaine read

Webb's poem. Unlike Burke and Wills or Leichhardt, Eyre's *survival*, and the fact that his mission to find the centre was a complete failure – he discovered nothing of economic value – are aspects of the Englishman's story that make it unique within the pantheon of explorer accounts.

Australian Modernists

By articulating the Australian post-war mythopoeic mission into the desert amidst the broader drives of modernism, 'Eyre All Alone' and *Aria* sit at the historical, conceptual and formal peak of a sandy double-crested wave. There are a number of important resonances between European modernism and the search for the centre performed by both Webb and Lumsdaine. W. B. Yeats's 'The Second Coming' (1920), where he wrote 'the centre cannot hold' (184), captures the sense of collapse and the existential alienation at the core of both Australian works. For Webb and Lumsdaine, like Yeats, the mythic centre cannot hold: it must be removed to a new location. Moreover, Webb's use of refrains throughout his series shows the stylistic influence of Yeats: 'A terrible beauty is born', from 'Easter 1916' is one of many instances of refrains. Longley states, 'Refrain has such structural importance to Yeats that sometimes, as MacNeice says […] "the refrain, far from being a mere decoration, is practically the focal point"' (166).

Refrains of imagined sound also resonate within nineteenth century and Modernist aesthetic valorizations aesthetic valorization of the idea of music, a form that emerged from the nineteenth century in a revered position among the arts. Walter Pater's axiomatic statement 'all art constantly aspires to the condition of music' (1893, 86) promotes music to the highest artistic pedestal. As Brad Bucknell explains, 'Pater is making a claim for "music" as the ideal to which any composition, poetic or otherwise, must strive' (2001, 115). Richard Wagner, held by many to be the greatest composer of the Romantic period and a forefather of modernism in music, reiterates Pater's ideas: 'The greatness of poets should be measured by what they leave unsaid, letting us breathe the thing unspeakable to ourselves in silence. It is musicians who bring this unspoken mystery to clarion tongue' (Wagner quoted in Goehr 1998, epigram). Bucknell argues that for writers like Ezra Pound, James Joyce and Gertrude Stein music 'refers obliquely to an art which transcends referential or lexical meaning, and which has the power of some kind of excessive, yet essential, element to which the literary may point, but to which it can never fully encompass' (1). For Bucknell this 'strange kind of recuperation of a romantic belief' (2) in the power of music means that it is not just 'a metaphorical solution to the representation of consciousness' but more importantly 'part of the larger question of the problem of representation in modernism itself' (3). This Modernist valorization of music, and the representation of a limit that it articulates, is taken up and transformed by Webb in 'Eyre All Alone'. Lumsdaine's *Aria* is also related to the modernism of Webb's poetic series, centrally the exploration of interiority. But rather than enacting Pater's movement beyond language, *Aria* explicitly relies on the text of Eyre's journal to represent the centre. Lumsdaine treats the text with extreme care, a relation to the historical Eyre that strengthens the connection across mediums.

The conceptual pivot between sound, Modernist interiority and its manifestation in Australian post-war mythic production is articulated by Judith Wright's formulation of the relationship between the settler society and the environment as 'the outer equivalent of an inner reality' (xi). The inability to neatly separate the 'inside' from the 'outside' underpins the many epistemological, phenomenological and representational challenges apparent in the work of Australian writers and composers in the post-war period. Wright's reading of the relation between the individual and their environment in Australian postcolonial work resonates with other key theorizations of interiority in and behind modernism, such as T. S. Eliot's 'objective correlative' (1921), John Ruskin's 'pathetic fallacy' (1856), or the concept of 'paysage moralise' (Emison, 1995), all of which describe the projection and reflection of emotion into the landscape.

Critics of both Webb and Lumsdaine agree that locating them in the crosshairs of 'Australian' and 'Modernist' is difficult: Webb's mystical religiosity puts him at odds with many Modernists (although not Eliot) (Ashcroft 1996; Brennan 2005; Davidson 2013). Beyond the key concern with interiority, the conceptual and technical difficulty of Webb's poetic *oeuvre*, and his historical time of activity (he published between 1940 and 1973), place him in the Modernist tradition. This is also apparent in his use of dramatic forms, which link to works like Eliot's 'Murder in the Cathedral' (1935). Foregrounded in earlier explorer poems like 'A Drum for Ben Boyd' (1948) and 'Leichhardt in Theatre' (1952), the figure of the explorer on the dramatic stage of history echoes throughout 'Eyre All Alone'.

Approaching Webb's poem series from a biographical perspective is to encounter his affinity with music. Both of Webb's parents were trained in the musical arts. His father Claude was a professional musician and the director of the North Sydney Academy of Music, and his mother Hazel, who died in 1927, was a singer. Born in Adelaide in 1925, following his mother's death and his father's institutionalization Webb was raised by his grandmother in North Sydney. An affection for music is revealed by several of his poems, with titles including 'Scherzo and Adagio of Bruckner's Ninth', 'Gustav Mahler', 'Brahms at Bruckner's Funeral' and 'Rondo Burleske: Mahler's Ninth'. These details amplify Webb's ear for sound: while the way he deploys sound in 'Eyre

All Alone' is unique in his *oeuvre*, music and sound are important conceptual elements evident throughout his poetry. Although 'Eyre All Alone' is already recognized in the ranks of post-war myth-makers thanks to the scholarship of Patricia Excell (1989) and Bill Ashcroft (1996), my analysis of the sequence provides a new perspective on the value and originality of Webb's relocation of the centre to the border.

Lumsdaine's life mirrors that of many expatriate artists: Born in Sydney in 1931, he lived with his parents and two elder brothers in Paddington, often visiting family farms inland (LeFanu, webpage). Lumsdaine was educated at Sydney University and the New South Wales Conservatorium of Music. Moving to England in 1953, he began studying with Matyas Seiber, and lived for a time with fellow expatriate Peter Porter, with whom he collaborated on the cantata *Annotations of Auschwitz* (1964). Lumsdaine spent much of his career in the UK: in 1970 he commenced teaching at Durham University, where he founded the Electronic Music Studio, and later at King's College, London. Some of his major works are *Kelly Ground* for solo piano (1966), *Flights* (1967) for two pianos, *Hagoromo* (1977) and *Mandala 5* (1988) and the cello concerto *A Garden of Earthly Delights* (1992). After making his first return trip to Australia in 1973, Lumsdaine made regular visits, and in addition to his acoustic and electro-acoustic compositions he produced several soundscape recordings, including *Cambewarra Mountain* (1995) and *Lake Emu* (1996). Lumsdaine has now ceased to compose.

Lumsdaine is also in excess of his branch of modernism. His expatriatism, examination of Australian landscapes and myths through both *Aria* and earlier compositions like *Kelly Ground* (1966), more recent soundscape recordings like *Cambewarra Mountain* (1990), and links with both Australian and a large constellation of English and European Modernists also place him somewhere in between the local, national and global. Lumsdaine's *Aria* can also be mapped through the optics of Modernist musical practice. Carl Dahlhaus defines modernism in art music as 'an obvious point of historical discontinuity' built on the 'breakaway mood of the 1890s and composers like Mahler, Strauss and Debussy' (1989, 334). This idea is backed by Daniel Albright's suggestion that such a mood constituted a 'testing of the limits of aesthetic construction' (2004, 11). The breadth of Lumsdaine's *oeuvre* shows the influence of central musical Modernists like Igor Stravinsky, John Cage, Pierre Boulez, Luciano Berio and Karlheinz Stockhausen. His experimentation with electro-acoustics and speakers, the influence of serialism, the use of improvisation and the soloistic musical language of the soprano, link *Aria* with these key European and American figures of musical modernism. My discussion of Lumsdaine's *Aria* augments the small amount of scholarship on the composer (Wiseman 1983; Schultz 1991; Hall 2003; LeFanu 2004; Hooper 2012), making a place for *Aria* among the range of nationally important post-war works that reconfigure the Australian desert geoimaginary, while also celebrating the fractured soundscape of the centre offered by the work.

The Desert Centre: Visionaries and the Wilderness

The desert landscapes evoked by Webb's and Lumsdaine's soundscapes and refrains are not just unorganized chaos, as Deleuze and Guattari's theorization of the first stage of the refrain implies. Nor are they scaffolds first erected by the Australian mytho-Modernists. The interlocking discourses surrounding the desert and the space of the centre map a diverse field of inquiry, binding strands of ecological, environmental, literary and biblical history, cultural geography and literary analysis. Mainland Australia is, geographically, dominated by desert environments. The Australian desert – sometimes referred to as the 'outback' – is a complex environmental, economic and mythic weave of ideas and histories. While 70 per cent of the overall space of the continent is defined as desert (Lynch 2007, 71), this statistic does not necessarily collate with the space of the desert as a post-war national geoimaginary. The scene of both 'heroic exploration and bitter pastoral disappointment' (Robin 2007, 100), in *How a Continent Created a Nation* (2007) Libby Robin describes how, dating back to the nineteenth century, deserts were defined as 'the places where there was no prospect of an agricultural economy. They were also the places where brave explorers regularly died. Exploration succeeded only under exceptional circumstances and great leadership' (100–101). Surveying the ecological and economic history of Australian spaces, Robin's work solidifies the link between economic motivations for rediscovery and the efforts of post-war poets and composers in re-imagining the space.

The non-Indigenous Australian engagement with the desert is a cohesive field and creative imperative to rival the output of any other period in post-settlement Australian history. Webb's poem and Lumsdaine's composition sit amidst a large range of now canonical works engaged with the 'discovery' of Australian desert centre space. Foremost in this cohort are visual artists Sidney Nolan, Arthur Boyd and Russell Drysdale, the poets Kenneth Slessor ('Five Visions of Captain Cook' – 1931), Douglas Stewart (*Voyager Poems* – 1931–60) and James McAuley (*Captain Quiros* – 1964), and the composers Barry Conyngham (*Edward John Eyre* – 1973), Peter Sculthorpe (the radio opera *Quiros* – 1982), Colin Brumby (*The Vision and the Gap* – 1985), Richard Meale (an opera adaption of White's novel *Voss* with a libretto by David Malouf – 1986) and Andrew Schultz (*Journey to Horseshoe Bend* – 2003). The novels marking this territory are headed by Patrick White's *Voss* (1957), alongside Randolph Stowe's *To the Islands* (1958) and *Tourmaline* (1963). This range of narratives align with Anthony J. Hassall's three types of quest: 'the voyage in search of Australia; the quest for 'home' in Europe; and the journey into the centre of the country' (1988, 390). All three types are Eurocentric in their approach.

Encompassing much post-war artistic production, the impulse towards a journey or quest was also discussed by historians such as Vance Palmer and Russell Ward. Palmer's *The Legend of the Nineties* (1954) and Ward's *The Australian Legend* (1958) describe the same mythopoeic moment, defining the Australian character in terms that foregrounded the white European masculinity of the explorer, bushman or bushranger, set in a landscape viewed primarily with an eye to economic opportunity. More recently, a series of texts including Carter's *The Road to Botany Bay: An Essay in Spatial History* (1988) and *Living in a New Country: History, Travelling and Language* (1992), Ryan's *The Cartographic Eye: How Explorers Saw Australia* (1996) and Haynes *Seeking the Centre* (1998) have begun to address the blindness of Palmer and Ward's histories, what W. E. H. Stanner called 'the great Australian silence' (1969) that suppressed the long history of Indigenous Australians.

The perspective of the explorer, both the historical and the re-imagined, overlooked and silenced Australian Indigenous people, their history and their connection to country. While the search for the centre was predominantly a non-Indigenous Australian preoccupation, there are several novels and memoirs, like Kim Scott's *Benang: From the Heart* (1999), and Kim Mahood's *Craft for a Dry Lake* (2000), that perform a similar return to the interior, although from a different cultural and historical approach. An increasing number of collections, published by Indigenous writers and storytellers in conjunction with community-run cooperatives like the Meningrida Literature Production Centre, have begun to emerge, such as *Voices from the Heart: Contemporary Aboriginal Poetry from Central Australia* edited by Roger Bennett (1995), and *Jumangkarni Wimi: Dreaming Stories from the Desert* (2003) compiled by Bruce Thomas (written in Warnman and Manyjilyjarra language with English translations). Meshing Dreaming stories with life writing and fictional forms, these works depict a desert space radically different from the prevailing representations produced by non-Indigenous Australians in the post-war years.

The divide between the long history of Indigenous connection with the desert and post-settlement experiences of European settlers and explorers is founded on the non-Indigenous importation of other ways of viewing and valuing desert spaces. Haynes discusses the prominence of the desert – 'A site of ancient myth, of spiritual dimension and cultural rebirth' (1998, 1) – in the 'collective imagination' of the Western world: 'For more centuries than European civilisation can lay claim to [the desert] has symbolised the land's endurance, provoking creative reappraisals of our place in Nature and the meaning of our existence' (1–2). Throughout *Seeking the Centre* Haynes explores the sedimentary layers of literature, visual art and film that have shaped the desert in the colonial and postcolonial Australian psyche. I would hasten to add that other art forms not covered in Haynes's study, such as art music, dance and theatre, have also been instrumental in accumulating the cultural capital of the centre. Haynes does recognize and explore Indigenous Australian desert mythologies and living traditions of knowledge, but her work shows that the concept of the centre as it applies to the two works by Webb and Lumsdaine emerges from European biblical and colonial depictions of the desert.

Haynes figures the centre as a site fundamentally stratified by several interconnected structures of meaning. Defining the 'two opposing prototypes' of what I term the desert continuum, Haynes says, 'One cluster of images, which we may call the wilderness image, presents the desert as harsh, infertile and punitive; the other, which can be identified as visionary, constructs it as a site of spiritual enlightenment' (26). The two prototypes are intimately related, both intertwined with the history of Western spiritual imagery and experience. John Rennie Short casts the visionary prototype in terms of the European romantic movement of poetry and philosophy in the late eighteenth and early nineteenth centuries. 'For the romantics, contact with the wilderness brought about not a bewilderment but a renewed contact with deeper psychological truths and a more pronounced spiritual awareness' (Short 1991, 10). Short's connection of Romanticism with the achievement of spiritual transcendence in the wilderness does not easily fit with the figure of Eyre, who is far from a Romantic poet-hero in his *Journals* and in Lumsdaine's *Aria*, although Webb's evocation of Eyre at times draws on such a literary tradition.

Short describes the two meanings of wilderness for the 'emerging agricultural community' (10) of the Judeo-Christian Bible, one characterizing the wilderness as 'a place of God's creation, a source of spiritual insight' the other as 'a place whose transformation by human actions allows the possibility of redemption' (10). The divine contradiction of the wilderness as 'sacred space' means that it is 'God's work to be contrasted with human sin' but at the same time, the 'human transformation of the wilderness is God-guided' (10–12). Short's discussion draws out the conflicting meanings and uses the desert can support, divided between its characterization as a site for the attainment of spiritual insight and its role as a testing ground for the achievement of human redemption. Underscoring this complexity, George Williams characterizes the wilderness 'as a place of protection, a place of contemplative retreat, again as one's inner nature or ground of being', and 'as the ground itself of the divine being' (1962, 4). Alternatively, negative interpretations of the wilderness figure it as 'the world of the unredeemed, as the wasteland, and as the realm or phase of punitive or purgative preparation for salvation' (Williams 1962, 5).

This is a fertile space for the creative exploration of mythic narratives that strike at the heart of how to imagine and realize one Australian landscape. While it is evident that other approaches to mapping space had an impact on Lumsdaine – his series of *Mandala* compositions (I–V, composed between 1968 and 1988), like Patrick White's *The Solid Mandala* (1966), show some influence from other traditions beyond Western colonialism – 'Eyre All Alone' and *Aria* remain within the bounds of the biblical/colonial nexus. Locating this mythopoeic imperative at the crossroads of wider artistic movements, Elizabeth McMahon argues that 'the movement into the centre is both a recognition of the possibility of a distinctively Australian interiority and the embrace of European modernity' (184). McMahon's tracing of the post-war search for authentic national identity and European modernity within Australia's continental interior returns us to Wright's 'outer equivalent of an inner reality'. The exploration of this outer/inner tension, and the combination of exultation and suffering experienced by Webb and Lumsdaine's Eyre, is a fundamental set of coordinates guiding my analysis: the conceptual and creative richness of these desert works are constantly drawn back into this spatial dynamic.

The Centre on the Border: 'Eyre All Alone'

Webb presents Eyre's journey in a sequence of 14 poems. The expedition is a great struggle: Eyre fails to achieve his initial objective of exploring the Australian continent from south to north, instead making a near-fatal crossing from east to west. Despite this, there are moments of transcendence and insight dispersed across Webb's poetic terrain, spaces for visionary enlightenment within the daily battle to survive. Discussing the central spatial and spiritual elements of Webb's poetry, Bill Ashcroft, Frances Devlin-Glass and Lyn McCredden suggest that 'the question for Webb was: How does this journey of spiritual contemplation transfer into Australian space?' (2009, 76). Webb's whole poetic opus can undoubtedly be viewed as an exploration of post-war spirituality and subjectivity. I open the close analysis of 'Eyre All Alone' with a brief discussion of 'South Australian Settler', a poem that provides a first mapping of the desert space of the series, as well as containing the first iteration of the pivotal 'Walk, walk' stanza and refrain. From there I follow Eyre into the horrific wilderness of 'April 29th' before arriving at the transcendent refrain in 'The Sea', the true centre of the poetic series.

Setting up the wilderness theme for the soundscape of the third poem 'April 29th' while also presenting a map of the imperial, economic and exploratory motivations that sit behind the profound spiritual and spatial discoveries of Eyre's journey, 'South Australian Settler' performs an important contextual function in 'Eyre All Alone'. First, the spatial tension between colonial power and the natural and 'unexplored' landscape is flagged: 'Our little township is a lesion / On the plump hinder parts of nothing' (Webb 2011, 265). Following this, Eyre mentions the hardships of the environment and weather, 'Scratching, scratching, / The moody nails of the sun', followed by a reference to the real and psychic distance to England: 'Our stony / Brain and gullet wobble corroboree / With London, tall lady Exeter, Broad Devon' (265). These issues resound with the existential questions forged by the pairing of the reality of a European existence in the Australian colonies and Webb's overarching personal religious questions, stated midway through the poem: 'We are isolated. Is man man?' (265).

'South Australian Settler' is brought to a close with the first use of the eight-line stanza 'Walk, walk', a ritualistic refrain repeated four times during the sequence. The regular appearance of the stanza is a constant reaffirmation of the wilderness character of Webb's desert. Built on a distinct spondaic rhythmic foot – 'Walk, walk' – in this propulsive opening, the wheels – or perhaps the feet – of the poem are put in motion. 'Walk, walk' emphasizes the dominant mode of locomotion: either horses, or as the journey grew in difficulty, human walking. The rhythm of this endless repetition is a poetic imitation and transposition into verse of this movement:

> Walk, walk. From dubious footfall one
> At Fowler's Bay the chosen must push on
> Towards promised fondlings, dancings of the Sound.
> Fourth plague, of flies, harries this bloodless ground.
> Cliff and salt balance-wheel of heathen planet
> Tick, twinkle in concert to devise our minute.
> But something on foot, and burning, nudges us
> Past bitter waters, sands of Exodus. (266)

A host of religious allusions populate this eight-line stanza. Excell lists the biblical references: 'the chosen' from Deuteronomy, and, from various parts of Exodus 'fourth plague, of flies', 'bloodless ground', 'burning' and 'bitter waters' (1989, 3). These references open up a space within the first scene of the sequence that emerges directly from the biblical desert of the Old Testament, the desert of the exiled and wandering Israelites. Webb's naming of Eyre's party as 'the chosen' is, as the poem unfolds, ironically fitting. While the historical Eyre was not an exile, his position on the reverse side of the globe to the imperial centre can be seen as such. The 'sands of Exodus' is a terrain through which 'the chosen', the colonial explorers, must travel, despite the profusion of visionary happenings along the way.

The principal sonic element in the 'Walk, walk' stanza is the 'dancings of the Sound'. The 'Sound' referred to is a geographical location, King George's Sound, the body of water adjacent to Albany, Western Australia. It is both the literal goal of Eyre's exploratory journey, and an ultimate, transcendent or ecstatic (considering the joyous implications of 'dancing') goal for Eyre as a visionary. Later in the sequence 'Sound' takes on a dual significance, resonant both in terms of a geographical site and a transcendental space. The biblical wilderness elements of Eyre's journey are already present in this opening poem, giving the reader's ears a hint of the soundscape that is soon to surround Eyre in the wilderness of 'April 29th'. In a move that mirrors the dynamics of discovery, neither the abject silence or sublime moments and sounds of transcendence that mark the centre of the poetic landscape are apparent at the start of the journey: they wait for Eyre at the re-placed centre on the border. But before Eyre can reach that space he must, like a prophet being tested by God, pass through many trials in the wilderness.

'April 29th'

The locus of Eyre's testing in the wilderness is the third poem of the sequence, 'April 29th'. The title, a reference the prosaic diary mode used in Eyre's *Journals*, details one of the few historical events that Webb explicitly refers to, that of the death of Baxter at the hands of two Aboriginal youths who accompanied Eyre on his expedition. The murder of Baxter, Eyre's overseer and the only other European member of the party, is an event that has a great impact on Eyre's state of mind, endowing a new sense of reality to the danger that he has already experienced. As such it is significant that 'April 29th' contains one of the most concentrated scenes of sonic activity of any poem in 'Eyre All Alone'. The first stanza features a haunting soundscape comprised of several sound elements, which I have highlighted:

> Moon-levee. This dame's weighty jowl
> And precipitous brows invite a *wild dog's howling*.
> For hours under her flag I must set course,
> Take countless *soundings of the giant horses*,
> While the *ocean coughs her non-committal oath*.
> Again the *fibroid wind and scrub choir* nothing
> Knit in *falsetto and raggedy bass* tonight,
> And rallying moodward are embryonic lightnings,
> *Whispers of thunder*, a tattered populace. (267)

The 'wild dog's howling' is a sign of animal communication through sound, although it is unclear what is being communicated, anxiety or territorial dominance? Whatever the case, it is a sonic response to the moonlight that washes over the scene. The familiar word 'soundings', meaning to measure the depth of water, is paired with the reoccurring image of the horse, here transformed into the surreal and monstrous 'giant horses', the imposing presence and pressure of history within Eyre's mind. Taking 'countless soundings of the giant horses', we imagine Eyre ceaselessly pondering the status of the expedition, its chances of success or failure and urgent need to find water – Eyre's main preoccupation as relayed in his *Journals*.

The next three lines are a harmony of natural sounds. The ocean, gendered female (an identity explored in later poems in the sequence), 'coughs her non-committal oath'. Indicating a lack of vigour, sickness, perhaps boredom, 'coughing' matches the indifferent tone of the ocean's voice, itself uttering an 'oath' that lends a note of animosity to Eyre's perception of his environment. Lines six and seven describe the wind in terms that accentuate texture and pitch. The 'fibroid wind and scrub choir nothing' gives a roughly woven character to the wind, and Eyre registers the 'choir', the multiple singers of the bush soundscape, as 'nothing', meaningless sound. Despite this, he is still able to note a high degree of detail, with the pitch-level personification of 'falsetto and raggedy bass' giving specificity to the sound of the wind. The final two lines of the stanza mobilize a light/sound combination, with the slightly unformed or diminished connotation of 'embryonic' taken up in the personification 'whispers of thunder'. 'Whisper' creates a sense of closeness, an intimacy that emphasizes the unsettling mood of a soundscape that seems to be emanating not from the outside, but from inside Eyre.

The remainder of 'April 29th' details Baxter's death – 'Well, Baxter, here you lie, bleeding and inert / [...] So, before God, we are together again' (268) – and the suspicious disappearance of two of Eyre's companions – 'two other parts of man have fled' (268). The final line of the poem features one last sound element: 'Daybreak, snigger of dawn. I am alone' (268). The description of this sound is consonant with the poems' weather harmony by conveying the hostility of the wilderness landscape. Underscoring the experience of real existential isolation, Eyre's final statement 'I am alone' resonates alongside both the original explorer *Journals* and David Lumsdaine's treatment of the material in *Aria for Edward John Eyre*. Despite Eyre's feeling of complete separation, he is, ironically, still with Wylie, not to mention the presence of local Aboriginal people. Eyre's isolation is from the Empire, and from the safety, authority and clearly defined subjectivity afforded by vision. The space opened in 'April 29th' is interior, a soundscape of isolation and spiritual doubt linking outside events with Eyre's interiority. This inside is not the inside of the heart, the soul or the centre; if anything, it is the inside of a paranoid ear linked to a desolate desert auditorium.

The road to the centre – via the wilderness of the soul in 'April 29th' – is one that almost defeats Webb's Eyre. This failure is confirmed in the sixth poem of the series, 'From the Centre'. The poem charts a false centre: the muddy salt-lake landscape is the antithesis of the mythical inland sea, a blockage to Eyre's progress that forces him to abandon his planned south/north continental crossing. The meeting with Hag Torrens, the metaphorical figure arising from the muddy salt-plain of Lake Torrens, is silent, a fact that highlights the sterility of the space, its failure as a site of transcendence, and the later sonic abundance of 'The Sea'. The refrain of the poem – 'pride' – evolves through the four stanzas, and the territory sounded is one that draws together Eyre's desire for conquest, the delusion of his mission, and his ultimate failure.

> The Centre has rolled me as a dice
> Into hot air above the tableland, face.
> Remains substantial (by God's grace)
> Some narrow pride. (270)

Despite Eyre's belief that he still retains 'some narrow pride', his experience of failure reduces him to a symbol of fate, a 'rolled' dice in the 'hot air above tableland', the tableland being a recurring symbol of the mapping of Eyre's consciousness onto the desert landscape. Compared to the outward projection of 'the gulls' (the refrain of 'The Sea'), here pride is a self-centred refrain.

Webb's Transcendent Centre on the Border

From the silence of the false centre to 'The Sea'. The seventh poem is the centrepiece of the sequence, both literally (it is number seven of fourteen) and conceptually. The experience of transcendence that the poem relates, fused with the constant sonic presence exemplified by the refrain of 'the gulls', relocates the centre from the geographical centre of the continent to its ocean/land boundary. In addition to this, the modification of the original order of events heightens the effect of Webb's repositioning of the centre to the border: the flat muddy lake of Hag Torrens is contrasted with the multileveled coastal space of 'maiden Bight', the feminine presence of 'The Sea'. The sonic absence and blockage of progress that Hag Torrens represents, a silent barrier, is resolved in the profusion of sound heard on the coast.

While the sea that gives the poem its title is the ocean of the Great Australian Bight, there is also a sense that it is the fabled inland sea that was thought to exist in the centre of Australia. This sea, which in reality only existed 100 million years ago, is here relocated and transformed into a zone of spiritual rehabilitation for Eyre. In a way this poem allows Webb to fulfil the wishes of the European explorers who dreamed of finding an inland sea. Describing the depiction of the sea in the journals of Eyre and fellow explorer Charles Sturt, Carter says, 'It's significance lay in its symbolic fertility as a hypothesis of exploration, as a device suggesting the journey's inner logic and, above all, as a means of bringing remote things close, vividly before the reader's inner eye' (1988, 92). Drawing on the symbolic utility of the watery inside / outside, Webb carries this richness from the *Journals* into the centre of his series. The relief experienced by Webb's Eyre is apparent in both the symbolism of his descent from the hardship of the cliffs down to the revitalizing seashore, and in the shift towards the idealized and romantic subject matter of the episode with Maiden Bight.

In addition to the sonic and spatial contrast between 'From the Centre' and 'The Sea', the register of the language used in the latter poem also transforms. Excell suggests 'The Sea' 'departs from the sequence's unifying pattern of imagery and maintains only a tenuous link with the representational world of Eyre's *Journals*' (94). Moving from the sparse dryness of the language used to describe Hag Torrens we are drenched by the sea images and coastal soundscape of 'maiden Bight': Ashcroft describes the poem as 'a dense and variegated saturation of the senses' (1996, 151). After the vacuous mud and failure of the meeting with Hag Torrens in 'From the Centre', the sea is rippling with symbolically charged sounds and images.

Webb plays on the tension created by the range of geographical and imaginary associations of the sea – as the mythical inland sea, as continental border, as the medium of movement (or escape) between continents and as a source of spiritual and bodily rejuvenation. Harmonizing all of these resonances, 'The Sea' is a complex overlay of mythic, symbolic and spatial meaning focused on a salience of sound. Even if historians (Dutton 1967, 1982; Evans 2005) regard his east/west journey as of little worth in terms of exploration and economics, Webb has indeed allowed Eyre to make a discovery – of the centre on the border. As Jacques Derrida states in his essay 'Structure, Sign and Play', 'the centre is at the centre of the totality, and yet, since the centre does not belong to the totality (is not part of the totality), the totality *has its centre elsewhere*. The centre is not the centre' (2008, 352). Derrida's theorization, like Webb's poem, questions the borders of the national structure, the position of its geoimaginary cartography, and the place of the Australian Modernist heart. Marking the replaced space of the centre as Maiden Bight, Webb uncoils the mythic centre onto the curved geography of Australia's vast southern central coastline. For Excell, 'If the Centre presided over by [Hag Torrens] is to be recognised as false, then the castle, dwelling place of Beauty, the Lady, the Sea, should represent its opposite – the true Centre' (95). The move from the hag to the maiden evokes many gendered oppositions – ugly/beautiful, barren/fertile, old/young – and while these resonate with debates on the feminine in Australian bush mythology, they are not carried beyond this poem. Webb's use of the personified figure is to anoint the poem, spatially and spiritually, as different to the rest of the series.

Outstripping the other figurative aspects that animate the poem, the defining feature of the centre in 'Eyre All Alone' is the sonic presence of 'the gulls', Webb's most resonant and muscular refrain. The gulls open a space between the markers that delineate the world of poem. They float between high and low, heaven and earth, inside and outside the continent. Discussing Webb as mystical religious poet, Excell suggests that the gulls 'function as mediators between God and man' (93). The sonic refrain of 'the gulls' also embodies the Modernist (and Romantic) conception of music as a form able to convey meaning and emotion beyond language. The refrain creates a rhythmic centre on the border, a space of transcendence both within and beyond the confines of the continent.

Pursuing the various articulations of the refrain through the poem reveals the different types of territory that are fashioned. By the end of the poem a multibordered spatiality enfolds the re-placed centre. The first stanza pinpoints the location of the action at the cliffs overlooking the sea and as the poem progresses Eyre moves from the tops of the cliffs down to the water's edge. This departure from high to low also operates in the construction of the architectural metaphor of the castle walls/cliffs, behind which beauty exists. Maiden Bight is decorated with several spiritual symbols. In this first stanza she is adorned with bells: 'Surf-bunches of your breast afloat in bells' (270). The ornate vision of waves seen as bunches of flowers is accompanied by an interconnected complex of sound, the important elements of which I have rendered in bold and italics:

> Old cranky **carillons creak** skyward, duly hover.
> And you **murmur** as a flight of **syllables**
> The résumé, steep and **voluble**, of **the gulls**. (270)

The 'carillons' – an instrument made of multiple bells, often housed in a church tower – is personified as cranky, hovering, like a squawking gull. The 'murmur' of the sea is itself described as a 'flight of syllables': the sounds of the sea and the gulls intermingle to produce a nimble harmony that infuses the space between the cliffs, high, and the sea, low.

The second stanza delineates a romantic domain. Eyre encounters the personified characters of the moon and sun, figures engaged in a daily-repeated love-triangle with the sea. Failing in his advances, the stanza ends with the sun unable to overcome the 'castle walls' of the sea. Instead, the sun, 'at sunset rolls in his blood under the gulls' (270). Here the gulls are a barrier, overhead, that encircles the action. The third stanza focuses on Eyre's descent from the tops of the cliffs down to the lower level of the water's edge. Again, the gulls form an overhead cover to the action occurring below. After reaching the sea, Eyre, the 'lovesick fool', experiences the 'brackish lips' of the seawater and his resolve is shaken: 'my honour reels' (270). The gull refrain has morphed into 'cynical halloos' that speak for Eyre's feelings of doubt. The fourth stanza begins by continuing to explore ideas of Maiden Bight's 'castle' and a glimpsed sighting of 'beauty'. Despite his failure to attain gratification – 'hardly an actual kiss' (270) – the gulls accompany Eyre's supplications: 'but could the whitest souls / Absorb these vespers, counterpoint of gulls' (271). Eyre's 'vespers' – an evening prayer – restate the religious atmospherics of this scene, but more importantly they form part of a woven counterpoint relationship with the gulls. Whether the explorers' prayers are private thoughts or voiced utterances, they are drawn out and into sonic partnership with the gulls and break down the interior/exterior binary that 'Eyre All Alone' dramatizes.

The final stanza is the spiritual climax of the episode at the sea. Eyre describes his costume: he is 'unwashed, in a corona of rotten clothing' (271), evoking the image of the eremite emerging from the desert, a common motif within Christian mythology that again locates 'Eyre All Alone' within that desert tradition. Contrasting with the stereotypical monochromatics of the desert, a fusion of colour and sound form a signal moment of epiphany for Eyre:

> Blue is the Sound, form, essence out of nothing
> Blue is Today harnessed, nodding at my heels
> Blue is the grave pure language of the gulls. (271)

Blue dominates the final lines of the poem. The colour of the ocean, blue is mobilized as both the goal of Eyre's journey, 'Blue is the Sound', and the abstract statement of visionary exaltation, the 'essence out of nothing'. Ashcroft argues that 'blue is the colour of the infinite in Webb's poetry' (152), while Excell suggests the three lines of blue are 'a summation, in direct and unequivocal terms, of what Eyre has learnt on the seashore' (91). Reconfiguring these strands of thought, I emphasize the final line of the stanza, where Webb links the infinite Blue with the 'grave pure language of the gulls'. The spatial and spiritual assemblage formed by the key words – Sound, form, essence and Today – is enfolded within the refrain. Discussing Deleuze and Guattari's refrain, Jacob Kreutzfeldt argues that it works 'in close dialogue with the ethological concept of "ritual" and "ritualisation"' (2012, 64). Webb's refrains are ritualistic and rhythmic in character, a point first evident in the 'walk walk' stanza and later reformulated in the refrain 'the gulls'. The ritualistic refrain creates a rhythmic structure of transcendence located not in the centre but on the border of the continent. This space of experiential abstraction is, for Webb, both a Modernist spatio-temporality and a deeply personal religious 'state' that strikes a chord with Pater's theorization of the sonic.

The remaining poems in the series only briefly resound the transcendent timbre of 'The Sea', in a way mimicking Eyre's departing footsteps as he 'walk walk[s]' away from the resonance of the centre on the border. Eyre's repeated questions to Wylie in the 10th poem 'Banksia' – 'can you hear the Sound' (272) – a line transformed by the conclusion of the poem into 'I hear the Sound' (273) – suggest an end to the state of fear and paranoia in 'April 29th'. Eyre is beginning to listen to his soundscape. Here Webb again plays on the literal and spiritual meaning of 'sound', but the lack of any correlation in the landscape – except, perhaps, the 'large agnostic ribaldries of an ocean' (272) – recalls the silence of the wilderness in 'From the Centre'. In creating both a soundscape of horror and a territory of epiphany through the refrain, the radical re-location of Webb's sound-immersed centre to the littoral border strikes a distinct harmony at the meeting of Modernist and Australian geoimaginings.

The Fractured Centre: *Aria for Edward John Eyre*

Composed 11 years after 'Eyre All Alone', there are as many similarities as there are differences between Webb and Lumsdaine's visions of Eyre's journey. In *Aria for Edward John Eyre*, Lumsdaine trains his attention on rearranging Eyre's words from the *Journal* to produce a hope-drained and fragmented narrative. In this sense *Aria* reflects the title 'Eyre All Alone' perhaps more closely than Webb's series of poems do: while Webb reimagines the whole journey, from Albany to King Georges Sound (he does omit parts), Lumsdaine focuses on the events leading up to the murder of Eyre's overseer Baxter. The work is dominated by Eyre's experience of isolation. Lumsdaine's treatment of the *Journal* meditates on desolation, fear, repetition, sand, flies and thirst. The continental landscape Eyre traverses is a wilderness, and neither the mythical inland sea or any space of transcendence are in evidence. Lumsdaine's Eyre exists in a profoundly fragmented territory, a soundscape stratified by the repeating lyrical refrains sounded by the narrators and the soprano.

Scored for soprano and double bass soloists, two narrators, three flutes, three clarinet/bass clarinets, French horn, trumpet, trombone, two percussionists, tape and two tape/volume operators, Lumsdaine's *Aria* is one of the most accomplished and underappreciated compositions to emerge in the post-war mythopoeic period. Locating it more exclusively in its musical field, *Aria* is also a fine example of 1970s era electro-acoustic experimentation. The work was commissioned by the BBC and written for soprano Jane Manning, double bassist Barry Guy and the London Sinfonietta, with its premier in 1973. Owing to the unusual nature of its orchestration and staging requirements, performance of the work has been very rare, although two recordings are in existence, by the Seymour Group and Gemini.[1]

The sonic character of *Aria* is shaped by and reflects Lumsdaine's masterful integration of a wide array of compositional techniques. These include, at a structural level, *Aria*'s foundation on the 'Gemini matrix' and the treatment of this content through small- and large-scale canonic structures (a method of imitation where ideas and material are repeated, inverted or elongated).[2] The soloistic roles of soprano and double bass are also notable, both for their sustained use of extended techniques and the utilization of varying degrees of improvisation in different sections. The sonic range of *Aria* is expanded by the integration of multiple pre-recorded tape tracks manipulated by two tape operators who control the tape material and its volume. Specially positioned speakers also surround the audience, a diagram of which is included in the score. *Aria*'s use of technology and its relationship to European Modernist composition offer other space-related strands of discussion that this work will not take up.

Couched in this soundscape, *Aria*'s text, the foundation of its depiction of the centre, is presented by the two narrators and the soprano. Despite my central concern with the text, I do not want to separate text and music into exclusive groups and will often make references to musical aspects of the work when such comments will clarify the accumulation of textual momentum and meaning. A key moment of this type of discussion is at the climax of the work. Text and music are intertwined across the complete terrain of *Aria*, and while the music carries or houses the text, without the text there would be no way to locate *Aria* in the mythic cartography of explorer-desert-wilderness.

The distinctive configuration of space in *Aria* aligns it with a branch of both Australian mythic production – Hassall's 'series of epic fragments' (395) – and modernism in art music, which according to Botstein 'demanded the shattering of expectations, conventions, categories, boundaries and limits' (1980, 869). A more radical theorization on fragmentation is offered by Derrida, whose statement describing the extreme isolation of the self – 'There is no world, there are only islands' (2011, 9) – resonates with Lumsdaine's Eyre in his journey through the centre. The fissured nature of Eyre's experience is evident in the gradual breakdown of his forward momentum through the desert, a defining aspect of the *Journals* that is emphasized by Lumsdaine's editing and setting or orchestration of the text. The re-arrangement of the *Journal* material entailed cutting words in sentences – or whole chunks of text – and changing the order of events. A document of approximately 1500 words is dispersed across the soprano and the narrators, and there is a number of ways the material is delivered, and recycled, by the three voices. The resistance to forward progression created by these manipulations is also supported by the medium of the work. Music is an art form in which temporality is a defining parameter and the tension between the forward motion of sound and the fractured and repetitious nature of Eyre's *Journal* casts the familiar mythic explorer narrative in a new light. The voicing of the many difficulties of the journey by the narrators and the soprano splinters Eyre's subjectivity and maps the complexity of the wilderness landscape.

I focus on the text of the soprano at two key moments: the beginning of the work, and at its climax. The centrality of the soprano to the exploration of the desert centre is already apparent in the naming of Lumsdaine's composition as an 'aria', defined by *Oxford Music Online* as 'any closed lyrical piece for solo voice [...] with or without instrumental accompaniment'. The text that is delivered by the soprano at these crucial points offers another optics that reveal the mechanics of fragmentation and interior/exterior construction at work with the narrators. The soprano's delivery of the first text of the work – 'I, I, I, will, wilderness' – semantically interweaves the interiority of the 'I' and the 'will' of the self, with the exteriority of the 'wilderness'. Such a complex of meanings, bound together within the voice of the soprano, launches *Aria* forth into the desert wilderness. As Deleuze and Guattari proclaim, 'One ventures from home on the thread of a tune' (344). Appropriately for Deleuze and Guattari, whose work often theorizes non-linearity and multiplicity, the 'tune' here inaugurates the splitting of Eyre's identity into three (soprano and two narrators). The soprano is a sonic entity very different in melodic, rhythmic and textual character from the narrators. Using this soloistic voice to deliver such an important text complicates and subverts a whole range of configurations that would position the non-melodic voices of the narrators, and the text they deliver, as separate from the abstract/non-texted sound of the rest of the ensemble. While the male-gendered voices of the two narrators represent the different levels of Eyre's interiority, through the conduit of the soprano Eyre's consciousness is located within the sonic spectrum of the instrumental ensemble. Extending the bounds of Eyre's subjectivity in this way recalls Pater's axiom on music and the arts while also broadening the continuum of sonic and textual fragmentation in the work.

'I, I, I, Will, Wilderness'

The opening of *Aria* foregrounds the soprano and the double bass, the two solo 'voices' in the sound-world of the work. Emerging from silence, the double bass bows a drone formed by a D harmonic in the treble clef, while the soprano blends her tone and dynamic with the double bass. At rehearsal letter B (track 2) a transformation is signaled by the shift of the soprano from wordless vocalizing to the repetition of 'I, I, I'. This movement is completed just before letter D (track 2: 2 min 3 sec) when the soprano sings 'I, I, I, will, wilderness'.

Following this introductory section of text from the soprano, the first entry of the two narrators occurs at letter D (track 3). Lumsdaine's reconfiguration of Eyre's *Journals* retains the original journal format, with the narrator beginning each diary section by announcing the date. The narration begins in the midst of the action on 28 January, 'after the toils, anxieties and privations of eight months' of exploration. This entry places the beginning of *Aria* after the failed attempt to cross Lake Eyre in a 'south to north' traversal of the continent. Eyre assures his patrons of the resolve of his party to complete the journey, and their stoic determination in the face of 'every hazard.' The next diary entry, dated 31 January, transforms the tone of Eyre's outlook: 'We […] we are now alone, myself, my overseer, and three native boys.' This pronouncement is repeated again and again once Eyre enters the fragmented centre midway through the work. The third diary entry, 3 March, describes the hardships of travel through the desert terrain, with complaints about the sand and flies, while in the fourth entry, 8 March, Eyre details the detours and misreadings of the landscape produced by the failure of sight. On 10 March, the fifth entry, Eyre turns his attention to the 'grandeur and sublimity' of the landscape, impressions tempered by an overriding sense of monotony: 'Hour after hour passed away, mile after mile was traversed, and yet no change was observable.' The sixth entry, 11 March, shifts scenery, with Eyre recounting the progress along the coast, and the discovery of water. The seventh entry, 12 March, notes the progress of the expedition: 'One hundred and thirty five miles of desert country' had been covered, despite the 'season of the year [being] most unfavourable'. In the eighth and ninth entries, 28 and 30 March, Eyre continues to describe his progress through difficult coastal terrain, his collection of water using a sponge, and the second discovery of a well. As the well is obviously maintained by local Aboriginal people, it is ironic that the arrival here leads to a recitation of a biblical text, from Isaiah, as close to a moment of transcendence as Lumsdaine's Eyre attains throughout his journey. The tenth entry, 27 April, denotes 'the last fearful push, which was to decide our fate'.

The broader trajectory of the work suggests it can be divided into two halves, the first characterized by the difficult advance leading up to the death of Baxter on 29 April, the centre. The second half repeats the earlier hardships of the journey before Baxter's murder in increasingly discontinuous combinations of certain key images and phrases, and apart from the final coda-like conclusion, no new journal material is introduced (for a period of about 18 min of a total 55 min) until Eyre arrives in Albany at the end of the work. Omitting all the incidents between the death of Baxter and the arrival of Eyre and Wylie at Albany – events like the meeting with a whaling vessel or the journey along the seashore – stresses the destabilizing effect of Baxter's death on Eyre. Baxter's death is a central locus, similar to the episode at the cliffs relayed in Webb's poem 'The Sea', from which the rest of the work unwinds.

There are four different 'delivery styles' used by the two narrators in *Aria*, all of which correlate to Eyre's ever-increasing levels of disorientation. The 'unison narrator' – where both narrators deliver the same text in unison – occurs only twice, and are brief moments of almost transcendence. For example, one section of unison narration is a biblical excerpt from Isaiah 41:17-19 (track 8: 1 min 45 sec): 'When the poor and needy seek water, and there is none, and their tongue faileth for thirst.' The doubling of the voices gives this text a greater dynamic presence. It is as if the 'unified' Eyre is reporting a triumph over the wilderness, making a statement that is both a prayer of thanks and a utopian fantasy. 'Dislocated narrator' is the dominant mode of the first half of the work, from the first entry of the narrators through to just before the murder of Baxter.

Narrator One: We,   we were now alone,   myself, my overseer,
Narrator Two: *We*   *were now alone. My*   *myself*

and three native boys.   The bridge was broken down behind us, and we must my
self   *the bridge was broken*

succeed   in reaching King George's Sound,   or perish.
        and   *we*   *must*   *perish*

The text of narrator two is abridged so that it conveys a kind of interior perspective, a private, perhaps psychological undertow of anxiety that exists within but is covered over by the fully realized public thoughts delivered by narrator one, Eyre's public persona.

The 'single narrator' marks Eyre's approach to the centre, the night of 29 April when Baxter is murdered (track 10 up to 1 min 38 sec), and it underscores Eyre's complete isolation in the wilderness. The text is extracted from the original *Journals* without internal editing: 'I found my poor overseer, lying on the ground, weltering in his blood, and in the last agonies of death.' Immediately following this, narrator two re-enters, delivering a text that has no direct relation to that of narrator one. This fourth style of delivery – 'antiphonic narrator' – juxtaposes two different texts. While narrator one is delivering the final pieces of new text, narrator two begins to recycle images from earlier diary entries, the sign of Eyre's move into the space of the centre. Such a *modus operandi* produces word combinations like 'the frightful/*the night*', 'bitterly cold and frosty/*which bit us dreadfully*' and 'intense bodily pain/*hour after hour*', unmasking Eyre's fear and amplifying the psychological horror of his situation (see track 10: 1 min 38 sec):

Narrator One: The frightful, the appalling truth now burst upon me,   that I was alone
Narrator Two: *The night   was   cold   and*

in the desert.   At the dead hour of night, in the wildest and most inhospitable
         the wind   blowing   hard

wastes of Australia,   with the fierce wind raging in unison with the scene of
         from the southwest

violence before me,   I was left with a single native. Three days had passed
   whilst scud and nimbus   were passing rapidly before the moon

since we left the last water,   and it was doubtful when we might find any
                cold   lakes   and   rivers

more.   Six hundred miles of country had to be traversed before I could hope to
      blowing hard   from the southwest   white sand
obtain the slightest aid or assistance,   whilst not a
                    it floated on the surface of the water covering

single drop of water or an ounce of flour had been left by the murderers.
our faces hair   eyes   and ears.   Pure white   scud and nimbus,

With an aching heart I passed this dreadful night. Every moment appeared to
the wind was cold Blowing *among the sandhills.* From massive

be protracted to an hour, and it seemed as if daylight would never appear.
battlements, stretching out before us in *lofty unbroken outline*

About midnight the wind ceased, and the weather became bitterly cold and frosty.
blowing swarms of large horseflies which bit us dreadfully

To mental anguish was now added intense bodily pain. Ages can
Hour after Hour, mile after mile,

never efface the horrors of this single night. A lifetime was crowded into
these vast plains were singular and deceptive

those few short hours.
threading in and out among the many.

The phrase 'a lifetime was crowded into those few short hours', almost exactly half way through the work, is a key to the map of Lumsdaine's centre. Resembling a nightmare phantasmagoria, this landscape is a spiralling web of interconnected desert images and sounds that are augmented, monstrous manifestations of selected images and sounds from the first half of the work. Through the fragmented centre of *Aria* this broken 'antiphonic narrator' delivery moves along a continuum between antiphony, a kind of disjointed and random call and response pattern, and polyphony, where both narrators are delivering different texts simultaneously. While narrator one is still conveying a coherent narrative, the discontinuous text of narrator two is pushed into the background, and as the 'antiphonic' delivery continues the syntactical sense of the text starts to break down, leaving a blend of forward momentum and fragmentation. The stasis that results from this combination is one of the unlikely achievements of a work about a colonial journey: the desire of the explorer for forward movement, new discovery and clarity of vision is repelled.

As the second half of *Aria* unfolds textual and musical materials are reanimated and recycled. The repetition of phrases stymies the diachronic footfall of The Explorer through space and the idealized linear narratives of history, where events precede one after the other. Instead, in *Aria* events and experiences reappear and, as the work 'moves forward', are broken apart and recombined into increasingly polymorphic images. The musical resources that comprise the sonic 'labyrinth' in the second half unfold according to complex canon forms, with reconfigured tone row matrix material from the first half. Labyrinth, the word used by Lumsdaine in the score to describe a range of aspects of *Aria*, from the process of tone row treatment to the name of the tape material (it also positions his work alongside the European avant-garde, Luciano Berio's *Laborintus II*, (1965) being the most obvious example). These compositional strategies are impossible to fully recognise on a first listening to *Aria*, an opacity consistent with the characteristic difficulty of Modernist works in general.

Commenting on the shaping of Eyre's journal text into the material we hear in *Aria*, Andrew Schultz suggests Lumsdaine's 'technique of subverting literal aspects of the text in favour of its underlying sense inevitably gives more power to the work than a direct 'word-by-word' setting could have done' (1991, 97). Such a setting diverts 'attention from the mundane', instead focusing 'on the spiritual quality of a quest in the wilderness' (97). Schultz argues that 'where the original text is obsessed with the passing of time (each date recorded like another nail in a coffin) Lumsdaine's score takes the listener into a world of remarkable stasis in which time seems irrelevant' (97–98). Elliptically circling back onto itself, *Aria*'s moebius-strip text foils the explorer's masterful line of sight by sounding a desert characterized by refraction and repetition. Like Webb's 'April 29th', the imagined sound of *Aria* produces a soundscape of introspection and paranoia.

The Soprano: Here! Here!

Although her text follows a different trajectory, the disjointed landscape articulated by the various forms of narrator delivery style is augmented by the work of the soprano. Singing simultaneously with the narrator, the soprano's layer of meaning and sound heighten the scattered state of Eyre's consciousness. The following is a collation of the soprano's text from the first half of *Aria*:

> Myself, my overseer, and three native boys, we were now, we were now alone, we were now alone. We were afflicted, we turned, we saw, we kept moving, we felt cooled and refreshed, we were fortunate, we were blessed, blessed, we were forced, forced, we progressed, we looking anxiously, we, we have now entered. I, I, I will open, I will make, will, wilderness.

The soprano text is drawn from a combination of material first heard in the 'we were now alone' journal entry on 31 January, as well as incorporating other text material from throughout *Aria*. Lumsdaine's treatment of the soprano's melodic material concentrates on pitch and intervallic movement, which in combination with the long duration over which the text is delivered (16 min of the work, between track 5: 0 min 40 sec and Track 9: 0 min 23 sec) makes it difficult for the listener to apprehend the content of what is sung. Specific events are deleted, with only descriptions of how Eyre and his party – 'we' is the most common word sung by the soprano – dealt with the journey. While a kind of forward momentum is provided by the narration, the soprano text, by simultaneously looping back, performs a ghostly haunting of the present by the past. Taken together, the two narrators and the soprano create a multilayered text that expands the time and space of the journey beyond a simple chronological progression, instead weaving a dense fabric of past/present, inside/outside, official/private and male/female.

The gateway to the complex spatio-temporality opened by the narrators and the soprano – the road leading directly to the fragmented centre of *Aria* – spans bars 45–277 (Beginning at track 10: 3 min 4 sec). Here the text of the soprano mirrors the 'antiphonic' delivery style of the two narrators, a patterning also matched by the increasing intensity and complexity of the instrumental and tape elements. In performance of *Aria* the textual content for the narrators is determined by the random choice of cards that hold short phrases of text: the disintegration of narrative sense created by this element of indeterminacy is echoed by the soprano text, the final section of which is transcribed below. The two narrators revert back to pre-scored text (beginning at track 13) and alternate between antiphony and unison styles of delivery. The tone of voice of the narrators also increases in urgency and volume to match the rest of the ensemble. While the narrators deliver short fragmented phrases, the soprano uses an even more disjointed syntax, characterized by the repetition of key words like 'blowing', 'I', 'blessed' and 'crying'. The use of anaphora – 'I will' – gives the text a liturgical tone, again linking back to the biblical origins of the desert as wilderness. The soprano text is as follows:

> I will open deep wells of crying, master, master, come here, hour after hour, mile after mile, running towards me and crying, we were now alone in the desert, at the dead hour of night, cold, scud and nimbus blowing before the moon, no change, blowing from massive battlements stretching out before us in lofty unbroken outline, blowing from deserts, blowing from the wilderness, I, I, I, will hear them, I, I, will not forsake them, running towards me and crying, Blessed, blessed by lakes, blessed by deserts, blessed by toils, anxieties privations, blessed, blessed

by honour duty, blessed by remote possibilities, blessed by fatigues difficulties, losses, blessed by risk and danger, yet he would willingly remain with me to the last, running towards me and crying, crying, crying, come, come here! here! here!

The climax of this section, and the whole work, is marked by the soprano's delivery of the word 'here' (track 14: 1 min 10 sec). With the score indication 'massive, as loud as possible', the soprano rises to the top of the ensemble texture with a high C sharp, the highest note sung in the work, before descending back down onto a G sharp. Moving away from the moment of 'here', the rhythmic and textural density of the ensemble follows a slowly unfolding downward trajectory, leading towards the end of the work, where the arrival of Eyre and Wylie at King George's Sound is narrated.

Aria's summit is a unique meeting of both ends of the desert continuum. The explanation of this contradiction lies with the origin of the soprano's text: 'Running towards me and crying, crying, crying, come, come here! here! here!' This text was uttered by Wylie, when he calls out to Eyre immediately after Baxter's murder: 'Oh master, oh master, come here.' Re-voiced by the soprano amidst the maelstrom of the ensemble, this is the ultimate statement of Eyre's abandonment in the wilderness centre, the refrain of *Aria* as fragmented centre. The moment stages the rupturing of the binary split between the otherness and exteriority of the wilderness image and the presence and interiority of visionary transcendence. Articulating such a pivotal landscape with the soprano also extends Eyre's subjectivity beyond a neatly demarcated self/other. With the narrators and the soprano articulating a statement of both isolation and presence in the wilderness, the soprano makes the defining assertion of these tensions, while also adding a female sonic signification to the male voices of the narrators.

Eyre's eventual arrival at King George's Sound provides a tidy end to the journey and the *Aria*, but the search for the mythical centre of the continent notated by Lumsdaine is one governed by labyrinthine repetition, disorientation and faulty forward momentum. Lumsdaine depicts an explorer immobilized in a space of utter desolation, bogged down under a cascade of fears that circle and taunt, dividing him against himself. This experience contrasts with Webb's Eyre, who is more confident and mobile, and the poem maps a larger variety of experience. But despite their profound differences, Lumsdaine's *Aria* is like Webb's 'Eyre All Alone' in its relocation of the centre. The paranoia of Webb's depiction of Baxter's murder, with its soundscape of horror, accompanies Lumsdaine's centre. Similarly, repetition of the refrain of 'the gulls', Webb's transcendent space of the centre on the border, is shared by Lumsdaine's method of editing the text and accentuating key words through the soprano. Drawing on well-established tropes – visual dominance, Indigenous absence and the centre as fetishistic focus – these two Modernist nationalist myths of the centre are nevertheless unique soundings of a key Australian geoimaginary.

Chapter Two

MIDNIGHT OIL: SOUNDING AUSTRALIAN ROCK AROUND THE BICENTENARY

Fifteen years after David Lumsdaine's *Aria* – and twenty-five years after Francis Webb's 'Eyre All Alone' – Midnight Oil captured the Australian public imagination by reimagining the centre as 'The Dead Heart'. The search for the centre became a journey into the monumental red expanse of Uluru – Indigenous country – charged with political urgency. Midnight Oil sounded the centre as a space becoming monumental. From the images of Uluru in their film clip for 'The Dead Heart' to their performance on the international stage of the Sydney Olympics closing ceremony, the band injected the national interior with the performative, explosive, multimedia energy of rock music, one of the defining mediums of twentieth-century popular culture. Mapped by Midnight Oil, the centre is more public, more political, more popular, more iconic and more inclusive.

Midnight Oil sit on the fulcrum of the Australian geo-becoming, between the post-war Modernist and nationalist oriented search for the centre, and the post-*Mabo*, postcolonial reorientation of that journey into the continental interior carried out by Alex Miller and later fully realized by Alexis Wright in *Carpentaria* in the 2000s. Over a career spanning the late 1970s to the present, The Oil's – like no other rock group in Australian popular music – worked to highlight Australian Indigenous people and, from an environmental perspective, to emphasize the value of Australian place. Following the band's movement from origins to authenticity, in this chapter we navigate from the continental coastline to the centre. In plotting this course, I examine three key moments and musical artefacts: starting with a discussion of Oz rock and the authenticity associated with that genre, I track the band through their groundbreaking 1986 Blackfella/Whitefella tour of remote Northern Territory and Western Australia, discuss the international success of the 1987 album *Diesel and Dust* and analyse the film clip for the song 'The Dead Heart' from that album. The Sydney Olympic Games closing ceremony performance, where the band made a powerful statement of postcolonial reconciliation that was broadcast internationally, closes the chapter.

Midnight Oil's focus on Australian Indigenous people and the environment, and their wider critique of globalized modernity and capitalistic ideology is imbricated within this series of events. Despite their position within that economic system – the band were signed with Columbia Records and Sony Records at different stages of their career, in addition to starting their own Powderworks label to release their early material – Midnight Oil often subverted the control of business, with numerous charity concerts and deals where recording royalties went straight to charity. For example, money from sales of the 1985 'Species Deceases' EP went into a trust to fund 'peace and disarmament activities' (Steggels 1992, 142) and the proceeds of 'The Dead Heart' single sales were directed back to the Indigenous community who they had worked with in the production of the film clip.

Two key concerns, with place and authenticity, are integral to the work of the band in forming an influential and valuable Australian continental geoimaginary. From the Northern Beaches of Sydney to the centre of the continent at Uluru and the 'international stage' of the Olympic closing ceremony, Midnight Oil's projection of Australian space was linked to their ethical and artistic authenticity. Committed to defending local, national and global landscapes from corporate and governmental injustice, this legitimacy runs like a spine through the career of the band. Tracing the authenticity inherent to Oz rock alongside the band's multifaceted representations of place – their multimedia search for the centre – I argue that Midnight Oil should be regarded as invaluable precursors of and contributors to the wider transformations of the Australian continental geoimaginary that continued to take place and deepen in the 1990s and 2000s. Considering the spatial and sonorous work of the band both from a micro perspective – within a single song – and from the career perspective – across the span of three pivotal events – Midnight Oil perform a musico-activist 'line of flight' out of the exclusionary and exploitative attitudes towards Indigenous people and the environment essential to colonial visions of the centre. While not wholly escaping the old structures of meaning associated with the search for the centre (as played out in Webb and Lumsdaine), Midnight Oil's work was a significant coming of age gesture, a step towards Australian postcolonial regeneration.

The historical and political terrain that surrounds Midnight Oil is characterized by a number of key events. Foremost among these was the outpouring of nationalist sentiment triggered by the 1988 Bicentenary celebrations, closely followed by the epoch-shifting claim to the Australian landscape signaled by the *Mabo* decision in 1992; four years later came the Wik decision, another significant moment in the land rights debate that prompted the Howard government to respond with the Ten Point Plan. The late 1990s saw a movement towards, and against, an apology, directly to the Indigenous 'Stolen Generations', and more generally for the history of government sanctioned abuse of Aboriginal people. Midnight Oil's performance at the 2000 Olympic closing ceremony was an exclamation mark within that ongoing discourse. Finally, the second half of Midnight Oil's career also aligns with the upheaval of 'The History Wars'. These events constitute a rugged landscape of competing and often opposed historical debates and political currents.

Working within this political and cultural context, Midnight Oil foregrounded the need for postcolonial reckoning. The band argued for the value of conserving the environment and questioned the ideology and policy of late capitalism and global military alliances. But despite this achievement, Midnight Oil did partially fall back into the familiar colonial mode of fetishising the centre and erasing the presence of Indigenous people, as my analysis of 'The Dead Heart' shows. Such a failure to match their activist and charity work reflects the historical position of the band, in the midst of the nationalist pride leading up to the 1988 Bicentenary, as well as the populist nature of the mediums in which they operated.

Origins in Rock

Midnight Oil's concern with place has always been prominent. The Oils (as they are known by their fans), based in Sydney throughout their career, were comprised of singer Peter Garrett, guitarists Jim Moginie and Martin Rotsey, drummer Rob Hirst and bassist Bones Hillman. Two other bassists also played in the band, Andrew James (1976–80) and Peter 'Giffo' Gifford (1980–87). Rob Hirst and Jim Moginie were the principle songwriters, with Garrett also often credited, and less frequently, the other members. The band produced 10 albums, but with the release of their fourth album *10, 9, 8, 7, 6, 5, 4, 3, 2, 1* (1982) the group started to reach a national and international audience. The album peaked at No. 3 on the Australian music charts and remained there for 171 weeks. Although earlier songs on their first three albums – *Midnight Oil* (1978), *Head Injuries* (1979) *Place Without a Postcard* (1981) – had expressed some anti-American and activist sentiments, *10–1* forcefully distilled such opinions in songs like 'Power and the Passion', 'U.S Forces' and 'Short Memory'. *Diesel and Dust* (1987) and its follow-up *Blue Sky Mining* (1990) saw the band reach an international audience through the strength of the 'Beds are Burning' single and extensive tours through North America and Europe.

The band's activism had not always been a central concern, but by the early 1980s Midnight Oil had begun to engage in public debates over nuclear disarmament and the environment in more ways than simply their lyrics and the 'rants' delivered by Garrett between songs at their gigs. While drummer Rob Hirst was elected co-spokesman, able to deliver the message and opinions of Midnight Oil to the media, it was Garrett who was most engaged in non-musical activism. In 1984 he ran in the federal election for the Nuclear Disarmament Party, as shown in the documentary *Midnight Oil: 1984* (2018, dir. Ray Argall). Garrett was the president of the Australian Conservation Foundation from 1989 to 1993 and 1998 to 2002 and between 1993 and 1998 was on the International Board of Greenpeace. After Midnight Oil ceased their regular musical activities in 2002, Garrett joined the Australian Labor Party and was elected in the federal seat of Kingsford Smith, standing down in 2013. Midnight Oil as 'socially conscious band' and the political career of Garrett are a strong non-musical demonstration of the ideals that underscored their creative output and drove their agenda for Australian social and political change.

The 'music scene' where Midnight Oil began their career – and its defining genre, Oz rock – grounds the emphasis on place that was later manifest in the activist work and musical representation of the band. The formative mythology of the band is intimately connected to a specific locale – Sydney, or even more precisely, the Antler Hotel in Narrabeen. The journey of The Oils from Sydney pub performances to the international stage of the Olympic closing ceremony is a familiar narrative of success. Like their contemporaries INXS (both groups were at one time 'stable mates' under the management of Gary Morris), Midnight Oil rehearsed a version of the local-to-global path trodden by many Australian bands, as much a product of British and American cultural and economic dominance as it was simply a need to expand the band's audience. The group in many ways refused to blindly follow this path towards international fame and fortune, a stance exemplified by the band turning down a performance at the Grammys so that Peter Garrett could honour his commitment to help with MC duties at the 1988 'Long March for Justice' rally.

While this local/global trajectory fits the long-term perspective of the band, it does not listen to the *sound* of Midnight Oil, or offer much in terms of specific historical, political or musical context. Looking and listening closely to The Oils reveals a paradox: how did such a 'political band' align with Oz rock, a genre associated with hyper masculinity and musical simplicity? Did Midnight Oil fit into this image at all, despite their emergence during the golden age of the genre? The most direct approach to this tangle of questions is to consider the fundamental importance of authenticity in rock music. Authenticity – genuineness, originality, legitimacy and artistic credibility – is the conceptual cornerstone of the cultural productions of popular music in the post-war era. Research into the politics of identity and representation, place, and nation has highlighted the complex and compromised relationship between authenticity and rock (Negus 1992; Whiteley 1997; Middleton 2006; Frith 2007). Furthermore, authenticity yokes rock music, specifically Oz rock, supposedly the first 'authentically Australian' popular music genre, to the centre. Undertaking their own search for the centre, Midnight Oil's exploration of this overdetermined landscape of mythic authenticity also accounted for the anxiety that permeated the non-Indigenous preoccupation with that landscape.

Rock music journalist Mark Mordue argues Midnight Oil occupied 'a critical and central position as the most widely heard radical voice for young people in Australia' (Mordue quoted in McMillan 1988, 7). This status can be attributed to the range of events that predate the formative years of key personnel in the band, including the Vietnam War, the rise and fall of the Whitlam government and the influence of feminist and Indigenous rights movements (Steggels 1992, 140). The socio-economic backgrounds of the band members – several had completed university degrees in law, arts and science – also helps to contextualize the political convictions of The Oils. Music journalist John O'Donnell sums up the integral tension between music and politics within the perception of the band: 'During the Eighties, possibly no popular artist working in any medium anywhere in the world blurred the lines between entertainment and "message" as much as Midnight Oil' (n.p.). The combination of 'entertainment' and 'message' puts Midnight Oil at odds with the majority of the other foundational practitioners of Oz rock – Cold Chisel, Men at Work, Rose Tattoo, Australian Crawl and The Angels – operating in the late 1970s and early 1980s.

Like O'Donnell and Steggels, Shane Homan argues 'an inclusionary political stance' that 'defied the borders of the Oz rock genre' (2003, 26–27) was the essential difference between Midnight Oil and their contemporaries. While the level of political rhetoric embedded in the music and performance of Midnight Oil was far different to that of, for example, Cold Chisel, a band that epitomized the golden age of Oz rock between 1975 and 1985, Homan argues that The Oils nevertheless shared with these contemporaries 'most of the fundamental Oz rock conventions'. These conventions primarily referred to 'fierce vocals with powerful drumming and raw, thoughtful guitar' (26). With each new album Midnight Oil evolved a nuanced style of rock while still remaining within the conventions outlined by Homan.

Homan argues that the gulf separating The Oil's from most other Oz rock acts was defined by 'approach to venue management [...] recording arrangements [...] and understandings of the 'pub rock apprenticeship' (diversifying tour schedules to include Aboriginal populations and various benefit concerts)' (26). These factors, particularly the way the band refused to compromise with booking agents and venues, linked Midnight Oil's legendary live performance with uncompromising attitudes to the music industry. Further distancing the band from Oz rock, Jon Stratton argues Midnight Oil was 'more of an Alternative Rock band than an Oz rock band, although The Oils clearly wanted to reach out politically to that suburban audience' (2006, 250). Stratton's mention of alternative rock raises another question mark about how to categorize Midnight Oil. It is not important – or possible – to get a definitive answer to whether or not The Oils were an Oz rock band, but their aspiration to move outside the spatial and ideological domain of that genre provides a set of contextual and generic coordinates that compliment the larger renovations of space they perform.

Steggels offers punk, a music and style movement that emerged in the UK and United States in the late 1970s, as an answer to the difficulty of placing the political energy of Midnight Oil. Drawing on Greil Marcus, Steggels discusses how British punk band The Clash 'rationalised the punk (anti) ideology by harnessing its anger and redirecting the attack back towards the establishment' (140). Instead of making blunt and attention-grabbing gestures based in adolescent violence and obscenity, the method of bands like The Sex Pistols, The Clash made eloquent social critique through the song/film clip/image assemblage. Relating his discussion back to The Oils, Steggels argues the 'cultural project of Midnight Oil is similar to [The Clash] in that they embrace the anger generated in the moment of punk and its iconoclastic (anti) stance'. Instead of following the path of highly political but largely underground genres like hardcore, they 'chose to remain within the world which it rejects in order to challenge the social establishment from within' (140). The social critique element central to punk in turn links with the broad category of protest music. While there are similarities between the anti-government message of Midnight Oil and an artist such as Bob Dylan, Dylan's choice of song form, with its roots in various genres of folk and the blues, differs quite radically from the vast majority of Midnight Oil songs.

Midnight Oil's links to the internationally mobile movement of punk or protest music position the band in a wider musical context, but the close association between the band and particular Sydney pubs, such as the Royal Antler Hotel in Narrabeen, reveals the grass-roots level of locality on which their early claims to authenticity are based. Commenting on the origins of the band and how their attitude towards music making and touring took shape, Rob Hirst says,

> I think it was born back at the Antler [...] where it was 110 degrees inside, where you had two thousand people with their shirts off and

beer getting thrown around. In this volatile environment what you had to do was deliver at all costs. The people that remember those shows remember them as being a band that played the songs three times faster than on record, that played them very savagely, that smashed up stages if they were inadequate, that yelled at members of the audience if they were abusive.

So having geographically removed ourselves from the pubs of Australia, we decided that we didn't need to be constrained to the three chords. It's an area we loved, but we could go further than that, we could explore and we needed to for our own sanity. (Hirst in O'Donnell n.p.)

In line with most commentary, Hirst figures the pub as the birthplace of both Oz rock and Midnight Oil, and the move out of that environment is seen as a necessary part of the band's musical development. While Hirst directly refers to his groups' refusal to perform on the established pub circuit because of the exploitative practices of promoters and lack of control over performance conditions, his comment also foreshadows the Blackfella/Whitefella tour, the genesis of the pivotal *Diesel and Dust* album. This trajectory out of the local and towards the national and international is synchronized to both the artistic development of the band and the emergence and foregrounding of a political consciousness. Starting the search for the centre of the continent, Midnight Oil was leaving Oz rock behind.

Looking closely at the cultural function of Oz rock reveals more of the political impetus behind Midnight Oil's eventual departure from the genre. As the name implies, Oz rock has often been described as a national music (Homan 2003; Stratton 2006). Discussing Oz rock as a national genre, Homan suggests that 'similar to the way that the term Britpop circulated within the British music industry and media in the 1990s, Oz rock codified a vernacular nationalism that extended beyond textual conventions' (30). As a localized source of national identity, Oz rock was, according to Stratton, used as a tool for nation building, and he figures the newly national reach of ABC television, and the start of the Australian Film Commission, as pivotal to the development and national dissemination of pop and rock music in the 1970s. This utility was 'something fostered deliberately by governments in respect of the Australian film industry but which happened more organically in Australian popular music' (Stratton 2006, 243).

Classic songs of this early 1980s 'nation building' imperative include 'Land Down Under' by Men at Work, 'Great Southern Land' by Icehouse and 'Sounds of Summer' by GANGgajang. 'Solid Rock' by Goanna is a more postcolonially aware song than most of its contemporaries, with stronger political affinities to Midnight Oil's music. Discussing Icehouse and the contemporary political timeframe of its release, Nicholas Birns states,

> The initial release of 'Great Southern Land' can be read as part of a pre-*Mabo* moment that might be said to comprise Thomas Keneally's novel *The Chant of Jimmie Blacksmith* (1972), or a film such as Peter Weir's *The Last Wave* (1977), in which Indigenous presence was noticeable, yet the emphasis was overwhelmingly on the discovery of Anglo-Celtic Australia. (2013, 295)

The 'pre-*Mabo* moment' of 'Great Southern Land' is in part shared by Midnight Oil songs like 'Beds Are Burning' and 'The Dead Heart', although these songs make a more complex engagement with land politics and race. In a pithy appellation to his discussion of the pre-*Mabo* moment, Birns adds, 'Of course, as a phrase "pre-*Mabo*" can of course mean "premonitory of *Mabo*" or "at a stage before *Mabo*".' It is in this premonitory mode, as discussed by Jacques Attali – 'music is prophetic and [...] social organization echoes it' (5) – that many of the sentiments of Midnight Oil's pre-*Mabo* career operate.

Despite the failings of their search for the centre, Midnight Oil's place in the pre- and post-*Mabo* national becoming resonates with Josh Kun's analysis of how popular music has the potential to work against exclusionary conceptions of the nation. 'While it may take root in national formations, impact national audiences, and impact the creation of national ideas and politics, [popular] music is always from somewhere else and is always en route to somewhere else' (20). Rather than redrawing national borders, as Kun's analysis of postnational formations in the United States suggests, Midnight Oil remaps previously ignored or exploited landscapes *within* the continent. The band attempted to amplify both the voices and traditions of Indigenous people, and the presence of issues that confound the progress of industrialized modernity. Bill Ashcroft's concept of 'transnation' – 'the fluid, migrating outside of the state that begins within the nation' (2011, 19) – describes this kind of line of flight. Ashcroft explains,

> The transnation occupies the space we might refer to as the 'nation,' distinct from the political structure of the state, which interpellates subjects as citizens. These subjects may indeed identify themselves as national, particularly in sport and war, but the transnation describes the excess of subject positions swirling within, around and beyond the state. (19)

Ashcroft's theorization of space redirects the imperative of Kun's postnation, although the two concepts are particularly concerned with the movements of unrecognized people and ideas in relation to the hegemonic nation state. In maintaining a focus on Australia, and a position for these subjects and spaces within and not solely in excess of the nation, Ashcroft's transnation moves Kun's valuable theorization of a popular music-centred spatiality closer to my analysis of Midnight Oil.

This outline of historical and political milieu sets the scene for the first part of my discussion of the three key works and moments that dominate Midnight Oil's revisionist map of the continent. Despite the deeply interconnected nature of these moments – for example, the song Midnight Oil performed at the Olympics, 'Beds Are Burning', was first realized on *Diesel and Dust*, an album that was inspired by the 'Blackfella/Whitefella' tour – I discuss them in chronological order because it enables me to comment on the relationship of each of the moments to its surrounding context. It also allows me to gauge the development of the band's aura of authenticity and thus plot the coordinates of their journey from Oz rock origins to transnational recognitions.

The Blackfella/Whitefella Tour

Undertaken in July 1986, the Blackfella/Whitefella tour encompassed performances throughout the remote regions of Northern Territory and Western Australia. Although it was not the first time the band had travelled to the Northern Territory – they had performed once before in Numbulwar – the length and breadth of the tour was a sizeable investment of time and energy, and there was no view towards making a profit. The primary aims of the tour were stated in a press release from the Federal Department of Aboriginal Affairs:

> Thousands of people in remote Northern Territory communities will now be able to see, for the first time, live performances by Midnight Oil and the Warumpi band.
>
> But apart from the music, Midnight Oil want the tour to be a bridge-building exercise for Aboriginal and non-Aboriginal Australians. The group has already expressed its wish to help expand community understanding of Aboriginal aspirations. (quoted in McMillan 1988, 9)

The statement is structured so that the entertainment aspect of the tour comes before the other objectives. 'Midnight Oil are a rock group first and political activist second. Entertainment is the medium through which their protest is voiced' (Steggels 1992, 144).

Accompanying The Oils was the acclaimed Aboriginal rock group the Warumpi Band, with George Burarrwanga on lead vocals, Gordon Butcher on drums, Sammy Butcher on guitar and bass and Neil Murray on guitar. Burarrwanga was a Yolngu man from Elcho Island in Arnhem Land, the Butcher brothers were Luritja men from the Western Desert near Alice Springs and Murray was a former schoolteacher, born in Victoria. The Warumpis were the first band to record rock music with Aboriginal language – 'Jailanguru Pakarnu' (Luritja for *Out from Jail*) – and released three albums with singles that included the racial equality anthem 'Blackfella/Whitefella', and 'My Island Home', a song written by Murray after visiting Burarrwanga's hometown of Galiwinki. Indigenous artist Christine Anu later covered 'My Island Home', and her performance of the song was perhaps the centrepiece of the Sydney Olympics closing ceremony.

From a financial perspective, Midnight Oil paid their own way (including numerous tour managers and other support staff) while their tour-mates the Warumpis obtained funding from sources such as the Aboriginal Arts Board. While the symbolism of the Indigenous Warumpi Band and the non-Indigenous Oil's touring through the central deserts and Top End together was significant, the choice of a touring partner was also pragmatic. The Warumpis were immensely popular in many of the towns on the tour schedule, and played a style of music – country rock – much loved by Indigenous audiences.

Andrew McMillan's account of the tour – *Strict Rules* (1988) – relates a unique cartography of central Australia; McMillan traveled with Midnight Oil to every town and community hall or makeshift venue through the six weeks they were on the road (and in the air). The list of the tour locations is an unlikely kind of musical map of central and northern Australia:

> It was the first weekend in July, 1986, and The Oils were about to embark on a tour unlike any ever attempted by a white band; a tour that would see them visiting Aboriginal communities like Mutitjulu, Docker River, Kintore, Pupunya and Yuendumu in the Western Desert, and Maningrida, Galiwinku, Yirrkala, Umbakumba, Numbulwar, Barunga, Wadeye and Nguiu in the subtropical wetlands of the top end. (McMillan 1988, 9)

In addition to this list of places, *Strict Rules* also contains a pictorial map that shows the circuitous route of the tour. Such a looped charting of space literally depicts the resistance to the flows of capital that a tour *not* organized around economic principles, a tour beyond the fringes of the continental east coast, represents. At the same time, this list of Aboriginal communities, mixed with a few mining towns, illustrates the diversity of Indigenous life experience. It is a demystification of the 'desert centre', a real encounter with Aboriginal people living away from the major population centres of the nation.

The success of the Blackfella/Whitefella tour is hard to measure in terms of its artistic and activist influence, but its symbolic value is undeniable. It also led to the production of a number of artefacts: the film clip for 'The Dead Heart' was in part filmed during the first days of the tour, a documentary was produced by ABC television and the band went on to record *Diesel and Dust*, their biggest selling album. In addition to the immediate and ongoing impact of the tour, its timing (1986) in relation to the 1988 Bicentenary and the 1992 *Mabo* land rights decision is important for considering Blackfella/Whitefella in the historical context of Midnight Oil's ongoing involvement with Indigenous Australia. As an act of acknowledgement and a sign of respect towards the sovereignty of Indigenous peoples and spaces – even if only on a level of their right to top-line entertainment – the tour was a precursor of the epoch-shifting events of 1992 and later. The tour also helped to sound a network of Australian places that may well have been ignored in the nationalistic jubilation of the Bicentenary.

Diesel and Dust and 'The Dead Heart'

If Blackfella/Whitefella established Midnight Oil's commitment to the people and places of Indigenous Australia, *Diesel and Dust* was the album where they presented such a map to the nation and the world. The popularity and influence of the album stretches into the present day. The album reached No. 1 on the Australian charts for 6 weeks, as well as No. 19 in the UK, No. 21 in the United States, No. 5 in Sweden and No. 7 in Switzerland. *Rolling Stone* also ranked the album No. 13 in their list of the top 100 best albums of the 1980s. In 2010 *Diesel and Dust* was rated as the No. 1 album in the book the *100 Best Australian Albums* by Creswell, Mathieson and O'Donnell. Triple J radio's 'Hottest 100 Australian Albums of All Time' 'Industry List' (voted by musicians) ranked the album No. 7, while its listeners voted it No. 33 on the equivalent poll. One characteristic description of *Diesel and Dust* is provided by Toby Creswell, who calls it the most 'Australian of their records to date [...] [remarkable] not only for its stories of the desert but for its unique sound' (Creswell 1990, 45). Creswell's claim, that the 'bass-and-drum patterns [...] [reflect] the endless highways and the impossible horizons of the outback' (45), is in keeping with the typically grandiose style favoured by *Rolling Stone*, but it nevertheless conveys how *Diesel and Dust* was considered musically groundbreaking and somehow sonically reflective of the Australian landscape. The highly speculative suggestion that musical sounds correlate to landscapes may be evocative (and good publicity) but it also draws on a tradition initiated by the

European explorers who characterized Australian deserts as featureless voids fenced only by sublime horizons (Ashcroft, McCredden, Devlin-Glass, 2009).

The album cover image used for *Diesel and Dust* resonates both with the wider Midnight Oil discography and, more specifically, the lyrical and visual imagery of 'The Dead Heart' film clip. The cover is one of several images within the Midnight Oil *oeuvre* where the desert is linked to the band. These images are all based around a desert landscape, with emphasis on flat horizons and the two-tone juxtaposition of blue sky and red/brown land. Variations on this theme include the album covers to *Place Without a Postcard, Red Sails in the Sunset, Diesel and Dust, Blue Sky Mining* and the most recent 'best of' compilation *Essential Oils* (2012), which features a desert landscape with a vintage petrol bowser sitting in the foreground, a play on the name of the album. As such, of the 11 studio albums, one-third are landscape themed, a proportion that does not account for the artwork of the numerous song single releases. For example, the single for 'Beds Are Burning' features a similar colour palette to *Diesel and Dust* – horizontal fields of black framing a fisheye perspective shot of the band standing on a red-dirt landscape with a white-to-blue stripe of sky. In this mode the horizon is highlighted, a representation keenly aware of the long tradition of European encounters with Australian desert environments. This type of image also occurs on *Place Without a Postcard*, where a topographic perspective is used, and on *Red Sails in the Sunset*, which features a large-scale landscape depicting the meeting and structural fusion of the desert and urban elements, such as the Sydney Harbour Bridge.

This desert imaginary is both reified and challenged in the film clip for 'The Dead Heart', a song included on *Diesel and Dust* but recorded before the Blackfella/Whitefella tour and the rest of the album. Midnight Oil had been invited by Mutitjulu community leaders (near Uluru, in the Northern Territory) to contribute a song to the soundtrack of *Uluru: An Anangu Story*, a documentary film on the return of Uluru to its traditional owners. As a gesture of gratitude the Mutitjulu permitted the band to film in front of Uluru, and part of this footage was used in the film clip for 'The Dead Heart'. The song plays out a complex and at times conflicting set of ideas about culture, the land and relations between Indigenous and non-Indigenous peoples. On the one hand, the genesis of the song in a request from the traditional owners of Uluru and the explicit permission granted by them for Uluru to be used in the film clip are evidence for the positive work of Midnight Oil in giving exposure to Indigenous perspectives and views. The agency of these Indigenous people in this transaction, and the existence of a real relationship between the band and the community, is also important. These facts lessen the sense that the band are appropriating the image of Uluru and merely profiting from its iconic historical (and touristic) position as symbolic of the centre.

The mythic power of Uluru is in part based on the colonial-era belief in the existence of an inland sea. 'Once execrated for its failure to provide an inland sea, the Centre is now the most exported image of Australia: in tourist offices around the world Uluru vies with the Sydney Opera House as *the* icon of the continent' (Haynes 3). Positioning Uluru as a focal point of 'The Dead Heart' film clip fetishizes its location in the centre of the continent, as well as its size and colour. The choice of the song's title – 'The Dead Heart' is one among a list of similar colonial terms, such as 'the red centre' or simply 'the centre' – explicitly upholds the colonial tradition of describing the desert as both a wilderness and a place of spiritual enlightenment. In addition, the lyrics, sung by Garrett, are delivered from an Aboriginal perspective, a problematic move that foregrounds both the privileged speaking position of Midnight Oil and the silenced voices of Indigenous people.

Close analysis of how the clip is constructed is useful for unpacking how it simultaneously upholds colonial imaginings and acknowledges Indigenous representations of place. Using a form of animation based on watercolour illustrations, the clip begins with a yellow sun rising amid a dark blue sky and land. Over 10 seconds this sun image morphs into a watercolour image of Uluru, before transforming into a photographic image of Uluru. This image (14 sec) is the iconic 'postcard' perspective and showcases the massive scale of the rock formation, its striking colour and the way it interrupts the flat horizon line of the surrounding landscape. The shot is held for around 13 seconds, a long time in the context of the clip. This basic schema – foregrounding the size and colour of Uluru and its impact on the surrounding landscape – is used throughout the clip, with many variations achieved through different perspectives and combinations of cross-fading and superimposition. In addition to images of Uluru, the clip is constructed from two other sets of images: a variety of different shots of the band performing near Uluru and a series of sand and charcoal drawings imitating Aboriginal rock and sand art. These stop-motion animation images are used throughout verses and as segues between different sets of images and their distinctive designs inject an explicitly Aboriginal aesthetic into 'The Dead Heart'.

The majority of the clip moves between combinations of these three groups of images, with several small additions of different types of shots that often synchronize with the lyrics. For example, with the delivery of the lyric 'we don't need protection' at the start of the third verse (1 min 58 sec), a rhythmic figure played on the drum kit is synced to a sped-up motion shot of an Aboriginal flag. A similar rhythmic effect is used at the end of the fourth verse lyrics (2 min 6 sec), this time using a fast zoom-in/zoom-out shot of Uluru. Another type of shot of the band, a night-time performance, is integrated towards the end of the clip (4 min 26 sec). The camera position takes the perspective of an audience member, with a small campfire in the foreground, children dancing and the white-light-illuminated band playing in the background. The final moments of the clip return to wide perspective landscape shots of Uluru (5 min 5 sec). Taken from an airborne viewpoint, Uluru fills the centre of the shot, surrounded by a sea-like expanse of brown/red/grey landscape and with a distant horizon line.

This brief exegesis of the film clip describes the variety of ways that Uluru and its surrounding landscape are depicted, in both a visual sense and in relation to the message conveyed by the lyrics. The reoccurring images of the clip – the massive red rhomboid form of Uluru, the colours of the rock in its landscape, the line of the horizon and the presence of the band around Uluru – form a complex and contradictory spatial representation. While the lyrics of the song make a strong statement in favour of Indigenous self-determination, the visual imagery of the clip is ambiguous. By explicitly drawing on and reifying the colonial mythology of 'the centre', the clip fails to subvert the fetishization of Uluru. Perhaps more telling is the failure to give physical embodiment to the people whose perspective the clip claims to voice.

In contrast to the visual production of 'The Dead Heart', close examination of the lyrics reveals Midnight Oil's attempt to speak from a collective Aboriginal perspective. The lyrics are as follows. Verse three has been omitted because it is the same as verse one.

> Verse One:
> We don't serve your country
> Don't serve your king
> Know your custom don't speak your tongue
> White man came took everyone
>
> Verse Two:
> We don't serve your country
> We don't serve your king
> White man listen to the songs we sing
> White man came took everything
>
> Verse Four:
> We don't need protection
> Don't need your hand
> Keep your promise on where we stand
> We will listen we'll understand

Chorus:
We carry in our hearts the true country
And that cannot be stolen
We follow in the steps of our ancestry
And that cannot be broken.

Break down section:
Mining companies, pastoral companies
Uranium companies
Collected companies
Got more right than people
Got more say than people

Forty thousand years can make a difference to the state of things
The dead heart lives here.[1]

Attempting to speak for an Indigenous Australian people who are separate from the rest of Australia and still in touch with their traditions and the 'true country', the general thrust of the lyrics is unambiguously a statement in favour of Indigenous sovereignty. Several parts of the lyrics, such as the chorus line 'and that cannot be stolen', pre-empt the emergence of the Stolen Generations as a national issue. The breakdown section lists various corporate entities, implying that they are not concerned with people and culture but only profit – this ignores the possibility that traditional owners may support and benefit from such business interests. Without considering the problems of delivery, the lyrics promote Indigenous unity and self-determination, affirming tradition and country in the face of environmental and economic pressures.

Comparing the two impulses of the film clip – the images and the lyrics – reveals a number of salient points around which a continental geoimaginary can crystallize. The basic misalignment between the lyrical message of the song and the visual representation of the clip is a reflection of the power held by images of the centre, the currency of the colonial history and rhetoric on which they are based and the difficulties for a non-Indigenous band to engage in such a debate. The lyrics convey a point of view – that of Indigenous Australia via Midnight Oil – while the images create a landscape for the 'viewing' of that opinion by an audience. These images have not been arranged in a way that allows the viewer to see anything beyond the familiar tropes of the centre, other than the spectacle of The Oil's performing in an unusually beautiful setting. For the viewer of the clip, the sublime colour and mystical size of Uluru simply repeats the trope of 'the centre' as central jewel of the continent. While the good intentions of the band are projected outwards via the lyrics, the visual landscape of the clip acts as a screen onto which the desires and expectations of the viewer are projected inward, from the coastal fringes to the centre of the continent. This problem of perspective – which perhaps is one that may be impossible to escape for anyone working in a visual medium – is in no way combated by the types of images Midnight Oil and Director Roy Argall assemble in the clip.

Lyrical analysis of the song shows that it does critique colonial cartographies when heard in isolation from the images, but the relationship between sound and image underscores the difficulty of representing the centre. The duel problems – how to move out of the colonial past and how to represent this move from a non-Indigenous perspective – are the defining tensions of 'The Dead Heart', and the contradictory forces (vision vs. sound) of the film clip medium are an ideal platform for the exploration of such a dilemma. Instead of attempting to present a solution, the achievement of the clip is its depiction of both Indigenous and non-Indigenous perspectives. Combining – almost juxtaposing – the message of the lyrics with the images of the centre works to affirm the presence of both histories and the power of both sets of images and concerns. The sentiment of an Indigenous point of view is made all the more stark when it is placed into the direct context of images that draw on colonial and touristic visions of the centre. The centre is still mythic, but it is also a homeland.

How are these two seemingly opposing conceptions of space – the mythic centre and the homeland – resolved? The clip positions Uluru as a synecdoche for Indigenous Australia, both for the people, who are absent, and their place(s), which is transformed into an iconic centrepiece. In other words, the lyrics speak for a collectivity of people, while the visual representation of the clip, dominated by Uluru, stands in as this collective. A similar type of use of iconic visual imagery is featured in the band's 1985 'Oils on the Water Goat Island concert': the stage was erected so that the band performed with the Sydney Harbour Bridge as the backdrop. A symbol of modernity, the Harbour Bridge is, along with the Opera House and the natural harbour on which they both sit, a defining landmark of Sydney. Beginning their set with the song 'The Best of Both Worlds', a song celebrating the existence of both modernity and Indigenous Australian history and culture, the performance has become one of the band's most well remembered.

Listening to the affirmative message of the lyrics and taking into account the good relations between Midnight Oil and the traditional owners of Uluru, it is difficult to excuse the absence of Aboriginal people in 'The Dead Heart' (other than a few children dancing at the end). Uluru as synecdoche is one way of thinking through this absence, as it serves as the marker of Indigenous presence within 'the dead heart' of the Australian continent – as

Garrett sings, 'The dead heart lives here.' Such a claim is a fundamentally essentialist and incorrect conception of contemporary Indigenous people and their place – only 20 per cent of Indigenous Australians live outside of urban areas (Australian Bureau of Statistics 2016 figures). While the lack of visual presence can be explained within the context of the clip as a whole – few people, other than the band, are in the clip at all – it nevertheless highlights the difficult historical terrain Midnight Oil's song is attempting to map. It also reinforces the obvious fact that images of Indigenous Australia were still too sensitive for mainstream non-Indigenous Australians to absorb via their televisions.

As the first non-Indigenous rock band to produce a film clip with such a depiction of Uluru, Midnight Oil's status as an activist band concerned with Australian place and its people is undeniable. That they took advantage of the mythic aura of Uluru, and produced a representation of the centre that failed to depict Aboriginal people, is also undeniable. But the difficulty of weighing these two sides against each other is somewhat irrelevant: in combination with the Blackfella/Whitefella tour and all their later activism, The Oil's became the most authentic activist band in mainstream Australian rock.

The Sydney Olympic Games Closing Ceremony

The performance of 'Beds Are Burning' during the closing ceremony of the Sydney 2000 Olympic Games enabled Midnight Oil to project the message of the song to a national and international audience. Alongside the lyrical and costume elements, the performance was a powerful statement of historical and political critique, an electrifying 'line of flight' towards postcolonial reconciliation launched in the face of conservative prime minister John Howard, the Australian nation and a world audience. The performance was only possible because it occurred after Blackfella/Whitefella, *Diesel and Dust* and 'The Dead Heart', when the band had accrued an unparalleled stockpile of cultural capital and general local and national popularity. In other words, no other mainstream Australian band could have done what Midnight Oil did. The historical position of the performance – post-1988 and *Mabo*, but in the midst of 'The History Wars' and the Howard era – also created the right conditions for 'Beds Are Burning'.

While the opening ceremony broadly narrativized Australian history and culture with segments depicting the Indigenous 'Dreamtime', the arrival of Europeans, and a variety of Australian national icons including the Hills Hoist washing line, lawnmowers, a Sidney Nolan-esque depiction of Ned Kelly and giant inflatable sculptures of Australian native animals, the closing ceremony focused more on popular music and entertainment. Song performances included leading Australian musicians Jimmy Barnes (from the defining Oz rock outfit Cold Chisel), Kylie Minogue, INXS (with Jon Stevens) and Christine Anu. The staging of Anu's performance of 'My Island Home', a song composed by Neil Murray of the Warumpi Band, featured an elaborately constructed hydraulic stage that transformed into a globe, with Anu positioned on top (McMahon, 2005, 2010). The performance of 'Beds Are Burning' embodies a similarly powerful politico-spatial statement that, like the sentiments of 'My Island Home', could have gone unnoticed to many of the millions of viewers unaware of the full meaning of the song or the reason for Midnight Oil's costume choice.

The lyrical content of 'Beds Are Burning' and the 'sorry suits' worn by the band – a plain black shirt and trousers with the word 'sorry' emblazoned onto a different part of each performers' outfit – constituted the only performance in the closing ceremony, a televisual event broadcast to around three and a half billion viewers worldwide, to overtly gesture towards the dispossession and suffering experienced by generations of Indigenous people. No mention of the political or historical resonance of the song was made by the Channel 7 commentary team. Critiquing the representational politics of the opening and closing ceremonies, Liz Reed has highlighted the superficiality of much of the Indigenous input and content. Reed argues,

> The entire Opening effected in important ways the erasure of Indigenous peoples from Australia's history, and when combined with the Closing Ceremony, presented an image of Australia as newly 'reconciled' to its past. This past, then, was represented as unproblematic [...] albeit unconsciously, the Olympic ceremonies indicated in different ways attempts to return to the pre-*Mabo* narrative: that is, to a representation of Aborigines as 'of the ancient past' and of Anglo-Australians as the new, the future. (2002, 96)

For Reed this return to the pre-*Mabo* narrative underpins a wide range of related criticisms of the representation of Aboriginal culture and Australian history in both the opening and closing ceremonies. Some of these problems include how a child-aged performer – whose presence was designed to symbolize the supposed youth of the Australian nation – 'leads' the song man Djakapurra across the bridge, the way *terra nullius* was reinforced through the progression of the historical narrative of the ceremony as a whole, the multiculturalism segment and the lack of media attention to the performances of Youth Yindi and Christine Anu in the closing ceremony (Reed). These grievances were partially rectified by Midnight Oil's performance. Reed anecdotally relates how 'the political statements of Savage Garden's Darren Hayes' Aboriginal flag t-shirt and Midnight Oil's performance [...] resonated with the Aborigines I talked with from the Kimberley area' (101).

As if answering the lack of recognition of the suppressed aspects of Australia's colonial history, the lyrics of 'Beds Are Burning' are direct in their questions: refrains are repeated throughout the chorus, such as 'how can we dance when our earth is turning?/ How can we dance when our beds are burning?' The statement in the bridge is even more direct:

> The time has come
> To say fair's fair
> To pay the rent
> To pay our share
> The time has come
> A fact's a fact
> It belongs to them
> Let's give it back [2]

Laetitia Vellutini argues the 'Beds Are Burning' performance 'hailed Indigenous Australia directly' (2003, 133) and Midnight Oil 'brought popular protest to one of the country's (and the world's) most iconic arenas, a place where symbols of nation are displayed' (133). With their stark simplicity and symbolism, the 'sorry suits' compensated for the lack of time for Garrett to address the crowd. The performance costume plays on the multimedia characteristics fundamental to popular music as a medium and cultural circuit of meaning: a pointed message, partly founded in their experiences on the Blackfella/Whitefella tour 14 years earlier, was conveyed through both televisual and textual mediums.

The performance at the closing ceremony allowed Midnight Oil to launch a postcolonial line of flight towards the mainstream acknowledgement of Indigenous Australia. This event was in many ways the pinnacle of the band's musico-activist energy, the moment when they offered up their unmatched relation to Australian space to both the nation and the world. Despite partially failing to erase the image of the centre formed by European explorer accounts and post-war Modernist nationalist concerns, with their ongoing activism and critique of global power structures, Midnight Oil did reform the continental geoimaginary. Breaking out of the restrictive space of Oz rock, the band used the sound/image package characteristic of popular music to assemble a continental geoimaginary, and their work in the 1980s was prophetic of the shifts that would take place in the early 1990s with the *Mabo* ruling.

Chapter Three

SOUND AND SILENCE: LISTENING AND RELATION IN THE NOVELS OF ALEX MILLER

To listen to the novelistic soundscapes of Australian writer Alex Miller is to encounter a refined postcolonial sounding of the Australian interior, one that creates complex links with other continental spaces while also making the defining move into the post-*Mabo* epoch. Such journeys are not into the geographic centre but to another influential geoimaginary, the bush. Over the course of his *oeuvre*, Miller's 'search' opens out an alternative space to the sandy desert-centred representations produced by Webb, Lumsdaine and Midnight Oil. The novelist's continental interior is a personally oriented (although not necessarily completely unique) geoimaginary with foundations in his first encounter with rural landscapes after emigrating to Australia from England and his subsequent work as a stockman on various cattle stations in Central Queensland and the Northern Territory (Miller in Dixon, 2012).

The soundscapes I examine in two of Miller's Central Queensland novels – *Journey to the Stone Country* (2002) and *Landscape of Farewell* (2007) – focus on the journey of an explorer-like figure, what Elizabeth McMahon, evoking Georg Lukacs's theory of 'transcendental homelessness', calls 'the wanderer'. McMahon argues this wanderer is 'only ever truly located when they enter into the centre of another, which [in Miller] is figured as being within a continental diversity' (2012, 125). Entering into the centre of another, for McMahon, is embedded within an 'anthropomorphic overlay' (127) between identity and geography, particularly the figure of the island. This intersection operates in multiple registers, in terms of sharing stories, traveling into country and forming friendships.

In Miller's novels, moving into the centre is as much about a journey into a physical, historical and mnemonic landscape as it is about the need to listen sympathetically to the cultural other. The two Central Queensland novels, published in the midst of the political and cultural turmoil of 'The History Wars', as well as work from earlier and later in his career, such as *The Tivington*

Nott (1989), *The Sitters* (1995) and *Autumn Laing* (2011), foreground the confrontation between the self and the other. This nexus of concerns with postcolonial identity aligns with and speaks to the post-*Mabo* era of spatial politics, a period that Ali Gumillya Baker and Gus Worby argue created a 'moral dilemma [...] in public consciousness' that 'has had profound and contradictory impacts on what it means to be Australian, Aboriginal, Indigenous, non-Indigenous, and sovereign' (2007, 31). Miller's novels have made a unique contribution to the conversation surrounding Indigenous and non-Indigenous Australian identity and belonging in the postcolonial era. Listening to the imagined sound of these novels enables me to amplify the complex postcolonial thematics – issues of otherness and cultural difference, land rights and historical trauma – that animate his work. In this critical imperative, I follow Miller's characters in the action of listening, of attention to and reflection on the relation to the other, to the self and the outside environment, both past, present and future. And as my analysis of Miller will show, paying heed to a soundscape can mean listening to silence, a unique imaginative amplitude whose expressive utility is unique among the pages of this book.

The relation between the sound or silence of a landscape and the characters that inhabit that space is at the core of how sound maps space and identity in Miller. Brendan LaBelle describes this functionality of sound as its 'intrinsically and unignorably relational' character (2006, ix). In a statement that expresses the connection between characters and their sonic environment implicit in the concept of the soundscape, LaBelle suggests sound 'emanates, propagates, communicates, vibrates, and agitates; it leaves a body and enters others; it binds and unhinges, harmonizes and traumatizes; it sends the body moving, the mind dreaming' (ix). Working through both environmental and bodily space, LaBelle's mobile and relational characterization of sound is extended by David Toop: 'What comes together through sound is emergent and passing time – a sense of duration, the field of memory, a fullness of space that lies beyond touch and out of sight, hidden from vision' (2010, xv). Temporality, spatiality, relationality – sound expands these parameters, and all are activated in Miller's soundscapes.

Toop also mentions the work of listening in uncovering space 'hidden from vision', and this is a reoccurring theme among theorists of the sonic. Sound phenomenologist Don Ihde argues, 'It is with the hearing of interiors that the possibilities of listening begin to open the way to those aspects which lie at the horizons of all visualist thinking' (2007, 70), suggesting that in the auditory the 'capacity of making present the *invisible* begins to stand out dramatically' (70). Ihde's discussion of sound and the auditory sense emphasizes the way that sound can transform the spatial presence of objects and actions and enable the listener to delve into, behind and beyond the visual surfaces of objects. For Miller the invisible is the space of forgotten or obscured history, but in addition to this, the imaginative function of memory and creativity are pivotal to this spatial revelation.

Uncovering and listening to suppressed violence and shame has ethical implications, a fact demonstrated in the heated debates of 'The History Wars' as well as the apology by the Kevin Rudd Labor government in 2008. More specifically, the call to listen is articulated by the 1997 *Report of the National Inquiry into the Separation of Aboriginal and Torres Strait Islander Children from Their Families*. Titled *Bringing Them Home*, the report states that 'having listened and understood, [the Australian community] commits itself to reconciliation' (7), what Brigitta Olubas and Lisa Greenwell call an ethics of listening (1999). The call to listen in Miller's novels resonates with these events. In sonic terms, this means the recognition not only of sound but also of silence. Ihde says, 'If there is an ethics of listening, then respect for silence must play a part in that ethics' (180). On the power of silence, Toop suggests, 'Through silence we come face to face with ourselves, but into silence sound may enter, intrude again, a question directed at tangible, visible reality' (xv). Silence draws us into ourselves, both in bodily and imaginative senses, but the implications of this listening practice are also far-reaching, affecting generations.

Equating sound with silence as if both are of equal weight is perhaps counter-intuitive – silence is commonly defined as the absence of sound – but John Cage's philosophy redrew the sonic borders. Cage's experience of an anechoic chamber was the catalyst for his influential theorization: 'After convincing oneself ignorantly that sound has, as its clearly defined opposite, silence [...] one enters an anechoic chamber [...] to discover that one hears two sounds of one's own unintentional making (nerve's systematic operation, blood's circulation)' (1961, 13). The silent environment of the anechoic chamber, perhaps unsurprisingly, prompts Cage into closer listening: with no sonic stimuli from the outside, his attention turns to the sounds produced by his body. Cage concludes that 'the situation one is clearly in is not objective (sound-silence) but rather subjective (sounds only), those intended and those others (so-called silence) not intended' (13–14). Cage's reformulation of sound, silence and listening in a sense does away with silence. Instead, there are only subjective sounds: the listener hears silence, which is, according to Cage, unintended sound.

Following Cage (and exemplified by Miller) silence is not nothing, is not the absence of sound. Instead, in the post-*Mabo* period that Miller's novels articulate, we have an ethical imperative to listen to silence. Miller's designation of 'silence' is therefore carefully crafted: his choice of word carries with it all the weight of 'The Great Australian Silence'. Drawing on W. E. H. Stanner's influential Boyer lectures *After the Dreaming* (1969), Jane Belfrage describes how, in the colonial invasion of Australia, 'foreign, 'deaf', visually-oriented knowledge practices of hand-written and printed texts usurped sovereignty in the knowledge soundscapes of the land' (2). The encounter between European and Indigenous resulted in the loss of ancient and sacred practices, many of which are explicitly sonic in their realization. 'As White Men mapped, renamed and stole the territories, they inscribed themselves and their knowledge systems upon the land and into text' (Belfrage, 2). For Belfrage, silence is the tonality of Australian colonial history, the product of an epistemological (but also a forced and violent) shift to the written. For Miller (working in a written and silent medium) silence is also a powerfully live descriptor of the unreconciled state of the present. In describing or assigning *silence*, Miller creates a sonic relation between the individual and the environment that emphasizes the mnemonic and historical depth of landscapes and characters.

Miller's use of silence is varied: the silence of historical guilt in *Landscape of Farewell* stands in contrast to the silence at the foundation of the central friendship of the novel, which can in turn be distinguished from the silence of the bush in *Autumn Laing* that emerges from explorer discourse on the mythical and unknown interior. While my earlier discussion of Cage and silence placed the presence and value of silence into the ear of the listener, it falls short of the complex historico-political valence conveyed by the imaginary silence (and sound) of the novelistic soundscapes in Miller's work. Addressing this colonial and postcolonial territory of silence, Iain Chambers describes 'the interval of the unsaid (and the unsayable)', suggesting that in 'acknowledging silence [...] the shadows of the subaltern are thrown across the transparency of words accustomed to ignoring the ontology of silence' (1996, 51). Chambers suggests in the 'historical performances and cultural speech that silence enacts, previous prescriptive grammars (individual, narcissistic and nationalist) are forced not merely into compromise, but also into interrogation, weakening, even dispersal' (52). Cultural outsiders, Miller's protagonists learn to listen to the silence of Indigenous characters once pushed to the colonial margin. While imagined silence dominates the soundscape of *Landscape of Farewell*, listening to the soundscapes of Miller's other novels, his wanderer characters – and by extension, his readers – are able to recognize this muted sonic space.

Expanding on the resonant relationship between the listener and the imagined sounds or silences of a soundscape, Jean-Luc Nancy's philosophy of sound and space helps me to move closer to the 'wanderer/other' friendships that occur in Miller's novels, particularly in *Stone Country* and *Landscape of Farewell*. In his essay *Listening* (2002), Nancy theorized the relation between the individual and the soundscape, what he calls the space of the 'referral', by making a distinction between hearing and listening. First, there is *hearing*, for example, hearing the many sounds which populate a landscape, like bird song, the human voices or the sound of a car: Nancy says that *hearing* 'strains towards a present sense beyond sound' (6). When we are *listening*, to the same soundscape, 'it is from sound itself that sense is offered' (6). So while hearing is occupied with the analysis and abstract naming of sounds, listening to these sounds is not about analysis, but immediate experience and bodily relation. Within Nancy's theorization hearing and listening necessarily take place simultaneously, but the distinction he makes encourages us to listen to the materiality of sound, and to think about how the 'sense' of sound has a certain way of structuring the connection between the self and the world. Nancy's listening/hearing theorization also works to recast the temporal relationship between the individual and the environment: instead of the relation of distance, separation and thus temporal dislocation that is produced by viewing a landscape, listening and hearing is immersive and simultaneous.

Although it has much wider implications within the context of his philosophical project, sense – the resonating materiality that one experiences in listening – is at the core of Nancy's idiosyncratic understanding of the structure of how a subjectivity is created through sound. The referral, what Ian James calls 'the passage of sense' (2006, 106), is the oscillating movement where sense touches the listener, and the listener is in turn open to sense, open to and in relation with the sonic world. Instead of a boundary between the self and the other, or the character and the landscape, the *sense* of sound produces both the character and its landscape, together. This relation between real sounds and listeners can be extended to imagined sounds and listeners who are readers. Nancy says, 'It is not only, for the sonorous body, to emit a sound, but it is also to stretch out, to carry itself and be resolved into vibrations that both return it to itself and place it outside itself' (8). Moving into and away from the 'sonorous body', sound, according to Nancy, shares with meaning 'the space of a referral, in which at the same time they refer to each other, and that, in a very general way, this space can be defined as the space of a self, a subject. A self is nothing other than a form or function of a referral' (8). In this movement of the referral is the idea that, through sound, to paraphrase Nancy, the self can both be returned to itself and placed outside itself. In other words, the referral breaks down the spatial and temporal boundaries that exist between the viewing, judging self and the inert, othered, landscape.

Foundational Soundscapes: *The Tivington Nott* and *The Sitters*

The soundscapes in *The Tivington Nott* and *The Sitters* – two of Miller's early novels – establish the through-running presence of sound in his *oeuvre*. Listening to these novels we notice the figure of the outsider and the work of memory – thematics realized with greater urgency in his later novels. To listen to the soundscapes of these two novels also expands the *imaginative* function of sound and silence.

The dramatic centrepiece of *The Tivington Nott*, Miller's second novel, is a deer hunt. Based on his experiences as a young man working on an estate in England, the novel is set in Somerset, on the borders of Exmoor. In what will become a familiar figure in Miller's novels, the young protagonist (Miller does not give him a name) is a newcomer and outsider in the community. He takes part in a hunt in an effort to prove his worth in a world of ancient traditions and class structures. Riding on his own, Miller's protagonist unexpectedly comes across a prized stag: 'Who knows what he might do? He looks to me to be capable of anything [...] The instant I tense up he barks again. I freeze. It is a sharp, urgent warning. A mad shout in the forest. And a wave of fear goes through me' (1989, 23–24). Robert Dixon suggests that at this moment 'Miller has opened a space for a different kind of encounter with nature, in which the boy establishes a relation to the stag on his own terms, independently of the ritual of the hunt' (2014, 16). Dixon goes on to discuss the ecological sublime, moving away from the sonic potential of this scene, but the 'different kind of encounter with nature' is one that positions sound as central to the dynamic between characters and landscapes. A superficial examination of this early soundscape shows how sonic elements and types of relations opened by sound – such as the alarm-like character of the stags' bark or an outsider experiencing a soundscape for the first time – reoccur in the later novels.

The startling 'bark' of the stag is like a shock wave that elicits a strong and immediate reaction from the youth. In the compressed space of three lines, Miller is able to load this animal sound with significance by calling it 'an urgent warning' and 'a mad shout in the forest'. In addition to this, the rhythm of the bark gives it an alarm-like function, as if the stag is broadcasting the presence of an intruder (a similar rhythmic description is used in *Stone Country*). In response to this sound, the boy freezes, as if the staccato bark has stopped time, a unique effect for such an ephemeral action. The sound of the stag also works spatially: the phrase 'mad shout in the forest' refers to the landscape in which the sound resounds, helping Miller to transform the character of the moor into something far wilder and stranger.

This scene from *The Tivington Nott* is in fact a closely voiced soundscape. First, it creates a relation between an individual and an environment: this is fundamental to the concept of soundscape. Each soundscape I encounter in this chapter, and throughout *Imagined Sound*, presents a slightly different type of relationship between sound, character and listener. It may be that the relation is just between a human character and the surrounding environment, or there may be more players, such as in this case, where the stag forms a third point with the protagonist and the surrounding environment. Looking back and forward into the surrounding chapters, this type of link is the most common: the inclusion of animal figures is also seen in other soundscapes in Miller's novels, as well as in the poetry of Webb and the novels of Flanagan and Wright. Such a reoccurrence attests to the attention these authors pay to depicting environmental detail, but it also highlights the role of the non-human in the formation of any soundscape.

Temporality offers another way into the operation of this soundscape. *The Tivington Nott* features perhaps the most immediate soundscape of any I discuss in this book. The reaction of the protagonist to the sound of the buck is immediate and affective. In addition to this, the sound does not spark any thought or reflection from the character (or narrator) relating to the past or future, as it does elsewhere, such as in the soundscape from *The Sitters* which I will discuss in a moment. The sound of the buck does not 'transport' the youth: instead, it roots him in the present. Instead of creating complex interconnections of time – most notably seen in my discussion of islands and archipelagos in Chapters Four, Five and Six – the immediacy of the sound in this scene makes it somewhat of an anomaly, both in Miller's work and throughout *Imagined Sound*. But while it does not prompt any profound reflections or insights for the character, the buck is nevertheless extremely important in the narrative: the refusal of the youth to report the presence of the animal to the other hunters gives him an advantage that he later uses to gain the respect of his peers. This moment therefore highlights the role of sound in revealing or amplifying integral moments in a narrative, a reoccurring characteristic of sound in all of the novelistic and poetic soundscape I discuss.

Like the stag soundscape from *The Tivington Nott*, a pivotal scene in *The Sitters* I will call the 'memory room' soundscape is another entry-point into my discussion of Miller. The scene stages a complex movement through different types and registers of space and time: from the imagination of an artist (again, Miller does not give him a name) into the experience and memory of the subject of the portrait he is painting. The soundscape illustrates Miller's subtle integration of themes of memory, loss and landscape, and features two reoccurring 'sonic characters' in my encounter with Miller, birdsong and silence. I quote the soundscape at length to show its detailed unraveling of space, time and memory.

> When a bird cries once from a branch in the tree, then again, and abruptly falls silent, its cries set something new in motion in the room, in the mind of the woman who is sitting on the bed and to whom there has been a mysterious call from the outside. The silence hangs during the interval after the bird's cry, waiting for her to reply, until the bird

> calls again, now from further away. The sound of the bird's call is being swallowed by distance and light as it flies further away from the house. It is becoming hollowed and echoing and more imaginary the further away it gets. It no longer calls for a reply. The cry of the bird is becoming part of the elaborate silence of the stringybark forest and the woman's thoughts, her uncertainty, her inability to reply. As it grows more indistinct and imaginary, for the woman who is sitting on the bed the call of the bird becomes a kind of lamentation for what is lost and cannot be recovered. She might have followed the call of the bird. A cry in which there is also a note of mockery, which makes the woman on the bed a little afraid, which has made her hesitate. So that fear has begun to be present in the room. When the bird has retreated and merged into the distance and into memory there remains, in the darkened room with the woman, a stirring complicated silence that might be difficult for her to distinguish from the sound of her own blood. This is the silence of strain and fatigue and worry. It is an undifferentiated silence. It is a silence that is the opposite of calm, graceful or beautiful music, and it is not just the absence of music. It is a silence in which the woman's uncertainty, her diffidence, has begun to oppress her. Her failure to decide [...] To locate this sound from her childhood. To deal with it. (1995, 63–64)

Representing, in words, a series of sound elements, an environment and the relation between those sounds and the people in that space, the 'memory room' soundscape opens a multileveled territory, both real and imaginary. Sound and silence weave a delicate fabric linking past and present, inside and outside.

Structurally, this soundscape is a cyclical examination of loss and memory. At the beginning of the paragraph the sound of the bird dominates, its rhythmic interjections linking and penetrating different spaces and temporalities of memory, explicitly creating a dimensionality, a 'distance'. Commentary on the disintegrating quality of the bird call is focalized through the artist, although the further into this soundscape we get the more that point of view becomes mixed with the perspective and memories of the 'sitter', Jessica. The relationship between the artist and the sitter is a reimagining of the wanderer/other relationships seen elsewhere in Miller's work. While sound can co-mingle the creative imaginings of the artist with the memories of the portrait subject, it also complicates the artist/sitter, subject/object, self/other relation. Instead of the object of the portrait being captured by the gaze of the artist, sound orients this scene around the depiction of the imaginative process while also empowering the sitter by sounding the uncoiling of her memory. As Dixon says in his discussion of the novel, *The Sitters* is 'concerned with being-in-time, with longing, absence and silence, and with the intimate connections between art, memory and death' (54). Sound and silence enable the sitter and the artist to explore the space of a memory, and the flexibility of its temporal weavings allows for this 'being-in-time' and for the complex relation of artist and subject.

In this soundscape memory is explicitly described as a process and movement: the 'sound of the bird's call' is 'swallowed by distance and light', 'becoming hollowed and echoing and more imaginary the further away it gets'. A distance is created in these lines. On one side, the resonance of the scene, and on the other, the narrator and reader.

As the soundscape unfolds, the spatial and imaginative work performed by sound is transformed into the work of silence. Two spaces – the inside room, the interior of Jessica and her memories and the outside landscape, opened by the bird call – are complicated by the mix of sound and silence. The 'silence hangs during the interval after the bird's cry, waiting for her to reply, until the bird calls again, now from further away'. This is a complex sonic moment in which Miller creates a relationship of equivalence between sound and silence. In the first third of the paragraph silence is like a background to the call of the bird, not connoting a void or soundless vacuum but instead delineating the space of the stringybark forest into which the bird, in flight, recedes. As the bird moves further into the forest the sound of its cry begins to change and integrate with the exterior silence, a process that foregrounds the connection between outside and inside. The narrator tells how 'the cry of the bird is becoming part of the elaborate silence of the stringybark forest and the woman's thoughts, her uncertainty, her inability to reply'. The movement of sound into silence implies a temporal immediacy. In this moment the silence of the stringybark forest, and exterior, is bound to the interiority of the women, a kind of 'objective correlative' (Eliot 1950, 7), an 'outer equivalent of an inner reality' (Wright, xi).

The silence of the second half of the paragraph weaves back into the intricate sonic web of the bird call from the beginning of the soundscape. 'When the bird has retreated and merged into the distance and into memory there remains, in the darkened room with the woman, a stirring complicated silence'. The movement of the bird call into an outside that is both the stringybark forest and the consciousness of the women meshes silence with different types of space. Sound also penetrates between the outside landscape and the interior of thought and memory: 'the bird has retreated and merged into the distance and into memory'. The sitter struggles to tell the difference between the exterior silence and the profoundly interior 'sound of her own blood', a sound recalling Cage's experience of bodily sound in the anechoic chamber.

Here Miller creates a counterpoint between two sounds – the bird call and silence – and the interaction of these sounds in the mesh of inside and outside is the most complex of his soundscapes.

The final quarter of the 'memory room', soundscape features a series of three sentences that all describe silence: 'It is an undifferentiated silence. It is a silence that is the opposite of calm, graceful or beautiful music, and it is not just the absence of music. It is a silence in which the woman's uncertainty, her diffidence, has begun to oppress her.' The parallelism of these lines is overbearing: the layers of description link the progress of the reader with the women's search for the childhood memory evoked by the bird. Such a relation between the experience of the reader and the character is also seen in the soundscape from *Stone Country*, where each discrete sound element is described in a way that imitates the temporality of the experience of 'real' listening. The 'darkened room' in which the woman sits also evokes the 'skull room' of Samuel Beckett's play *Endgame* (1957), or Proust's childhood bedroom in the 'Swann's Way' volume of *In Search of Time Lost* (1913–27), comparisons that locate Miller in wider literary ranks.

Stone Country Soundscapes

The stag and memory room soundscapes highlight the work of silence, the spatio-temporal interplay between different spaces and times, and several key thematic resonances across Miller's *oeuvre*, such as the use of birdsong and the figure of the outsider or wanderer. A crucial absence from these two soundscapes is meaningful engagement with the spatial politics of the Central Queensland novels. Related 'like cousins', *Stone Country* and *Landscape of Farewell* are at the centre of how Miller uses sound to explore Australian colonial and postcolonial space.[1] The sound-worlds of both novels are focalized through the perspectives of wanderer figures whose experiences in the explicitly postcolonial, post-*Mabo* landscape of Central Queensland emphasize their political, historical and cultural difference and displacement.

In *Stone Country*, Annabelle Beck, an Anglo-Australian anthropologist, makes the journey back to the country of her parents, and of her own childhood, with the help of Bo Rennie, an Aboriginal cultural adviser and former stockman. Annabelle's journey into a landscape drenched in sound leads her to an encounter with the past – of Aboriginal dispossession and murder, partly carried out by her own ancestors – while also showing her the way forward. In *Landscape of Farewell*, Max Otto, a German history academic, faces up to the possible involvement of his father in World War II war crimes, his own grief from the recent death of his wife and the bitterness of moral failure in the aftermath of his academic career. Meeting feisty Indigenous intellectual Vita,

Max is persuaded to visit the similarly grieving Aboriginal advocate Dougald Gnapun, who lives in the same Central Queensland setting as *Stone Country*.

The distinctive sounds and prominent silences of Dougald's landscape provoke Max to embark on an emotional and physical journey where he rediscovers his own self-worth through writing, composing and actually becoming, through fiction, the ancestor of his friend Dougald. While Annabelle's soundscape is not so redolent with silence, through listening she can grapple with the complexity of her own cultural inheritance while forming a romantic relationship with Bo. Max becomes involved in a different kind of sonic relation with Dougald, one that is based on silence but which nevertheless leads to the two men forming a close and healing friendship. Through listening, Miller's wanderers, Annabelle and Max, are able to exist in the landscape in a different way. Instead of inhabiting a relation of self/other, they, to use Nancy's idiom, 'stretch out' and are touched by the sonic landscape. Listening to these Central Queensland soundscapes reveals complex interpersonal connections between characters, but it also shows the fundamental need to recover, uncover and reclaim lost or dispossessed homelands. Miller's exploration of the centre of the continent is located in the relation between these characters as they journey into, reclaim and share knowledge and ownership of the land with their Indigenous friends.

The following soundscape in *Stone Country* is the most sonically rich and varied of all of Miller's soundscapes, equal to anything found in Wright's *Carpentaria*. This scene, 'Annabelle's soundscape', is from early in the novel, when Annabelle makes her initial trip into the Central Queensland landscape and encounters Bo for the first time:

> Bo stood by the open door of the truck. From the sandalwood ridge behind him a friarbird repeated its ardent cry again and again, warning off the intruders, Ar-coo! Ar-coo! Ar-coo!
>
> Bo turned and walked down the hill towards the Pajero. The volume of the music increased, the voice of 2PAC pursuing him along the slope, *I shall not fear no man but God, though I walk through the valley of death* [...] The girl's laughter, rich, youthful, sensuous. A liberation in some deep amusement. The dry groundcover crackling beneath Bo's boots, releasing the musty odours of dead time. (2002, 55)

Within the context of the novel this soundscape reveals a significant amount of information about each of the characters. With the benefit of hindsight we can see that the scene also shapes the path of the narrative: after meeting Bo, the course of Annabelle's life is completely altered. This soundscape makes it clear that Annabelle, the perspective through which we hear the soundscape, is an outsider who at this stage of the narrative has little connection with the landscape or the other characters. But the soundscape also foreshadows the relationships she will share with Bo, Arner and Trace. In the terms of Nancy's theorization of *listening*, Annabelle is actually existent in the sonorous space of the referral, even before she is fully aware of her position.

Listening to the discrete elements in this soundscape reveals how different sounds create lines of connection with Annabelle. There are four sound elements: (1) the sound of the friarbird's song, 'its ardent cry again and again, warning off the intruders, Ar-coo! Ar-coo! Ar-coo!'; (2) the sound of 'the voice of 2PAC', with lyrical content that is notably included and accentuated by its italicization; (3) the sound of the 'girl's laughter, rich, youthful, sensuous' and (4) the sound of the 'dry groundcover crackling under Bo's boots, releasing the musty odours of dead time'. The friarbird's song is, through its enthusiastic repetition, a warning or alarm, similar to the sound of the buck in *The Twington Nott*. The sense of its cry 'Ar-coo', emanating from the natural part of the soundscape, touches on and amplifies Annabelle's feeling that she is an outsider. The voice of 2PAC is an element that would seem, in comparison with the friarbird, to be out of place, but when 2PAC sings about the *valley of death* he is voicing Arner's negative state of mind. Through this sonic medium Arner projects his feelings of apathy, while also cloaking his own silence beneath the hip-hop. The music gives his attitude an aggressive sonic character; the form that this takes is 'the steady beat of the bass' which is combined with the 'fierce' tone of 2PAC's voice, elsewhere described as 'crying forth his bitter desire for revenge' (123).

In direct opposition to Arner's sonic presence is the laughter of his sister Trace, described as being 'rich, youthful, [and] sensuous'. From a compositional point of view, it is as if Miller is filling out a two-part human-harmony in this soundscape: Arner is the bass and Trace is the soprano. While the friarbird and 2PAC make Annabelle feel unwelcome and out of place, the sound of Trace's laughter identifies her as someone who is open to Annabelle for friendship. The final sound element, the crackling of the groundcover under Bo's boots, is a double-sense combination in that its sonic presence calls forth an imagined olfactory sensation, 'the musty odours of dead time'. Even though Annabelle has only just met Bo, his movement through the landscape gives her an indication, through the imagined 'smell of time', both of his knowledge of the land and his connection to its past. While Annabelle may feel that she is an outsider, the Nancian 'sense of sound' positions her as part of the back and forth referral motion of the sounds that populate this space. In one sense she may be a newcomer, but the relation created by the soundscape will not let her distance herself. It draws her into a relation of being with another – Bo, as well as Trace and Arner – and Annabelle has a presence within and relation to the soundscape. The various sounds resonate around and within her, creating her as subject with an increasing understanding of the landscape, its past and its Indigenous caretakers.

As the narrative progresses, Bo, the most sonically present character to the landscape, becomes intimately connected to Annabelle, both in terms of their romantic relationship and the slightly utopian ending of the novel on Verbena Station. It is no surprise that sound and listening are instrumental to this conclusion:

> When she woke beside him later, the bush beyond their camp was still and silent. She lay awake listening. She realised she could not hear the thump of Arner's music. Bo stirred beside her. 'Arner's not playing his music,' she said. They lay in the dark, listening.
>
> 'That boy's gotta sleep sometime,' he said.
>
> 'It's a sign to you.'
>
> He was silent a moment, then, 'I guess you're right.' (364)

This soundscape, from the final pages of the novel, is a sonic resolution to the dissonance present in Annabelle's first experience with Arner. The absence of Arner's music reveals the silence of the bush, an atmosphere of openness and peace.

The sounds in these soundscapes develop and link both character details and the landscape, and the various types of sound create different layers of space that exist simultaneously. Demarcating a territory built from the 'fierce' tone of 2PAC's voice and the regular drum/bass pulsations that characterize hip hop music, the 'sense' of Arner's music is particularly arresting. In a broader sense, Miller's inclusion of Arner's music throughout the novel highlights the complexity of the spaces he is depicting. Arner is a young Indigenous Australian man who is learning about his culture and country from his uncle Bo. The presence of his music, with its strong iteration of African-American ghetto life and gang masculinity, endows the Central Queensland landscape with a spatially distant element. While Arner's music may be his attempt to erect a sonic barrier, the aggressive attitude of 2PAC's lyrics also help Miller to allude to the presence of Aboriginal colonial histories of oppression and dispossession within this landscape. Although this sound element is more global than local in comparison to the birdsong or the crackling of groundcover, it powerfully connects the disparate space that spans the United States and Australia and resonates between the historical and emotional character of this shared experience. Given the importance of music to Arner, his decision to stop listening to it at the end of the novel is material evidence that he is beginning to reconcile his differences with Annabelle and Bo.

Landscapes of Silence

In comparison to the prodigious sound of *Stone Country*, *Landscape of Farewell* is a novel of distant rumbling, but more predominantly, of silence. Although there is no indication of an exact chronology that calibrate the narratives of either of Miller's 'cousin' novels, I think of *Landscape of Farewell* as coming after the events of *Stone Country*. The central reason for this is the transformation of sound: the mining issue that is explored, but not audibly emphasized in the start of *Stone Country*, is sonically manifest in *Landscape of Farewell* as the ever-present rumbling of the mine: Max repeatedly mentions how 'the air trembled with the distant thunder of the mine' (2007, 121). This menacing machine ambience is distinctively minimal, quite unlike the intricate soundscapes that resound throughout *Stone Country*, but it nevertheless ties the landscape to wider issues of environmentalism and economic development.

Commenting on the Central Queensland novels, Miller has stated, 'My own displacement from one side of the world to the other, my loss of culture and home, is dealt with silently in my empathy with the displacement and dispossession experienced by the book's principle characters, black and white' (Miller quoted in Dixon 2012, 97). Arguing the Central Queensland novels 'are not just about the displacement of their Indigenous characters', Dixon suggests 'the sense of personal and cultural displacement of the authorial consciousness that allows the stories of *other* displaced people to be realised sympathetically in story' (97) is also of central importance. I echo Dixon here in highlighting Miller's choice of the word 'silently', but this silence is not just implicit or unstated. Silence is literal, working between characters and in the soundscapes they inhabit, a materiality whose presence binds the immediate situations of the characters with larger historical contexts. It is the heartbeat that animates the friendship of Max Otto and Dougald Gnapun, and it also links the two Central Queensland novels: In *Stone Country*, Annabelle is struck by Dougald's characteristic silence, 'the enormous weight of his silence in its presence, indeed the gravitas of his silence' (94). Similarly, in *Landscape of Farewell* Max notes how Dougald 'inhabited a deep and very private silence of his own – as some poet has expressed it, *listening to his own depth*' (67).

The landscape in which Miller sets Max and Dougald's friendship is one that resonates. Arriving at Dougald's house in the town of Mount Nebo, Max listens, 'The enormous silence of the landscape was suddenly close and oppressive, the unrelieved solitude of the forlorn township in the ocean of scrub, the abandoned machines rusting into the ground' (117). For Max this silence expresses the isolation and dysfunction associated with old age. But on a deeper emotional level this soundscape resonates with the silence that exists at the core of Max's relationship with his father. Thinking of this parental relationship, Max says, 'No matter how much we say about these things, no matter how truthful we are, no matter how ruthlessly we expose the terrible detail of those events, there will always remain something we cannot say [...] something left in the silence' (49). Dixon suggests that, over the course of the novel, Max moves through a process to becoming 'fully conscious of the link between the German and Australian silences' (144). As I will explore in a moment, a key stage of this becoming conscious of silence occurs with Max writing Dougald's own history of massacre.

The mutual respect and eventual friendship that emerges from Dougald and Max's individual histories exemplifies the sonic, and silent, journey into the 'centre of another' (McMahon 2012, 125). This passage through silence has multiple spatio-temporal resonances. The silence of the landscape resounds both between the two elderly men in their emotional and physical present, and between Max and Dougald's geographically distant individual pasts. Dougald's silence signals the broader Australian Aboriginal experience of colonization, Belfrage's 'Great Australian Silence'. Reflecting on his childhood wartime experiences and the suppression of guilt in the post-war years, Max remembers how 'a capacity for deep silence was revealed within each of us, like a cavern we had not known existed before' (227). This silent interior space recalls the 'memory room' soundscape from *The Sitters*, but here the context has been broadened to encompass two of the most horrific stages of European and Australian history.

To continue his journey into the continent – into both the self-knowledge of the present (with Dougald) and into the shame of the past (with his father) – Max writes the story of Dougald's ancestor Gnapun, a creative task of historical fiction that, for Bill Ashcroft, expresses 'the ultimate agency of utopian reconciliation' (2011, 34). In writing this story, sound and silence, and the act of listening, collapse the spatial boundaries of nation and the temporal distance of history separating Max and Dougald. Sound and silence are also integral as a kind of preparation for composition: the sense of sound touches Max when Dougald first tells him the story of his ancestor Gnapun: 'As I lay there in my bed in the silence after he had gone, listening to the moaning of the wind in the scrubs and the creaking of the embers of my fire, his voice was still sounding in my ears' (165–66). Listening to the soundscape of his small room, Max is aware of how the sound of Dougald's voice resonates within him, touching and inspiring him to compose the story. This same spatio-temporal movement, while only a small element of this novel, is at the foundations of the vocal refrains I discuss in relation to Flanagan and Bird in Chapter Five, and Baecastuff's *Mutiny Music* in Chapter Six.

'Massacre' is the story that Max writes after hearing Dougald's oral history of an Aboriginal massacre of European settlers. In this story Max comes to hear and listen to the resonance of the bush through the 'ears of another', Gnapun. The world of this history, in contrast to the present time of the novel, is filled with much more dramatic sound, including the 'shrieking silence of the cicada chorus' and 'the listening scrub' (180–86). The most striking example of Max's sonic embodiment of Gnapun occurs when he writes: 'I shall give the cry of the Wylah, the funeral black cockatoo, for you all know that his is the bird of my spirit and you will recognise my command in its cry above the clamour of these people' (194). The sacred sound of the totemic bird is a call to arms that, while only existent in the past tense of the story, helps to break the silence of Max and Dougald's present and push them into their journey in search of Gnapun's burial ground. It is also a profound sonic becoming for Max, both becoming-other and becoming-animal. Max is transported by the act of writing, away from his place in the present and into the past, into an Indigenous experience of colonization. But at the same time, the massacre at the centre of Gnapun's story (and the centre of his continent) is also at the heart of Max and his father's Europe. This realization is rendered through sound; 'It rang like a bell in my head: *So you have identified yourself at last with the perpetrator of a massacre*' (215). Again, the sonic element of the alarm bell is featured. Max realizes that 'with his gift of the story of his great-grandfather, Dougald had unknowingly instructed me in my own way forward' (227). For Max 'the wanderer', the silence of Dougald's continental landscape allows him to approach the dissonance in his own history, buried in the European continent. This way forward leads to the final journey undertaken by the duo, in search of the burial ground of Dougald's ancestors.

A Return to Silence

Part of the achievement of Miller's search for the continental centre in *Landscape of Farewell* and *Stone Country* is the subtle examination of a post-*Mabo* landscape. This meeting of Indigenous and non-Indigenous is not important to *The Tivington Nott* or *The Sitters*, although the antecedents of how Miller orchestrates issues of belonging, otherness and silence are buried in these earlier soundscapes. The final soundscape I want to discuss in this chapter, from *Autumn Laing*, travels back to a pre-*Mabo* landscape, and, in a sense, to the territory explored by Webb and Lumsdaine in Chapter One. While this is a return to an earlier time in Australian spatial politics – a digression also flagged by the references to the explorer narratives of Leichhardt and Eyre in the novel – Miller's use of silence, and the imperative of the search for the centre, connects this soundscape from *Autumn Laing* to the sound and silence present in the rest of his *oeuvre*. Perhaps just as importantly, Miller's use of silence to mark the beginning of an epoch of artistic discovery of 'the centre' points to the adaptability and importance of silence to his work.

Autumn Laing is the *kunstlerroman* of an artist, Pat Donlon, and his relationship with art patron Autumn Laing. The novel is based on the real relationship between Sidney Nolan, a figure at the forefront of the 'search for the centre' in the 1950s and one of Australia's greatest artists, and Sunday Reed, an important art patron who helped Nolen early in his career. In a period of imaginative gestation – recalling novelist Patrick White's reading of Eyre's *Journals* before his return to Australia to eventually produce *Voss* in the mid-1950s – Donlon immerses himself in the accounts of the European confrontation with the Australian landscape provided by the journals of the explorers. Describing his impression of the journals, Pat says,

> 'Isn't it beautiful? Don't you feel it? Out there a thousand miles from another white man and these people seeing Charley coming along. Never having seen anything like him before. Standing up and gazing at him. Can't you just feel the silence of that moment? The whole of Australia is in that silence.' He looked down at the book in his lap. 'What a great thing that is. That silence. It calls to you, doesn't it?' (2011, 356–57)

Pat's statement – 'The whole of Australia is in that silence' – records the exact moment of contact between the European explorer (in this case Charles Sturt) and Indigenous Australia. The silence of this frontier meeting is an inversion of the 'sound in between', the sonic encounter of colonial and Indigenous people theorized by Paul Carter, which I discuss in more detail in Chapter Five. Instead of a 'coo-ee' exchange, Pat imagines a silent greeting. Perhaps this is a reflection of the silence of his chosen medium of painting, but it is also a product of the explorer accounts, which emphasized the monotony, silence and desolation of some Australian landscapes, themes that are explored by Webb and Lumsdaine. Miller – through his character Pat – has given this moment a silence that references both the imagined reality (and shock) of that meeting and the Australian Gothic tradition and Marcus Clarke, whose discussion of the 'weird melancholy' of the Australian bush mentions both silent forests and silent plains. This type of soundscape echoes between Miller's novels, underlining his penchant for realizing Australian landscapes with highly charged silence.

Reflecting on Don's time at a Central Queensland cattle station, Autumn Laing considers the mythic idea of the Australian 'outback': 'In truth the outback is not a place but is the Australian imagination itself. It is always elsewhere. A steady thunder of silence is imposed on the inhabitants of this island by the impossible weight of isolation in space and history' (415). Like so many of the landscapes described by Miller, Autumn's thoughts on the outback are suffused with silence. Here the silence is linked to 'the impossible weight of isolation in space and history', a phrase that refers to the real experience of remote farm life while also linking with Belfrage's discussion of the history of colonial violence towards Indigenous people. *Autumn Laing* is largely concerned with old age and the formation of the Modernist artist, and the 'ethics of listening' (Ihde) put forward by the novel reiterate the historical ignorance of the Modernist 'discovery' of the centre. Despite this, the relationship between the artist Don and the Australian landscape is, like *The Twington Nott*, *The Sitters* and the two Central Queensland novels, a meeting between self and other, a relation founded in and inspired by sound and silence.

Part Two

LISTENING TO ISLANDS AND ARCHIPELAGOS

songs are 'a crying out' (2); they are narratives of 'brutish suffering' (2) that sound the 'where am I?' question of the deject and the exile.

The border insecurity signaled by Kristeva's abject accentuates the movements between the nineteenth-century convict experience related in the three songs. Listening to this unique harmony of imagined sound we can hear how the abject undermines the innately fascist tendencies of the nationalistic use of the convict mythology (Livett 2007). At the same time, the songs open a landscape of abject otherness within the carceral foundations of the nation, positioning the figure of the deject and outsider as central to the spatial relations underpinning the convict myth. The convicts and outsiders in these songs manifest the impurity of an abject figure that moves in excess, both across the boundaries of the continent and across a global network of carceral spaces – Ireland, Van Dieman's Land, Moreton Bay, Guantanamo Bay and Manhattan. The ability of the archipelago to house such spatial tensions, to in effect map the landscapes *between* the island and the mainland and between islands, casts it as an ideal way of conceptualizing the global transhistorical movement, and subsequent space of abject otherness within the borders of the national imaginary, sounded by the songs by the Drones and Liddiard.

The antecedents of the three songs also emphasize the mirroring between conceptual archipelagos and their musico-historical contexts. Spread throughout a wider Drones musical *oeuvre* characterized by loud, raucous, noisy rock music – with vocals often delivered in a screamed or howled manner and electrified and distortion-tinged instrumentation – the three convict songs exist like an archipelago of aesthetically 'softer' folk songs within the larger Drones/Liddiard songbook. Spanning a global network encompassing the nineteenth-century folk song and broadside ballad tradition from the British Isles, the American folk tradition with Woody Guthrie and later Bob Dylan, and the great contemporary Australian singer-songwriters like Archie Roach, Paul Kelly, Nick Cave, and rock bands like the Beasts of Bourbon and the Scientists, the space between the musical 'ancestors' of the songs pushes the archipelagic relation further. The shared content and form of the three songs are currents that can give the listener and reader a wider sense of continuity as they traverse their sonic and lyrical terrain, another kind of archipelagic relation, not unlike Edouard Glissant's rhizomatic 'system of communication' (quoted in DeLoughrey 2001, 41) sitting just behind, or just beneath the surface of my main focus on remapping the convict myth.

'Words' from Exile

Sounding an arching trajectory across the transhistorical continuum of the three songs, I will begin with the carceral wilderness of Van Diemen's Land described in 'Words'. Here the abject exile embodied by both the Executioner and the 'Cannibal Convict' Pearce establishes the spatial economy of the island, a space that stands 'for paradise and purgatory', a place 'where we quarantine the pestilence and exile the subversive' (Gillis 2004, 3). The doubled character of the island is a through-running refrain in island theory. For Godfrey Baldacchino, the island indexes 'local *and* global realities, of interior *and* exterior references of meaning' (2005, 248). Defined by Elizabeth McMahon as a territory marked by 'circumscription and singularity', with 'borders that fend off contamination and infiltration' (2005, 21), for John Gillis the island 'has been the West's favourite location for visions of both the past and future [...] it is there that we most readily imagine origins and extinctions' (3). As Rod Edmond and Vanessa Smith suggest, the 'particular features of the island [...] its boundedness and discretion, its microscopicality – render it available to ideal colonial fantasies and extreme colonial realities' (2003, 6). Preparing the ground for the more concentrated discussion of lyrical abjection in 'Sixteen Straws' and 'D', the grotesque reality encountered in 'Words' also resounds in the Tasmanian novels of Flanagan and Bird, which explicitly take up the theme of island origin and extinction.

Pearce is the initial figure of exile in 'Words' and his experience describes a triple movement within the British convict archipelago that is also a scaling-down progression from large to small and centre to margin. After being transported from Ireland to Van Diemen's Land in 1819, a major transoceanic displacement, Pearce was incarcerated on Sarah Island. This transferal from the larger island of Tasmania to the tiny Sarah Island, within Macquarie Harbour on Tasmania's west coast, performs a miniature repetition of the archipelagic relation already realized between Ireland and Van Diemen's Land. Each movement along the chain of islands is an attempt to place Pearce under more severe punishment, relocations that also maroon Pearce further and further outside civilized colonial space. Escaping into the Tasmanian wilderness and murdering his companions for the purposes of cannibalism, he is forced to partake in a supreme act of abjection. The centralized power structures of the colonizer become so distorted in their reach to the colonial periphery that the subjects of punishment self-administer and deal out the harshest of penalties to fellow convicts.

The retelling of Pearce's story by the Drones takes the perhaps counter-intuitive perspective of a kind of dramatic monologue delivered by the Executioner, the man charged with delivering the death sentence. The six stanzas of the song express the Executioner's feelings of ambivalence and anger towards Pearce, the other 'death row boys', and the colonial authorities. The Executioner gives particular attention to what he sees as the hypocrisy of the chaplain, here figured as a metonym for colonial society. Stanzas two and five begin with the same lines: 'Well your chaplain loves you/ Death row boys/ More than he loves me.' Stanza five continues:

> He abandons you to prayer
> Turns so he won't see
> You standing alone
> As you were all along
> To descend fear first
> Abscond from the earth
> Alone

The Executioner's contempt for and alienation from all parties involved in the colonial system doubles the sense of alienation that is already apparent with Pearce. While the experience of exile pervades the whole song, particularly Pearce's abject cannibalism – conveyed in the Executioner's question 'and tell me how do we taste?' – the theme is stated most succinctly in the final short stanza: 'We were meant to meet/Your exile is reached/ You're home.' The Executioner's final words mark a complex spatial figuration: according to the Executioner, Pearce is at home in exile. Additionally, the first line of the final paragraph – 'we were meant to meet' – suggests that Pearce is also fated to encounter the Executioner, and therefore the convict is, in a sense, at home on the scaffold, the machinery of death. The paradoxical idea of 'exile as home' expressed by the Executioner resonates with Kristeva's theorization of the foreigner: 'Not belonging to any place, any time, any love. A lost origin, the impossibility to take root [...] The space of the foreigner is a moving train, a plane in flight, the very transition that precludes stopping' (7–8). The first lines of the song – 'Now that it's time to go/ Can you see the chariots/ Swinging low' (a reference to the African American spiritual composition 'Swing Low, Sweet Chariot') – are also consonant with Kristeva's discussion of the foreigner's space as rootless, as a 'moving train, a plane in flight'. The abject swinging motion of execution by hanging that awaits Pearce casts him as a foreigner and exile in life. Despite the stasis of death, Pearce still exhibits some small level of mobility, even if it is only a macabre sway in mid-air.

'Words' resonates within the archipelagic connectivity at play in the larger framework of the three songs through its mobilization of a number of tensions: home vs. exile, life vs. death and human vs. cannibal. From a broad geographic perspective, the landscape of Van Diemen's Land – one of the most far-flung and mythically hellish outposts of the British Empire – is placed in opposition to the colonial centre, from where Pearce is exiled. From Ireland to Van Diemen's Land, from one island to another, and from one archipelago to another: this centre/margin dynamic is complicated by the Executioner. His criticism of Pearce, the other Irish death row boys and the chaplain displaces the typical convict hero vs. colonial power structure and offers a second point of opposition with the centre. On the surface the narrative of 'colonial/penal exile marooned on an island' plays easily to the set of island tropes – insularity, the reification of borders and resistance to contamination – discussed by McMahon, Baldacchino and Gillis. But the abject undertone of Pearce's cannibalism and the decentering perspective of the strangely moral figure of the Executioner accentuates the paradoxical traits of the island. The positioning of the Executioner as the teller of this colonial tale supplants Pearce as the sole representative of the underdog and outsider. Instead of the overtly abject figuration taken by the Drones and Liddiard in their other convict and outsider songs, 'Words' delivers a colonial myth through a fresh set of eyes. The Executioner – an actor deployed by 'the System' to perform its most omnipotent judgements on the ultimate figure of abjection, the cannibal Pearce – others himself by taking neither the side of the oppressed or the oppressor.

'I Was a Native of Erin's Island'

'Sixteen Straws' moves the spatial concerns of 'Words' to Moreton Bay. Based on the real events that also inspired Jessica Anderson's 1975 novel *The Commandant*, 'Sixteen Straws' is a strophic ballad-style song that draws on the lyrical content, but not melody or chord structure, of 'Moreton Bay'. Through five verses the song tells of the cruelty and brutality of the colonial penal system, of the grim desperation of convicts attempting to escape lives of misery and of frontier violence involving the surprise attack by local Aboriginal people on the infamous Commandant Logan. The perverse degradation of nineteenth-century convict life is summed up in the convict O'Brien's speech, mid-way through the third verse. Appealing to the inverted logic of his fellow convicts, O'Brien asks, 'Why should we grasp at the/ Straws of our lives/ When we're only condemned by our will to survive?' Equating life to the insignificant 'straws' of the title of the song typifies the moral and ethical distortion created by colonial systems of power.

The first two verses of 'Sixteen Straws' transplant lyrics directly from 'Moreton Bay'. Included is a list of the various 'places of condemnation' that the convict protagonist has survived:

> I was a native of Erin's Island [...]
> I've been a prisoner at Port Macquarie
> Norfolk Island and Emu Plains
> At Castle Hill and cursed Toongabbie
> At all of these settlements

> I've worked in chains
> But of all of the places of condemnation
> At each penal station in New South Wales
> To Moreton Bay I've found no equal
> The tyranny there makes all the rest pale

This list of locations describes a nineteenth-century penal archipelago that, in its orientation according to convict experience, spreads across the globe. What Liddiard then adds to the bare bones of the narrative of 'Moreton Bay' is his own exploration of a landscape that, peppered with abject imagery, expands the bounds of the Australian convict mythology.

The chief flogger drinking a bucket of blood-infused water after his inhuman exertions – a moment of the song which proved so popular with the audience at the Drones concert – is one of many abject and violent images that identify the porosity of the convict body under punishment. Another related instance is the consequences of a conspiracy hatched by two convicts, the Jew and O'Brien, who formulate a plan to murder Commandant Logan. In an obvious reference to Rufus Dawes in Marcus Clarke's classic *For the Term of His Natural Life* (1874), when the convict protagonist informs the authorities of the plan the Jew and O'Brien are severely punished with 300 lashes. 'O'Brien came off his triangle/ With exposed shoulder blades/ His skin never healed/ He turned morbid and strange.' The next episode recounted by the protagonist is of his unlucky selection of the long straw in the death pact: '14 pairs of eyes watched me/ Pounding a shiv through his heart/ And for a few moments there was no/ Stopping the blood.' The intricate movements of displacement and othering that feature in 'Words' are again apparent in 'Sixteen Straws'. The archetypical outsider figure of 'the Jew', while at once rehearsing Kristeva's thesis on the fascist tendency latent within the abject, amplifies a second, more marginal experience of otherness, outside even that abject landscape inhabited by the rest of the convicts in the song. The Jew is in fact the most deformed and abject character in 'Sixteen Straws': 'The Jew had one hand/ He was a violent man/ He'd worn the twenty-pound iron's since before time began.' Sounding a current of anti-Semitism within the otherness already opened by the national convict myth, the Drones have their convict protagonist, an Irishman, murder the Jew.

Following the death pact episode the remaining prisoners must be transported from their workstation back to the authorities to face punishment. The sequence where the convicts attempt to escape captivity on the whaleboat *en route* to Moreton Bay also features a set of violent images, including 'A red coat squirting blood/ Through a hole in his chin' and the protagonist's recollection: 'I've seen ghoulish things/ Men shot limb from limb/ O'Brien was dead/ There were pieces of him.' The protagonist also learns of the demise of Logan, who, hunting the escaped convicts, happens upon a group of local Aboriginal people and 'took a spear through the brain'. These images provide an often-explicit depiction of the abject state of convict bodies and the general brutality of the early colonial period in Australia. The malleability and disintegration of these bodies under the impact of the colonial penal system accentuates their rejected, expelled position from the imperial centre and the forced exile from their homelands. 'Sixteen Straws' maps an outsider cartography, crowded with antipodean inversions exemplified by the game that gives the song its title. In reinventing and extending 'Moreton Bay' as 'Sixteen Straws', the Drones re-inscribe a nineteenth-century landscape of exile, opening an abject space of otherness within the convict story. This reverberation, literally voiced by the crowd at the Metro, picks up the tones of otherness and displacement heard in 'Words' and places them not on Van Diemen's Land or Sarah Island but on the 'island continent' encased within an archipelagic webbing of 'places of condemnation'.

Twentieth-Century Abjection

The final link in the 'Drones-ipelago' transports the figure of the outsider from the early nineteenth century into the late twentieth and early twenty-first century, just prior to the 11 September terrorist attacks in the United States. 'D' also shifts from the encroaching wilderness of the Tasmanian and New South Wales penal settlements in 'Words' and 'Sixteen Straws' to an urban fringe wasteland. Mixing Liddiard's Western Australian childhood with a purely fictional reconstruction of David Hick's early years, 'D' is a dramatic and dynamic song describing the development of a modern outsider, from adolescence to young adulthood, that builds to a more explosive sonic conclusion than 'Words' or 'Sixteen Straws'. The finals minutes of the song – produced by only Liddiard's vocals and steel string acoustic guitar – are a sonic maelstrom that moves the lyrical focus from D to Cliff, a resident of Brooklyn, New York. Despite possessing the affluent trappings afforded by wealth and opportunity and living in one of the centres of the industrialized world, Cliff's existence is a nightmare. His story, conveyed through a powerful vocal/lyrical refrain, resonates across the transhistorical global archipelago sounded by the three songs.

'D' is divided into four verses that relay experiences and images progressing in scale from extreme locality through to the global events of 9/11, an event that is figured in terms of worldwide media networks. The opening verse of the song is populated by specific, everyday objects that are given an abject character. Liddiard intones a horrific landscape that completely subverts any notion of the innocence of childhood. Wandering through his environment, the young D kills birds, makes bombs, tries to imagine his absent mother and plays with disused toys, finding a King Kong doll that 'roars ants when he shakes it'. Rehearsing a childhood not available to him, so much of what D experiences is abject. He sees a 'Phillishave full of hair clippings', hears 'the sound of his father fucking through the evening' and watches an appalling pornographic video depicting 'two girls on a farm somewhere/ Playing with a Labrador'. The centrepiece of this scene, by far the most abject image of the song, undermines the sanctity of an Australian national icon. While exploring, D

> Finds a severed kangaroo hind leg
> Just laying in a clearing
> There's a tendon or a tapeworm
> That retracts after a kick
> Finds a new stink that nearly makes him puke
> When he pokes it with a stick

The episode is completed when D – who is both intrigued and repelled by the perverse form and smell of the kangaroo leg – returns home via the 'dog door'. This opening verse creates an extremely detailed picture of the outsider landscape of D. Some of the objects, like the 'Hills Hoist' or 'Tip Top bread', are icons of Australian culture, specific to the domestic space and time they evoke. The kangaroo leg operates as a metonym: separated from its body, it deconstructs the wholeness of nature. An animal unique to Australia, this kangaroo is not 'Skippy' from the (now deeply nostalgic) children's television programme of the same name (1968–70), not the bounding marsupial painted onto Qantas planes or the namesake of so many proud Australian sporting teams, like the Boomers (basketball), the Wallabies (rugby union), the Kangaroos (rugby league), Socceroos or Hockeyroos. Nor is it fit to be consumed as an Indigenous food source. Instead, the kangaroo's abjection is multiple, both a sign of death and the home of a parasite. D's construction of a pipe bomb that 'fizzes like a feral cat he's seen, slithers like the snake he killed' only emphasizes the animal hostility of the environment.

Further episodes of D's unfortunate life are narrated. His father dies; he continues to live in the socio-economic underbelly. D's flirtation with fascism – in the form of a friend, Werner, 'whose father was SS' – is an echo of the fascist sentiments heard in 'Sixteen Straws', although 'D thinks Hitler's obsolete/ And Werner's practice too relaxed.' Another side to D's exploration of fascism is revealed when he starts drinking 'cheap cask wine with old black fellas/ living in the park/ One has a tattoo of a swastika made with a candle, soap and spoons'. The perversity of this image seems to strike a chord of pity in D: the Aboriginal man describes himself as a 'half cast [...] brought up on a mission', he 'became a Viet vet' and 'Ain't got a single tooth to chew'. In response to this, D 'gives him the bayonet' he had bought earlier. This is the only act of kindness relayed in the entire song – or 'Words' and 'Sixteen Straws' – and it stands as a moment of connection between two figures on the fringes of society. Aboriginal Australia is peripheral to the songs by the Drones and Liddiard, and its presence here, and in 'Sixteen Straws', reminds us of the larger colonial effort towards silencing the first Australians. Including Aboriginal 'minor characters' adds depth to the landscape of abjection opened by the songs, assigning it to more than a purely white colonialist locus.

Unlike the colonial violence and convict bodies in 'Words' and 'Sixteen Straws', the abjection in 'D' describes an animalistic urban wasteland populated by domestic sounds and images that are disgusting in their closeness and variety. Young D is exiled from the institution of family and wanders beyond the boundaries of a safe childhood backyard. All this leads to his later outsider experiences, where the historical figure of David Hicks is subjected to the suspension of human rights through his incarceration at Guantanamo Bay in the United States controlled territory in Cuba. The abject instability founded in childhood and adolescence is played out on a global scale through D/Hicks's shackled movement between the island continent of Australia and the ambivalence of the Cuban island in the Caribbean archipelago, a space with its own long and complex history of colonialism, slavery and postcolonial regeneration.

The fourth verse of 'D' moves from this deeply embedded (almost hidden) Australian landscape and zooms out to a broader perspective. In a change that underscores the global character of the mapping performed by the song, another location – New York City – is brought into view. Here Liddiard shifts from narrating the experiences of D, who we leave as he attempts suicide after being abandoned by Werner:

> 'D goes to find his .22
> But there ain't no shells at all
> He finds 5 valium in a Winfield pack
> In a duffel bag in the hall
> Then sits in front of the TV screen
> Washes it all down with a bottle

A new character – Cliff – is introduced. From an economic and material perspective, he is the polar opposite to D: 'Cliff has a beautiful wife/ He's insured for his life.' In contrast to D's place on the periphery, Cliff lives in an economic and cultural centre. Despite this difference, the two characters do share an important similarity: they are both deeply engaged in global (Western) media networks and this techno-archipelagic link, where abjection and radicalization butt up against fear and paranoia, is the key to making sense of Liddiard's switch of perspective in the last quarter of the song. The coda of the song explicitly places the action at the time of 9/11 – 'But now we interrupt this broadcast/ To bring you breaking news/ There is a building in Manhattan/ And it's burning' – and in this sense D and Cliff are like two sides of a coin. One is radicalized, abjectified and decentred, and the other is caught in a heart of darkness in the centre. Cliff, in his nightmare Brooklyn, is like the continent to which D, the deject outside, is both attracted and repulsed.

Television is the linking force spanning the extreme distances of this global archipelago. Earlier in the song D follows a news story on TV: 'There's a man gone crazy/ He stole an APC from an army base/ And closed down half the city.' In Brooklyn, Cliff watches sloganistic television commercials that reflect the pressures and preoccupations of Western modernity. Liddiard sings, 'Yeah Just Do It, Have A Break, yes Life Is Good/ Because You're Worth It/ Maybe She was Born With It?' Unlike the abjection of D's world, media advertising emphasizes fetish items, but the abject reality of this culture is still recognized: 'You are driving the Jeep Cherokee/ Burning Arabs for fuel/ But you are driving the Jeep Cherokee/ And that's good enough for you.' Cruising the American highways of opportunity, the Jeep Cherokee runs on the fumes of the abjected Arab – Middle East is another location on the global carceral archipelago. Cliff's world is one undergirded by exploitation of the other, and, as we see in the final epilogue to the song, the full horror of this reality is about to be performed in the real and symbolic violence of 9/11 and the ensuing 'War on Terror' in Iraq and Afghanistan.

Where the opening third of 'D' maps an abject Australian wasteland surrounded by the mists of childhood and adolescence, the last section of the song creates a nightmare zone positioned just before 9/11. Liddiard does this through a lyrical refrain built from the line 'you are living in a nightmare', a phrase that appears in an earlier verse that relates the death of D's father. This refrain works in conjunction with sonic intensification: Liddiard sings the whole Cliff section up one octave from the rest of the song, his voice takes on a harsher tone, and his guitar playing is more aggressive and percussive. Delivering the following lyrics in this way serves to build the momentum of the song to boiling point.

> You are living in a nightmare,
> Let them Balkanize the East
> No one says a word these days,

> They turn the other cheek
> You are living in a nightmare
> You can't trust a ceasefire bid
> And any wall they build around Gaza
> Will be begging for a lid
> You are living in a nightmare
> You can't bribe a want of doubt
> You are living in a nightmare
> You can't bribe your way out of

The repetition of 'you are living in a nightmare' is the crux of this refrain. The second person 'you' changes the direction of the address: instead of telling a story about a character (D, or Cliff), Liddiard is more directly addressing the listener, like he is diagnosing a wrong or making an accusation. At the same time, and just as importantly for the refrain, this perspective allows interior access to Cliff: the lyrics also operate as if Cliff is addressing himself. This doubling within the refrain creates an overlapping personal/public territory that extends the horizon of the abject landscape opened in the childhood and adolescence scenes with D. The two spaces – D in Australia and Cliff in Brooklyn – sit at either end of Liddiard's song and relate to each other as periphery and centre. Within the temporality of the song the nightmare-scape of Cliff's existence emerges out of D's misery – a causality mirrored in the link between the ultimate horror of 9/11 and the abjection and radicalization behind it. Cliff is not a deject, but, via the global networks of the media, the reverberations of D's experience of rejection reach across the globe. This mobility continues the global carceral journeys – between Ireland, the British archipelago, Van Diemen's Land and Moreton Bay – sounded by the figures of Alexander Pearce and the Executioner, and later with the characters in 'Sixteen Straws'.

Stretched between the nation as both continent and (global carceral) archipelago, the mapping of Australian space performed by the Drones and Liddiard occupies a unique position in *Imagined Sound*. Escaping continental bonds, these songs sound a global carceral territory at the foundations of the non-Indigenous experience of the Australian landscape. From the nineteenth-century convict frontier through to the contemporary urban space of the modern deject, this music remaps the landscape of one of Australia's central myths. It is a timely contribution to the evolution of the convict narrative. Returning to the scene of performance at the Metro, the audience response to the abject lyrical flourishes that mark 'Sixteen Straws' (but also 'Words' and 'D') recognizes the creative individuality and performance skill of the Drones and Liddiard. Eliciting such a chorus of voices in response to a foundational Australian myth is no mean feat.

Chapter Five

ECHOES BETWEEN VAN DIEMEN'S LAND AND TASMANIA: THE SPACE OF THE ISLAND IN RICHARD FLANAGAN'S *DEATH OF A RIVER GUIDE* AND CARMEL BIRD'S *CAPE GRIMM*

Exploring colonial history, contemporary trauma and the geoimaginary of the island, Richard Flanagan's *Death of a River Guide* (1994) and Carmel Bird's *Cape Grimm* (2004) embed genealogical narratives within revisionist historical fiction. The novels search for origins – of family, space and culture. Extending maps of the present back into the colonial past, they uncover the landscapes of violent contact between colonial settlers and Aboriginal people. Reading these two novels we listen to how imagined sound creates a spatio-temporal continuum bridging the chasm between the present and a lost and repressed past. This portal – created by two soundscapes in each novel – is explicitly figured in both works as the violent resonance of the clash between colonial and Indigenous culture, events that are sounded and re-sounded in traumatic echoes that link the past to the present.

My close listening analysis of the soundscapes at the foundations of both *River Guide* and *Cape Grimm* takes up Georg Lukacs's thesis on the historical novel – that it involves 'not the retelling of great historical events, but the poetic awakening of the people who figured in those events' (1962, 42) – and shows how this poetic awakening is also a sonic haunting. The return of the repressed via sound coheres most powerfully around the form of a scream. Circumscribing the geoimaginaries of the novels, the scream echoes across time and space to reveal within the separate hidden histories of *River Guide* and *Cape Grimm* a deeply entrenched tonality of trauma that places the island of Van Diemen's Land/Tasmania between familiar island coordinates, origin and extinction. The experiences of trauma co-mingling between soundscapes past and present is as much a product of the island as it is a reinscription of the complexity of that geoimaginary: the island produces the soundscape and the soundscape produces the island.

Flanagan and Bird's imagining of the island also pushes against the historical and aesthetic dynamic, apparent in the tradition of Australian Gothic literature, that positions Indigenous Australian history, and the sound of that history, as other. Overlaying Australian Gothic and sociological theorizations of temporality and haunting with the spatial configuration of the island, the soundscapes in *River Guide* and *Cape Grimm* present Van Diemen's Land/Tasmania as a staging ground capable of supporting the conflicting but nevertheless productive tensions that pierce the local/national/international landscapes and past/present histories of the novels.

River Guide, Flanagan's first work of fiction, tells the story of Aljaz Cosini and his family history in Tasmania and Slovenia. Aljaz is prompted to recount the multiple strands of his genealogy by the situation he finds himself in. Due to an accident that occurs while he is employed in the position of head river guide – leading a group of 'punters' (river adventure tourists) – he is trapped underwater by the flooding Franklin River. Aljaz proclaims, 'I have been granted visions – grand, great, wild sweeping visions. My mind rattles with them as they are born to me. And I must share them, or their magic will become as a burden' (10). These visions are of his birth, the migration of his mother and father from the 'old world' of Europe to Tasmania, and the mythical, hidden and violent events that populate his ancestry at the foundations of colonial contact. The colonial soundscape in *River Guide* depicts the rape of an Indigenous woman, Black Pearl, by a sealer. This is connected to a second soundscape occurring before the colonial scene in the narrative order of the novel, where Aljaz hears a band playing in a Hobart pub. Although *River Guide* has by far the most sonic material of Flanagan's five novels, sound does have a small role in his second novel *The Sound of One Hand Clapping* (1997), with the sublime howling of the rugged Tasmanian landscape harmonizing with the experience of Flanagan's migrant worker Bojan. The retelling of history, specifically Tasmanian history in relation to its recent ecological, migrant and convict past, is an ongoing concern for Flanagan.

Alongside *The White Garden* (1996), *The Red Shoes* (1998) and *Child of the Twilight* (2010), *Cape Grimm* is the third in a series of novels examining what Carmel Bird calls 'charismatic people' (quoted in Salas 2006, 100). The work oscillates between three intersecting phases of genealogical history, all involving the Mean family: the arrival-via-shipwreck of Magnus and Minerva in the 1850s, the birth and life of Caleb Mean and the relationship of Paul Van Loon and Virginia Mean. Paul and Virginia echo French novelist Bernardin de Saint-Pierre's influential novel *Paul et Virginie* (1788), not only in name but in terms of character and theme. Island isolation and innocent incest link Saint-Pierre's novel, set on the French colonial island of Mauritius, with Bird's contemporary setting. The theme of innocence, central to Saint-Pierre's novel, is transformed from a type of knowledge and sexual awakening into historical knowledge through sound in *Cape Grimm* (Henderson 2000, 2002). Amplifying the island resonances shared by *Cape Grimm* and its antecedent *Paul et Virginie*, Ian Henderson suggests, 'Saint-Pierre's *Paul et Virginie* is really a critique of the notion of the New World as a place for starting life "afresh"' (2002, 92). *Cape Grimm* and its mapping of family history and death explicitly takes up this problematic. Bird's Virginia, the survivor of a contemporary mass murder in the isolated North West Tasmanian town of Skye, has a dream that reveals a forgotten part of the early history of European and Indigenous Australian contact: she witnesses a sequence of events depicting colonial violence and the genocide of local Indigenous people. The corresponding contemporary soundscape of the Skye genocide replays this impulse to extinction. Positioned within Bird's larger body of work, genealogy, convict history and the island landscapes of Tasmania, particularly its isolated North Western corner, are reoccurring themes, although sound does not feature significantly in any of her other novels.

A unique aspect of Flanagan and Bird's soundscapes in *River Guide* and *Cape Grimm* is the listening perspective. Recalling Truax, whose definition of soundscape places specific 'emphasis on how [the soundscape] is perceived or understood by the individual, or by society' (126), in these two Tasmanian novels there are several 'listening perspectives' or points of view (perhaps more pertinently, points of imaginary hearing). The reader experiences each soundscape from this perspective, a position that registers differences in narrative style, structure, characterization and location, a spectrum that reflects the spatio-temporal complexity of the narratives being told by Flanagan and Bird. The value of a close listening approach lies in its ability to engage with the entanglements of space and time resonant within the novels and projected by their soundscapes. In addition to issues of perspective, I approach the specific structure of imagined sound in the two novels through Deleuze and Guattari's refrain, the rhythmic repetition of which enunciates the overlapping spaces of the past and present in Flanagan's novel. Paul Carter's concept of 'the sound in between' also enables me to examine how the past is linked to the present through sound, specifically through the echoes of the frontier meeting-through-sound of Indigenous and colonizer that feature in Bird's novel.

Gothic, Haunted, Suppressed: Island Soundscapes

In addition to these sound concepts – the soundscape, refrain and 'sound in between' – the unstable time and uncanny resonance of the haunting, the spectral and the traditions of the Australian Gothic also reconcile the distance between Van Diemen's Land and Tasmania. The 'difficult liminal states, transgression of boundaries, and spatial oppressions' (Ng 2007, 149) of the Australian Gothic tradition have long contended with the ghosts of a colonial past that Tasmania, and the rest of Australia, has attempted to forget. Jim Davidson argues that the Gothic is 'a way of looking at Tasmania as least as old as Marcus Clarke' (1989, 310): Clarke's *For the Term of His Natural Life* (1874) is often cited as one of the finest Gothic works of literature produced by an Australian (Turcotte 1998; Ng 2007; Gelder and Weaver 2007). While *Natural Life* is a canonical work of this genre, more pertinent to Flanagan and Bird's novels is Clarke's *Preface to the Poems of Adam Lindsay Gordon* (1876), a short but foundational evocation of the Australian Gothic and the experience of the 'weird melancholy' of the bush:

> The savage winds shout among the rock clefts [...] Flights of white cockatoos stream out, shrieking like evil souls [...] the mopokes burst out into horrible peals of semi-human laughter [...] The lonely horseman riding between the moonlight and the day sees vast shadows creeping across the shelterless and silent plains, hears strange noises in the primeval forest [...] the dweller in the wilderness [...] becomes familiar with the beauty of loneliness. Whispered to by the myriad tongues of the wilderness, he learns the language of the barren and the uncouth. (Clarke 1970, n.p.)

The sonic elements in this text extracted from the middle of Clarke's *Preface* are numerous, encompassing the ghoulish sounds of the supernatural and the vast silences of the wilderness. Ken Gelder and Rachel Weaver's suggestion that 'the colonial Australian Gothic especially relishes the aural effects of the bush' (2007, 4) voices the ongoing influence of the sounds emanating from Clarke's 'primeval forest'.

Despite its value in terms of sound, Clarke's description of the Australian Gothic landscape suppresses what Gelder and Weaver see as the defining feature of the Gothic in its Australian context. They argue that 'the colonial Australian Gothic is intimately tied to the violence of settler life' (9), Gelder suggests that both the colonial legacy of 'dispossession and killing of Aboriginal people' and the 'foundational systems of punishment and incarceration [...] [continue] to shadow Australian cultural production [and] keep the Australian Gothic very much alive' (2007, 122). A nexus of historical and fictionalized instances of this colonial violence are central narrative events in *River Guide* and *Cape Grimm*: both novels can in this sense be branded Australian Gothic historical fiction in the tradition opened by Clarke's sound-filled *Preface*.

Relocating the scene of the Australian Gothic to a time frame contemporary with the composition of *River Guide* and *Cape Grimm*, literary critic Judy

Newman extends Gelder and Weaver's discussions to the postcolonial Gothic. According to Newman, 'Postcolonial Gothic [...] is Janus-faced. At its heart lies the unresolved conflict between imperial power and the former colony, which the mystery at the centre of the plot both figures and conceals' (86). Newman's characterization of the colonial and postcolonial within *River Guide* and *Cape Grimm* as 'Janus-faced' resonates closely with my listening to a transhistorical continuum of imagined sound in the novels. Newman also casts this temporal relation in terms of sound, suggesting the discourse 'establishes a dynamic between the unspoken and the "spoken for"' (1994, 86). This energy, which is at the core of the novels, also speaks to the sonic forms favoured by Flanagan and Bird, vocalization and screaming. The connection between soundscapes and the events they narrate and surround is a temporal shift that links, through sound, the postcolonial present of each novel to its colonial past. In this shift the suppressed or forgotten violence at the foundations of the two related Tasmanian landscapes is heard.

Commenting on the temporality of such a haunted landscape, David Bunn suggests that time 'is experienced in a peculiar way. The settler landscape cannot afford the Romantic luxury of bathing in the past [...] because the past is the domain of the Other, and history is the history of dispossession' (1994, 143). *River Guide* and *Cape Grimm* both orchestrate this history of dispossession. The novels also attempt to navigate this landscape without harking back to a lost utopia. The soundscapes from the colonial past in each novel depict a history of violence, but through the sonic connection with the soundscapes of the present, the past is not marked purely as an historical space for hiding or commemorating violent encounters with Indigenous Australians, forgotten people that are unknowable, designated 'other'. Instead, through the sound of this past as it resonates within the present, these encounters on the colonial frontier are sites of common, if violent, foundation and grounding. Like Henry Reynolds's recent call for the recognition of the Frontier Wars (2013), the novels by Flanagan and Bird enable us to listen to and recognize the bloody foundations of Australian history.

As we will hear in the close listening below, the sounds that emerge out of the past in *River Guide* and *Cape Grimm* are distinctly ghostly evocations of events forgotten or repressed. Avery Gordon's concept of haunting provides another useful thematic and structural plank linking the Australian Gothic and the transhistorical continuum in sound. Gordon argues, 'Haunting raises specters, and it alters the experience of being in linear time, alters the way we normally separate and sequence the past, the present and the future' (2011, 2). The non-linearity of the haunting is seen in the looping, interrelated content of both soundscapes – in the return of the song structures and the screams from the past to the present in *River Guide* and

Cape Grimm respectively, as well as more generally, in the narrative structure of both novels. The spectral – what Jacques Derrida characterizes as 'the experience of the non-present, of the non-living present in the living present (of the spectral), of that which lives on' (1994, 254) – takes both visual and auditory form in Flanagan's and Bird's novels. Gordon's characterization of haunting as 'not about invisibility or unknowability per se, it refers us to what's living and breathing in the place hidden from view: people, places, histories, knowledge, memories, ways of life, ideas' (3) speaks directly to the obscured or silenced histories made audible in the soundscapes of *River Guide* and *Cape Grimm*. This history is a spectral resonance within the present. While reconfiguring linear temporality and remapping historical space, the sonic hauntings of these novels also broadcast a challenge to visual dominance, to the colonial formation and control of the landscape via the imperial eye of the explorer, cartographer, soldier and jailer (Pratt 1992; Columpar 2002; Arnold 2006).

Van Diemen's Land and Tasmania: Islands within Islands

The histories revealed by sound in *River Guide* and *Cape Grimm* chart the early colonial period, when Tasmania was called Van Diemen's Land. The change of the name Van Diemen's Land to Tasmania, which took place on 1 January 1856, exemplifies Davidson's suggestion that 'Tasmania is the only state which systematically set about erasing its first half-century: under a new name, it was determined to be born again' (307). This conscious attempt to forget and erase the contamination of the past, of the origin, is the island geoimaginary *par excellence*. Tasmania, and the 'spectre' of the island's former guise, Van Diemen's Land, position the novels within a web of interlocking spatial and thematic discourses that characterize the island as capable of grounding and *sounding* turbulent histories and contradicting ideas.

Examining what he calls the 'master metaphor' (3) of the island, John Gillis argues the 'island is capable of representing a multitude of things [...] fragmentation and vulnerability but also wholeness and safety [...] loss but also recovery [...] [it] can represent both separation and continuity, isolation and connection' (3). Of particular relevance here is the tension, played out in myriad ways in Flanagan and Bird, between symbolic quarantine and exile of subversive elements, otherwise known as convictism, vs. the 'welcome' of immigrants from 'old Europe' (River Guide), South America and the British Isles (Cape Grimm). Godfrey Baldacchino designates the island in terms of both spatial and temporal movement, key aspects of the novels that are voiced as issues of immigration, travel and narrative movement across time. As Baldacchino says, the island 'confronts us as a juxtaposition and confluence of [...] local *and* global realities, of interior *and* exterior references of meaning, of having *roots* at home while also deploying *routes* away from home. An island *is* a world, yet an island *engages* the world' (248). Forming a transhistorical continuum between past/present or origin/extinction, the imagined sound of *River Guide* and *Cape Grimm* accentuates the always-connected nature of Baldacchino's 'nervous duality' (248) while also amplifying the forgotten or silenced parts of a colonial history founded on power dynamics of European/Indigenous, winner/loser, official/outsider and recorded/suppressed. Davidson's suggestion that 'Gothic Tasmania proves to be a synthesizing vision, since it can accommodate disjunctions between the past and present' (310) both addresses the competing forces at play within the island and gestures towards my own discussion of a transhistorical continuum through sound.

The wider cultural impact of the retelling and uncovering of Australian colonial history performed in *River Guide* and *Cape Grimm* is closely aligned with the often-heated confrontations of 'The History Wars' in the 1990s and 2000s, and both the publication dates, content and Tasmanian setting of *River Guide* and *Cape Grimm* place the novels in the midst of this struggle. The effort of the works to reimagine and resound this difficult and bloody history link them with other similarly themed novels published in the period, such as Peter Carey's *True History of the Kelly Gang* (2000) or Kate Grenville's *The Secret River* (2005). But the use of soundscape in *River Guide* and *Cape Grimm* sets them apart from these contemporaries, gesturing towards a large number of works in different media, such as Peter Sculthorpe's *Quamby* (2000), a composition that draws on the same history as *Cape Grimm*, or Ros Bandt's sound work *Mungo* (1992) which mixes the voices of local Aboriginal elders with soundscape recordings and Aeolian harp.

Like all historical fiction, *River Guide* and *Cape Grimm* are driven by the creative tension between imagining the private lives of fictional characters and the real historical figures and events at their foundation. In his influential study *The Historical Novel* (1937) Georg Lukacs argues, 'Really great historical art' consists of 'bringing the past to life as the prehistory of the present, in giving poetic life to those historical, social and human forces which, in the course of a long evolution, have made our present-day life what it is' (53). The colonial soundscapes in *River Guide* and *Cape Grimm* are the sonic realization of Lukacs's 'prehistory of the present': structural and textural aspects of historical soundscapes echo within the contemporary soundscapes by literally and sonically 'bringing the past to life'. In *River Guide* the explicitly historical content includes the rape of Indigenous women by sealers, as well as the more immediate contexts of European immigration to Australia and the Franklin River protest movement. *Cape Grimm* gives even more specificity to the integration of historical events with fictional content, overlaying the massacres at

Cape Grim and Quamby Bluff with an account of the eccentric inhabitants of a fictional town in North-Western Tasmania.

Colonial Soundscapes

My approach to the soundscapes of *River Guide* and *Cape Grimm* is to listen to them in the reverse order to which they occur in the narrative of each novel. Rather than figuring it as a pivotal moment that other events proceed from, the inverted configuration chosen by Flanagan and Bird emphasizes the silenced nature of the histories they write. Instead, we will first listen to the colonial soundscape, the origin, hidden deep in the pages of these narratives before encountering the ghostly return. Such as reordering reveals the continuum fashioned by the echoing of sounds, the causality of events, from past to present.

Each small section of *River Guide* is given a title, and the colonial soundscape is called 'Black Pearl 1829'. It is one of the last visions Aljaz has before he drowns in the river.

> The woman being raped begins to sing a strange and forlorn song. Her song sounds the emptiness of the beach and the ocean, echoes the distant cry of the sea eagle, calls for the return screech of the black cockatoo. 'Shut up, Black Pearl', warns the sealer as he thrusts in and out. 'Shut up'.
>
> But Black Pearl continues to sing to her brother the blue-tongued lizard, her mother the river, her father the rocks, her sister the crayfish that smells of woman [...] On and on the song goes, and after the sealer pukes and then falls asleep in a stupor, the two other women come over and lie together with Black Pearl. They lie together on the land on which they once stood with pride. As they warm each other on the beach, they join in the low song that seems to cover all the sand. The song and the sound of the waves become one and on and on it goes, and though the women are now asleep the black cockatoo and the sea eagle sing. The wind in the boobiallas passes the song on to the wind in the gums, who teaches it to the wind in the myrtles and celery top pines, who then sings it to the river and to the rocks. (315–16)

This soundscape is sonically profuse and full of detail. It opens a similar landscape and time – the littoral beach in the early nineteenth century – to what we hear in *Cape Grimm*. Despite the parallels, the violence here is more graphic, and the personal significance of this event to the contemporary listener, Aljaz, is also more explicit. Following all the other revelations he has already had about his ancestors, in this scene Aljaz understands that Black Pearl is the matriarch of one branch of his family: 'I realise I am witness to the conception of Auntie Ellie's mother and to the genesis of all that I am' (316). This genealogical epiphany is at the core *River Guide*'s exploration of suppressed colonial and family history.

From the ocean and rocks up to a variety of birds and tree species, the song of Black Pearl sounds a multileveled local natural environment. Although Black Pearl is being assaulted, her song is both a defensive refrain against the violence and a sonic analogue with her surroundings. She both 'sounds the emptiness' of the local space while also eliciting responses from birds and plants that appear to be of totemic importance. The scene shows Black Pearl's song directly addressing animals and parts of the environment: the bluetongue lizard, the river, the rocks, the crayfish. Sound here embodies family and totemic ties, orienting Black Pearl in the midst of her country. In the second half of the scene Black Pearl is joined in her song by two other women. The song 'covers' the sand, 'becomes one' with the sound of the waves and, after the women sleep, this momentum is carried by the black cockatoo and the sea eagle, who then pass it onto the 'wind' that moves between several species of tree, before finally arriving at the river and rocks. Initiated by Black Pearl, the movement of her song signals something of the multilayered and interconnected nature of an Indigenous Australian worldview thrown into violent contact with sealing, a commercial aspect of colonialism. Because it is *imagined* sound we as readers do not know what Black Pearl's song sounds like, but the way that it is taken up by so many elements of the surrounding ecology gives a sense that it is beyond conventional harmony/melody parameters. It is a song of imagined sound that, in its consonance with the environment, shares timbres and textures with many animal, plant and environmental sounds.

In *Cape Grimm* the foundational scene of colonial violence is focalized through the perspective of Virginia Mean. Virginia is one of only three survivors of the fire that destroys Skye, the insular community founded by the ancestor of Virginia's cousin and lover, Caleb Mean. Orchestrated by Caleb, the fire results in his incarceration in a mental facility, while Virginia is so traumatized as to be rendered mute. Encouraged by her carer Father Fox, Virginia keeps a journal, where she records this dream:

> I am sitting in the cave that is a place to which I go, a special secret place. The black girl swims up to me, and whispers a word that sounds like 'Mercy' over and over again. Even though she is far below me in the water I can hear her whispering moans and sounds and words as they climb through the air towards me, up the cliff. Ladders of whispered words ascend the split and crumbling battered flecky stoneface of the crenellated cliff [...] We look out to the horizon and we see tall ghost

ships sailing alone with purpose and intent just behind a scrim of dull-grey drizzling gauze. We see small flashes of the red coats of the soldiers, we hear the sound of guns, the rough cries of the men in chains [...] Like George Augustus Robinson, I hear the shrieks of the mothers, the cries of the children, the agony of the men. And I see the people, and I see the massacres, and they move across and through the phantom landscape of my sight. (2004, 180–82)

This scene, and the name of the novel, reference the Cape Grim massacre that took place on 28 February 1828, when around 30 Pennemukeer people were murdered. George Augustus Robinson, charged by the colonial governor with resituating the remaining Indigenous inhabitants of Tasmania, reported that the bodies of those killed were also thrown from a 60-meter cliff: this is also alluded to in Caleb's plan to ride off the cliff with Virginia after the fire has killed the rest of his followers.

The sonic aspects of this dream soundscape are numerous. Foremost are the whispered pleas of the Indigenous woman named Mannaginni, who Virginia later thinks may be Truganini, an Indigenous woman made famous as the mythical 'last Tasmanian', a false title considering the continued presence of Indigenous people on Tasmania to this day. Mannaginni 'whispers a word that sounds like "Mercy"', perhaps a reference to the Tasmanian landmark Quamby Bluff, reportedly the site of another Indigenous massacre by colonialists. These sounds are repeated 'over and over again', appearing to fill the entire area. Housed within the soundscape, this is a refrain that sounds the horror of the Indigenous experience of colonial violence. The sounds 'climb through the air towards me, up the cliff'. It is as if the sound has an agency of its own: 'Ladders of whispered words ascend the split and crumbling battered flecky stoneface of the crenellated cliff.'

This first part of the soundscape is dominated by the multiple meanings of the word 'mercy'. Carter has theorized sonic misinterpretation at the frontier meeting of colonists and Indigenous people, calling words like 'mercy', or, to use his example of 'cooee', 'sounds in between' (1992). The resonance of such words fill the material space of the frontier, and despite the fact that they are incorrectly interpreted by the colonists (and Virginia, in her dream), they are a form of first contact communication. As Virginia enters another part of the dream, she joins with Mannaginni in perceiving the violent sounds of colonial invasion and convict occupation, 'the sound of guns, the rough cries of the men in chains'. By mentioning the similarity of listening perspective to Robinson – 'like Robison I hear' – the scale of the events Virginia witnesses are augmented, from a personal vision to a wider historical scope. Alongside Robinson, Virginia hears the screams of a whole people: 'The shrieks of the mothers, the cries of the children, the agony of the men' accompanies her visions of 'the massacres'. This is not one scene but a tableau or compilation of suffering.

Soundscapes Return

The contemporary soundscape in *River Guide* revoices some of this harmony of suffering while transposing it into a different register and perspective. The soundscape takes place in the last third of the novel, after the majority of the various stories of family history have been told by Aljaz, but before the soundscape of Black Pearl. Aljaz is in a pub listening to a band:

> When Aljaz heard the sound that then screeched forth from Shag's guitar he knew what Shag was playing upon that guitar, knew that fat old man wanted to make those strings scream: *If you leave you can never be free.*
>
> It was a dreadful noise, but there was something in it that even then I recognised. Now I know it was not a new song, but a song I had unknowingly carried within me for a long time. But what was it? Once more I hear the lead singer, shouting, screaming, joining Shag's guitar. Even back there in the bar Aljaz felt compelled to watch the singer's hands, outstretched as if he were being electrocuted, watch the fat on his face wobble and his forehead sweat and a few thin streaks of hairs that crossed it grow wet with exertion. He screamed it out until he looked worse than some animal in agony. He was no longer singing for the crowd or for the lousy money those behind the ringing till would give the band at the end of the night. Nobody in that bar knew, but I know it now. That he was not even singing for himself. That he was singing out of himself and out of his soul and out of a memory of loss so big and so deep and so hurting that it could not be seen or described but only screamed out. (257)

For Aljaz the sound of the band conveys the emotional anguish he experienced on his return to Tasmania after several years of running from a past that included the death of his child and the breakdown of a relationship with the mother of that child, Couta Ho. The relation of this soundscape to that life experience and familial loss reverses the operation of the earlier soundscape of Black Pearl, whose rape by the sealer, while at once an experience carrying with it a profound deprivation of human dignity, is a point of origin for Aljaz and his ancestors. To Aljaz, the 'sound that [...] screeched forth from Shag's guitar' represents the lesson of his travels: '*If you leave you can never be free*'. This italicized sentence is Aljaz's own commentary on the sound of Shag's guitar and its presence shows the position in hindsight that Aljaz inhabits throughout the novel as he reflects on his life and ancestors from beneath the floodwaters of the Franklin River.

In his commentary on this soundscape Aljaz plainly addresses the temporal continuity produced by the sonic link between colonial past and the present: 'I knew it was not a new song, but a song I had unknowingly carried within me for a long time.' This internalization of the song structure likens sound to a form of genetic inheritance – a genealogical refrain. Linking this contemporary scene with the song of Black Pearl highlights the complex movement of temporality at play in the duel resonances of these soundscapes: Aljaz's acknowledgement of Black Pearl's song – 'I knew it was not a new song' – comes before he bears witness to it in the colonial scene at the end of the novel, therefore proleptically anticipating the impact of Black Pearl's song on the sounds of the present. The capacity of the song to connect disparate moments is viewed by Aljaz as surpassing the immediate context of the performance – 'He was not even singing for himself [...] he was singing out of himself and out of his soul and out of a memory of loss so big and so deep and so hurting that it could not be seen or described but only screamed out.' This description features two different functions of polysyndeton: 'out of' is used to exaggerate the ability of the song to transcend the normal limits of self and memory. The repetition of the adverbial intensifier 'so' simultaneously amplifies the extreme nature of the emotions and histories being mobilized within the song and gestures towards a depth of transhistorical space, to the haunted island of Van Diemen's Land. The repetition of 'so' also gives dramatic and rhythmic forward propulsion to Aljaz's memory. These aspects of Flanagan's language are like the rhythmic operations of a refrain, in this sense mimicking the repetition of musical structures in the rock music Aljaz is listening to in the pub.

The singer Shag is described as an almost inhuman figure – he looks 'as if he were being electrocuted' – like 'some animal in agony'. Shag's singing is more specifically labeled as screaming, a description that draws on the common characterizations of rock music (the present) and the trauma of Tasmanian colonial history (the past). The scream works to both describe and embody the emotional and historical space of the past and the present: 'It could not be seen or described but only screamed out.' This can also be understood in terms of Pater's influential ideas on the power of music to exceed the bounds of language. Using sound to map a landscape beyond language, the scream is therefore the central element of this soundscape and it carries within its net of texture and volume a raft of temporal and spatial meanings and connections.

There are multiple links between the contemporary and colonial soundscapes, between the song of Shag and the song of Black Pearl. Both evoke trauma and resonate within spaces that are immediate while also expanding beyond, and both are uttered by people rather than, as in *Cape Grimm*, initially emanating from nature. The most noticeable similarity is structural: the sounds comprising each soundscape take the form of a song. The two songs gather together space and time, functioning as a refrain that aligns the temporally disparate island spaces. The filial structure headed by Black Pearl is the lynchpin of *River Guide*, both in terms of Aljaz's impulse to uncover his family history and to understand his life leading up to the present. Heard as a refrain, Black Pearl's song is the sonorous foundation of the novel, binding the themes of colonial violence and genealogy and grounding these themes within the overlapping landscapes of Van Dieman's Land/Tasmania. Imagined sound echoes between the past and the present: Shag's refrain re-harmonizes and re-sounds this hidden history, while also voicing the contemporary trauma of Aljaz's life.

The two soundscapes in *Cape Grimm* offer less of a clear structural transmission between past and present. One of the asymmetries in Bird's novel is the listening perspective – in the dream soundscape we hear the sounds through Virginia, whereas in the soundscape of the Skye mass murder/suicide, the narrator, Paul Van Loon, describes Caleb listening:

> Without looking back Caleb rode his horse through government boundaries to the top of the cliff that is Cape Grimm, the cliff near the weather station. There he watched and listened as the congregation down in his village died in the trap of flames. The cries of death carried in the cold starry air; gold and crimson and strangely malachite and indigo the flames leapt towards the heavens; sparks and flurries of flying charcoal glowed, glittered, floated, spurted into the darkness as the little town leapt up into the sky. A glimpse of hell, a sudden view of a fairy-land lit by the sizzling fat of human bodies, accompanied by the whinnies and shrieks and moans of children choking in crawling billows and wraiths of smoke, lungs and eyes filled with stinging poison. (58)

This soundscape resounds with the 'cries of death'. Colour features heavily – gold, crimson, malachite, indigo – and Paul does not hesitate to make his own suggestions as to the images the fire can evoke: 'A glimpse of hell, a sudden view of a fairy-land'. The mention of colour is a significant point of difference to the other three soundscapes, while at the same time drawing this moment, and the novel, back into the wider tradition of the Gothic novel. This elevated and superhuman landscape, paradoxically drawn as either a hell or a fairy-land, sits atop the island and fires this scene with biblical bombast. The way that the elements of the soundscape are 'carried in the cold starry air' also harmonizes with the upward motion of the flames in the 'little town'.

Like the contemporary soundscape in *River Guide*, the pivotal sonic feature here is the scream: the 'whinnies and shrieks and moans of children choking in crawling billows and wraiths of smoke'. Paul's description of this sound through the use of polysyndeton gives it an element of Gothic horror, particularly in conjunction with the ghostly form of the smoke, described as 'wraiths'. Recounting the fire years after it took place, Paul relates how 'later on some firefighters said the noises, shaped by the remoteness and the darkness, the noises were one of the most terrible parts of the whole conflagration' (59). The repetition of 'noise' gives an indefinable character to the sound of the fire, accentuating the way that this disturbing resonance is said to be 'shaped' by a similarly immeasurable spatiality, again inflected by polysyndeton: 'the remoteness and the darkness'. The ominous extension of space created by the repetition of 'the' layers the two spatial signifiers 'remoteness' and 'darkness'. Like in Shag's song, this tropological language creates the repeating rhythms of a refrain. The screams of Caleb's victims become disembodied and float, ghost-like.

The interweaving of the scream and colour in the Skye soundscape is reminiscent of Edvard Munch's painting *The Scream* (1895), a hauntingly resonant Modernist embodiment of the alienated subject. Commenting on the startling nature of Munch's visual representation of sound, Steven Conner discusses how 'the power of utterance is represented by its very capacity to bend and buckle visual and spatial forms' (2001, 11). Fredrick Jameson also describes the interface between the visible and audible in *The Scream*: 'The visible world now becomes the wall of the monad on which this "scream running through nature" (Munch's words) is recorded and transcribed' (1999, 129). In *River Guide* and *Cape Grimm* this 'scream running though nature' is also a soundscape reaching from the colonial to the postcolonial.

Despite the overarching similarities between *River Guide* and *Cape Grimm*, most notably their burial of the colonial *after* the contemporary, there are several differences, of structure, perspective and location, which reflect the unique characters, narrative styles and overall objectives of Flanagan and Bird. In *River Guide*, Flanagan explicitly forms his soundscapes into song refrains that gather together a set of experiences imbricated within a genealogical territory spanning a 150-year period. Bird's soundscapes, while working across a similar time frame, do not create a personal structure communicating individual traumas passed down through generations. Instead this trauma resonates in terms of a whole community and sounds a larger landscape of extinction and absence. The intimate connections heard in *River Guide* – the recurrent appearance of totemic animals evoked in several different time periods in Aljaz's memories in addition to the song of Black Pearl – are transposed into a broader historical resonance in *Cape Grimm*. This structural difference on the level of sound also relates to variations in listening perspective between the two novels. Flanagan's repeating refrains are heard exclusively by Aljaz – again, a reflection of *River Guide's* genealogical narrative – while Bird's soundscapes are split between Virginia (colonial soundscape) and Paul (contemporary soundscape), members of an extinct community rather than a family. Geographically, both soundscapes in *Cape Grimm* occur on the elevated littoral space of the cliffs of North West Tasmania and reveal Bird's concern with that region of Tasmania, whereas Flanagan's scope in *River Guide* encompasses the whole island, with the colonial soundscape located on an unspecified beach and the contemporary sounds emanating from a pub in Hobart.

River Guide and *Cape Grimm* map island histories from the frontier meeting of Indigenous people and European colonists. Both meditate on the beginnings and endings of family and community. The soundscapes in each novel hold together both the past and the present. These are Tasmanian landscapes where muted, traumatic histories buried in the Van Diemonian past are uncovered: colonial horror-scapes that resonate within contemporary times are transposed into modern sound-forms. The past–present island continuum created by the imagined sound that haunts these novels opens an intersecting landscape of local, national and international movements and narratives. In these two Tasmanian novels imagined sound carries trauma and enables it to pierce the 'Great Australian Silence' as a scream or a song. Reemerging in the present, imagined sound links origin to extinction, Indigenous to European, colonial to postcolonial and silenced to sounded.

Chapter Six

A SONIC PASSAGE BETWEEN ISLANDS: *MUTINY MUSIC* BY BAECASTUFF

Journeying between islands and across history, *Mutiny Music* is a 12-part suite conceived by saxophonist Rick Robertson, first performed in 2006 by his band Baecastuff, an ARIA award nominated Australian contemporary jazz ensemble. The work narrates the series of historical events at the foundations of two Pacific Sea Islands, Pitcairn and Norfolk. Beginning with the mutiny on the *Bounty* in 1789, the development of the community on Pitcairn Island, through to the arrival of the Pitcairners on Norfolk Island in 1856, *Mutiny Music* tells a story of shared history and culture in the relation between islands.

The suite uses a variety of materials to perform this mythic story: musical symbolism, hymn forms that emerged with the cultural and religious growth of the islands, songs built from speech samples – the very sounds of human life on the islands – and abstract musical interpretations of the narrative. Listening to the imagined sound of these different musical forms, *Mutiny Music* is a 'tidalectics' (Brathwaite 1999) or 'archipelography' (DeLoughrey 2001), a remapping characterized by the tide-like forces of history and spatial relation. Josh Kun's neat description of popular music as producing 'maps that move' (2005, 22) is apt for a work about movement and relation delivered in a medium characterized by just these elements. Celebrating a rich and unique history and culture, *Mutiny Music* plots the location of two small and isolated islands in the Pacific Ocean and in doing this sounds an archipelago encompassing and in excess of the nation from where the work is performed and recorded. Sounding a Pacific archipelago the suite provides an alternative to the convict narrative surrounding Norfolk Island. At the same time *Mutiny Music* decentres the cultural and historical dominance of the continent of Australia: in this jazz archipelography, Australia is just one link in a global historio-musical chain.

Despite the relative simplicity of the narrative as it is told by Robertson and Baecastuff, *Mutiny Music* does not attempt to provide a 'definitive' account of history, a final statement pinning down and locating the originary time and space of Pitcairn and Norfolk. Instead, through its musical composition and narrative structure, the suite remaps the joint historical and cultural mythology of Pitcairn and Norfolk by exploring the geoimaginative dynamics of the Pacific regionality in which the two islands are embedded. The dense spatio-temporal weave of these archipelagic relations take the form of interconnected layers of technological, linguistic, structural and instrumental content that resist and even subvert a basic chronological history. Perhaps the most striking feature of this range of sound is the speech sample, an overdetermined sonic node within the musical texture of *Mutiny Music* that evokes the dislocations, tensions and re-routings at the centre of the work. By testing the narrative fabric of the mythology on which it is based *Mutiny Music* also opens a space for the contemporaneity of the real Pacific archipelago out of which the work emerges in the moment of performance. This musical form makes *Mutiny Music* a unique contemporary iteration of a representational field that reaches back to the foundations of Western exploration and colonialism. Offering a sonic cartography of an unrecognized island/archipelago formation, its history and the many filaments of its pan-Pacific ties, the suite is a singular musical assemblage that gauges colonial and contemporary spatial dynamics and explores tensions between globality and locality.

Formed in 1996 by Robertson and Phil Slater (who had both just returned from an international tour with popular Australian acid jazz and funk band d.i.g.), Baecastuff has been described as a vehicle for exploring the musical intersection between '70's Miles Davis, Dave Holland, Ornette Coleman and Jan Garbarek' combined with 'modern rhythms such as Jungle and Drum'n'Bass' (Baecastuff website). While these influences are still clearly audible, since that time Baecastuff have crafted a unique ensemble sound based on the highly individual styles of the players. The current members of the group are recognized leaders in their instrumental fields: Robertson (saxophones), Slater (trumpet), Matt McMahon (piano/keyboards), Simon Barker (drums), Alex Hewetson (electric bass) and Aykho Akhrif (percussion). The band has produced three albums, *One Hand Clapping* (1997), *Big Swell* (1999) and *Out of this World* (2001), the first of which was nominated for an Australian Recording Industry Award (ARIA). The name Baecastuff is a Norfolk word referring to a tobacco weed that grows on the island, a playful title that highlights an interconnection of place and language.

According to the brief description of *Mutiny Music* published on the Baecastuff website the work explores four central concepts – narrative, history, language and geography.

> *Mutiny Music* is a modern music show based on the story, music and culture that developed as a direct consequence of the Mutiny on the

Bounty and the clash of Tahitian and English cultures which developed into the language and song of the Pitcairn and Norfolk islanders.[1]

Approaching *Mutiny Music* from the perspective of island and archipelago studies realigns those concepts, suggesting another three themes that are central to my critical close listening. Firstly, the suite is fundamentally concerned with narrating a story of movement, between islands, cultures and across time. Secondly, transgression, in terms both of the event of the mutiny overturning social hierarchies and the later racial segregation that occurred on Pitcairn Island, is also central to the history the work recounts. Thirdly, the relationship between Pitcairn and Norfolk Island is also one that problematizes ideas of origin.

A vital and unique aspect of *Mutiny Music*'s construction of an archipelago is its performance in the present. In its recorded studio form, twelve compositions comprise *Mutiny Music*. Baecastuff does not always present this precise number of pieces – some performances, such as at Notes, a club venue in Newtown, Sydney, have featured 13. The discussion and analysis in this chapter is based on the official studio recording, released in 2016.[2]

The venue for the first performance of *Mutiny Music* that I attended in 2012 was a small jazz club, 505, in Surry Hills, Sydney. Witnessing a performance of *Mutiny Music* amplified the inherent malleability of the work, particularly its resistance to the idea of a set narrative structure. Technical difficulties resulted in a situation where none of the speech samples could be triggered (by Robertson, from a laptop on stage) and the band was forced to play the four speech sample pieces with that component missing. The silencing of one central element did not mean that the performance could not proceed: the technical hiccup hardly caused much of a delay, probably a testament to the professionalism of the players. This fact strengthens the importance of musical performance – the present moment – above narrative chronology as the central concern of *Mutiny Music*. In other words, while retelling the story narrated by *Mutiny Music* is important, so is putting on a live musical performance. As Robertson emphasized in his discussion of sound sample choice, sound, rather than textual meaning, is the guiding principle of the work. This sentiment is underscored by the fact that the complete semantic meaning of the speech samples is only available to Norfolk-Pitcairn speakers therefore giving the musical qualities and the exotic sound of the samples greater prominence to many listeners.

At performances where suitable space and technology are available, such as Notes or the Campbelltown Arts Centre, a series of images that depict the mutiny and the two islands are projected onto a screen behind or above the band while they play. The packaging of the CD also features similar images.

Although the historical accuracy of the images often strays from the space-time boundaries set out by the titles of each piece in the programme, the visual display enhances the sense of place and history being evoked by the work. In addition, Robertson gives a small spoken introduction to the work at the beginning of the performance, and he may or may not introduce the names of the songs and give commentary on the development of the narrative throughout the performance. At the 505 performance Robertson distributed a programme containing historical information and a 'program of events' that listed the narrative events in the order that they occurred. These two pages of printed information (much of which is included with the CD) provided some historical and narrative context and allowed audience members to gain an understanding, although diffuse, of the context, and, to a lesser extent, the narrative of *Mutiny Music*. These efforts by Robertson show that some narrative detail is important to the overall project of the work, even if it is only enough information to raise a basic awareness of the events which *Mutiny Music* depict.

This brief discussion of performance highlights a synecdochic tension between the telling of the narrative in the suite and the intricacy of the historical events on which it is based. It also reveals the subjective listening position of the audience, and the malleable nature of live performance. *Mutiny Music* is a part that refers to a whole history and narrative which can only be conceived of from a location outside a purely 'listening position' in relation to the work. This position outside, where the whole constellation of interlocking narrative, historical and material discourses can come into focus, could be called the place of close listening analysis.

Maps That Move: Islands and Archipelagoes, Theory and Mythology

Investigating tidalectic themes of movement, relation and origin, *Mutiny Music* uses a musical form to confront the problem of how to retell history, specifically spatial history. The literal 'sounding' offered by the suite is a complex layering of multiple times and spaces that produces a unique cartography of a historical and mythic terrain. Tony Mitchell, in a discussion of Māori popular music and depictions of place, coined the term 'sonic pyschogeography' – the 'exploration of identity through emotional attachments and connections to place' (2009, 146) – to describe this type of work. And while the suite's stated aims are benign, *Mutiny Music* exemplifies the role of popular music to challenge norms and boundaries. Josh Kun argues that 'through music, space is constructed and de-constructed, shaped and shattered, filled up and hollowed out. Music creates space in which cultures get both contested and consolidated and both sounded and silenced' (22). *Mutiny Music* performs this contestation, what Kun calls 'double acts of delinquency that question both the geopolitical boundaries of the modern nation-state and the disciplinary boundaries that govern its study in the academy' (22). As Kun points out in his discussion of popular music and the construction (or de-construction) of national space in a US context, the need to traverse disciplinary boundaries in my analysis of *Mutiny Music* leads me to take an interdisciplinary approach to the work. Kun's discussion also figures delinquency – or transgression – as essential to the project of musical 'construction and de-construction' of space. *Mutiny Music*'s expansion of the web of relation traced by the basic movement of people between the British Isles, Tahiti, Pitcairn Island and Norfolk Island to include a global web of places and sonic influences epitomizes Kun's musical delinquency.

Vital to the expanded archipelago of *Mutiny Music* are the Cook Islands, which provide Baecastuff with access to the only Polynesian drumming culture to survive the impact of Christian missionaries who began to arrive in the eighteenth century. Across the globe, the British Isles was the port of origin for the mutineers and so has a stake in the formation of the community on Pitcairn and Norfolk. The imperial and commercial centre of the world when the mutiny occurred, the British Isles is sonically represented several times through the work, including the hornpipe melody in 'Return to Tahiti' and the military drum patterns in the final piece 'Kingston'. Across the Atlantic, the origin of both the hymns included in *Mutiny Music* is the United States. The United States is also the origin of the musical language – jazz – used by the players in Baecastuff, a defining aspect of the way that the work is presented. Philip Hayward's *Bounty Chords* (2006), an account of the history and music of the two islands, also describes how musical life on the islands was influenced by the gifting of instruments such as harmoniums and pianos from visiting ships, another relation to the outside world.

Finally, Australia is an important link in the archipelago sounded by *Mutiny Music*, the place where the members of Baecastuff live. The relocation of Robertson from Norfolk Island to Sydney around the age of 16 is a familiar story for people that live on small islands. In light of *Mutiny Music*'s dynamic narrative of relation between islands, such a biographical fact underscores the importance and prevalence of movement and spatial interrelation for island peoples and their history. In addition to these concerns it is worth briefly noting the resonance between the historical period represented by the work and the themes of transgression and origin. The contemporaneity of both the American War of Independence and the French Revolution, two epoch-shifting events in the background to the mutiny on the *Bounty*, can easily be linked to the Pitcairn Islanders' rejection of aspects of the British Empire.

Emerging from and in response to the historically contemporaneous unfolding of colonialism, several key theorizations of island and archipelagic space underpin the historical and spatial network of *Mutiny Music*. The island reverie of Gilles Deleuze – 'Dreaming of islands [...] is dreaming of pulling away [...] of being lost and alone [...] of starting from scratch, recreating, beginning anew' (2002, 10) – focuses on a dialectic of movements towards and away, of separation, and origins. Daniel Niles and Godfrey Baldacchino echo this with their discussion of 'seamless flows of matter and energy'. Islands can 'help us to perceive how [a global] flux is resolved in particular places' (2011, 1). Deleuzian in its discussion of movement and energy, this statement pragmatically positions the island as a watermark towards measuring global concerns with climate change and human geography. In a gesture towards the interconnection characteristic of the archipelago, Deleuze's island moves, both in attraction to and repulsion from the mainland: 'Some islands drift away from the continent, but the island is also that toward which one drifts; other islands originated in the ocean, but *the island is also the origin*, radical and absolute' (10). For Deleuze, as with other theorists like John Gillis, the island can be a place of origin as much as it can be a site of desolation.

Telling a story imbricated in the relation between islands, archipelagic dynamics are central to the landscapes of *Mutiny Music*. Characterized by Elaine Stratford et al. as 'abstract and material relations of movement and rest' (2011, 122), Chris Bongie locates the archipelago 'between the solitary confines of the islands that constitute it and the expansive territory of the mainland towards which it points' (1999, 89). Both of these definitions evoke images of sea travel, the experience of isolation, and a certain spatial orientation and desire. Edward Brathwaite's concept of 'tidalectics', described by Elizabeth DeLoughrey as a 'the complex and shifting entanglement between sea and land, diaspora and indigeneity, and routes and roots' (2007, 2), complements these theorizations of the archipelago. Discussing Pacific Island conceptions of space and navigation, DeLoughrey suggests that unlike 'western models of passive and empty space such as *terra* and *aqua nullius*', the 'concepts of tidalectics and moving islands foreground alter/native models of reckoning space and time that require an active and participatory engagement with the island seascape' (3). As a musical performance composed of various complex compositional layers, *Mutiny Music* is an explicitly 'active and participatory' way of valuing and depicting island space. A work of swirling oceanic tides and distant islands, in *Mutiny Music* the archipelago is filled by sound.

Edouard Glissant's theorization of the colonial and postcolonial space of the Caribbean also resonates with this archipelagic geoimaginary. Considering the importance of the development of creole language and the central role of creative works in the realization of postcolonial regeneration, Glissant's conception of island space, movement and what he calls 'errantry' (33) – the constant travel and relation between places – speaks directly to the matrix of concerns raised by *Mutiny Music*. Within the complementary harmony of Glissant's ideas, *Mutiny Music* is a 'symphony of errantry'. Glissant's concept of relation – which he describes as 'a new and original dimension allowing each person to be there and elsewhere, rooted and open, lost in the mountains and free beneath the sea, in harmony and in errantry' (1997, 33) – also harmonizes with Brathwaite's 'tidalectics', both emerging out of encounters with the Caribbean archipelago. The persistence of movement as a central force within these theorizations of islands and archipelagos is, I suggest, easily and successfully realized in the rhythmic and affective energies of the idiosyncratic form of jazz-influenced music performed by Baecastuff in *Mutiny Music*.

Coexistent with these theorizations of islands and archipelagos as powerful and recurrent geoimaginary formations, the joint mythology of Pitcairn and Norfolk has been greatly affected by the numerous literary and filmic retellings of the *Bounty* story. This relationship between representation and history creates a kind of self-perpetuating feedback loop: as Bernard Smith relates, the actual event of the '*Bounty* mutiny did much to sustain in the minds of Europeans a romantic view of Pacific Island life' (1985, 327). Accounts of the mutiny prompted poets like Mary Russell Mitford and Lord Byron to compose 'Christina, The Maid of the South Seas' (1811) and 'The Island, or, Christian and his Comrades' (1823). As Maria Amoamo suggests: 'Pitcairn is a Pacific island inextricably bound to literary myth and imagination through various tropes of literature' (2013, 121). For Amoamo, the 'trope of island paradise/utopia' based on the Bounty story has a 'romantic cachet' – the 'story is not myth, but has served to mythologise Pitcairn. Perceptions of "utopia" and "paradise" have persisted in popularised anthropology and geography, as well as tourism' (108).

Phillip Hayward's study of Norfolk and Pitcairn Island music, dance and cultural heritage figures the number of written and visual representations of Pitcairn and Norfolk as between 2500 and 3000 (213). 'Such a number principally attests to the enduring fascination of the drama of the *Bounty* saga, and the willingness of generations of writers to speculate upon, interpret and revise earlier accounts' (Hayward, 13). Hayward argues that two films – *In the Wake of the Bounty* (Dir. Charles Chauvel, 1933) and *The Mutiny on the Bounty* (Dir. Frank Lloyd, 1935), the latter of which starred Clarke Gable as Fletcher Christian and Charles Laughton as Captain Bligh – had a significant impact on the formation of Norfolk Island cultural politics in the years following their release, despite the problematic construction of Tahitian identity and historically inaccurate music in these Hollywood productions (85–92). Seen in this silver-screened light, *Mutiny Music* is a current manifestation of a long impulse to retell the story of the mutiny on the *Bounty*.

Many of the basic facts of the early history of Pitcairn and Norfolk are embedded within national histories, island mythologies and, thanks to the aforementioned films, well known in the popular imagination. The people who lived on Pitcairn Island were originally partly comprised of mutineers from the British ship HMS *Bounty*: the vessel left England in 1787 bound for the Pacific island of Tahiti on a mission to obtain breadfruit for trading in the West Indies. After staying in Tahiti for an extended length of time due to unfavourable weather conditions, the *Bounty* set sail only for the mutiny to take place on 28 April 1789, not long after leaving Tahiti. Led by Fletcher Christian, the mutineers forced Captain Bligh and the sailors loyal to him into a longboat – Bligh did eventually get to safety – and set sail for Tahiti, where they were joined by a group of five male and twelve female Polynesians. Historians disagree over whether the Polynesians were forced or tricked into joining the mutineers (Dening 1992; Alexander 2003). After unsuccessfully attempting to settle on the island of Tubuai, the group eventually found Pitcairn Island in 1790. A small, uninhabited island that had been incorrectly charted and was therefore somewhat hidden or lost, Pitcairn served as a hiding place from the British authorities for the next 18 years. The community was eventually discovered – again, by accident – by the United States whaling ship *Topaz* in 1808.

Life on Pitcairn Island was far from idyllic: after only three years all the Polynesian men and five of the original mutineers had died in violent disagreements. The production of alcohol led to more deaths and by 1800 the only survivors were Alexander Smith, nine women and twenty children. Hayward says, 'Smith's isolation and the fate of his fellow mutineers appear to have prompted a profound change as he turned to religion and endeavored to be the pastor and patriarch of the small community' (24). Such a profound change rehearses the familiar image of the island as a site of origin, renewal and purity, a place small enough to be ruled over by the individual. Eventually Pitcairn Island became too small to sustain its population. In 1829, 87 Pitcairners moved to Tahiti, but almost 20 per cent died after six months, a catastrophic loss. In 1856 the Pitcairners relocated to Norfolk Island on the ship HMS *Morayshire* after being granted residency rights by Queen Victoria. The island had been used as a penal colony on two separate occasions (1794 to 1814 and 1825 to 1855). The wholesale relocation of 175 people from Pitcairn Island constitutes a radical re-routing of the historical narrative of Norfolk Island.

Mutiny Analysis

Instead of the grim carceral abjection and abandonment of Norfolk Island *qua* convictism, *Mutiny Music* re-figures the island as a homeland, directly connected to a temporally distant Pitcairn Island via language, culture, history, and real/imagined sound. A more detailed map of this contemporary jazz 'archipelography' shows it is built from four levels of material. The *narrative* is primarily conveyed through the titles of the songs, as well as the contextual printed material distributed at performances. Emerging from and working in conjunction with the narrative level is *musical symbolism*, which includes forms and structures that convey the narrative instrumentally, rather than through song titles or language, such as percussion pieces like 'Return to Tahiti' or songs that use hymn forms, like 'Ship of Fame'. The third level is *speech samples*, which feature in four pieces. Speech samples operate in semantic terms, through the linguistic meaning of the phrases used, while also giving sonic materiality or texture and a specific, if overdetermined, spatio-temporality to the work. *Abstract musical elements* – melodic, harmonic, textural, durational, improvisational – constitute the fourth level of the work. While they are integrated within the three other levels I have designated, these musical elements are dependent on a musical network – jazz – that exceeds the historico-narrative and spatial discourse discussed above. The performance of *Mutiny Music* by the six players in Baecastuff animates a complex web of musical relations. The instrumental materiality, player interaction and improvisation, and harmonic and melodic building blocks that constitute Baecastuff's idiosyncratic approach to performance are another set of conceptual and analytical challenges and a different contextual conversation to what is undertaken in this chapter.

Mutiny Music

1. 'The Mutiny' – Composition by Rick Robertson.
2. 'Return to Tahiti' – Composition by Simon Barker, horn arrangements by Phil Slater. Drawing on Cook Island drumming patterns, the piece begins with drums and other percussion before a hornpipe melody is introduced at the conclusion, played on saxophone and trumpet.
3. 'Search for Sanctuary' – Traditional, arrangement by Baecastuff.
4. 'Come Ye Blessed' – Tradition, arrangement by Baecastuff. A hymn originating on Pitcairn Island – it is also known as 'Pitcairn Anthem' – this is the official anthem of Pitcairn Island and the unofficial equivalent on Norfolk Island.
5. 'Gut Evrything Yu Want Deya' – speech sample piece. Composition by Rick Robertson, horn arrangement by Phil Slater.

6. 'Hue Hue' – speech sample piece. Composition by Rick Robertson.
7. 'Mauatua' – percussion feature, no trumpet/sax/piano/bass. Composition by Simon Barker.
8. 'Gethsemane' – traditional Norfolk Island hymn. Composition by Driver Christian and George Hunn Nobbs, arrangement by Baecastuff.
9. 'Daun I Goa' – speech sample piece. Composition by Rick Robertson.
10. 'Dem Da Mus Gwen It Et' – speech sample piece. Composition by Rick Robertson.
11. 'Ship of Fame' – Traditional. Arrangement by Baecastuff.
12. 'Kingston' – Composition by Rick Robertson.

Aligning the historical narrative told by *Mutiny Music* with the 12 pieces, the suite begins with the mutiny on the Bounty ('The Mutiny'), followed by the return of the mutineers to Tahiti, symbolized by a percussion piece ('Return to Tahiti'). The next piece, 'Search for Sanctuary', depicts the search for Pitcairn across the expanses of the Pacific Ocean. Alongside the last piece 'Kingston', 'Search for Sanctuary' is a creative interpretation of a waterscape of movement. The original composition of these pieces, without any hymn structures or speech samples, draws an interesting link between a kind of 'unmoored' spatial dynamic evoked and the creativity of the composer and performers in musically representing an archipelagic seascape.

'Come Ye Blessed' symbolizes the arrival of the *Bounty* at Pitcairn Island. 'Come Ye Blessed' is one of the most culturally important hymns from Pitcairn and Norfolk Island, and perhaps this, along with its title, is the reason for its position as first hymn in the suite. The next seven pieces correlate to a depiction of life on Pitcairn Island. 'Gut Evrything You Want Deya', the first composition to use speech samples, represents life on Pitcairn Island and the development of the distinctive culture. The second speech sample piece is titled 'Hue Hue': this Norfolk/Pitcairn phrase refers to something distasteful. 'Mauatau', a second percussion feature, continues the theme of discontent sounded among the Polynesian members of the Pitcairn community in 'Hue Hue'. Mauatau was one of several names of the Tahitian wife of Fletcher Christian. The ensuing compositions – the traditional hymn 'Gethsemane', and the two speech sample pieces 'Dem Da Mus Gwen It Et' and 'Daun I Goa' – sound the unique harmony, texture and melody of Pitcairn-Norfolk voice and hymnody, emphasizing the 'everyday-ness' of island life on Pitcairn. 'Ship of Fame', another traditional Pitcairn-Norfolk hymn, represents the voyage of the *Morayshire* from Pitcairn Island to Norfolk Island in 1856. The final piece of *Mutiny Music*, 'Kingston', represents the arrival to Norfolk.

Three representative compositions – 'Return to Tahiti', 'Pitcairn Anthem' and 'Gut Everything You Want Deya' – illustrate the interconnection of the narrative, musical symbolism and speech sample levels of the work. The pieces align or misalign with the narrative time of *Mutiny Music* in ways that create different types of archipelagic relation. 'Return to Tahiti' expands the territory of the narrative to include more Pacific islands, 'Come Ye Blessed' is perhaps the most exact replica of the musicality of the island, its historical context underscoring island to island connection, and 'Gut Everything You Want Deya' plays with temporality while explicitly linking Pitcairn and Norfolk. Some musicological analysis of the speech samples in 'Gut Everything You Want Deya' is also included so as to enable a deeper engagement with the construction of space.

'Return to Tahiti' and 'Come Ye Blessed'

The anachronism inherent to the use of the voice samples, while not central to what *Mutiny Music* is trying to achieve, is nevertheless a part of any historical fiction. 'Return to Tahiti', the second composition of *Mutiny Music*, contains a related type of inconsistency which again epitomizes tidalectic relation between islands. The piece utilizes Cook Island percussion rhythmic structures, and, with the use of log drums, timbres that explicitly place *Mutiny Music* within the Pacific Islands. Beginning with the exchange between Akhrif's congas and Barker's drum set, as the piece progresses a hornpipe melody is played by soprano saxophone and trumpet, a combination of Polynesian and British musical traditions. Baecastuff's drummer, Simon Barker, learnt some of the characteristic rhythms of Cook Island percussion so as to more fully engage with the musical traditions being referred to. The use of log drums to augment the standard drum set often used by Barker is a more recent development in the performance of the work, and it is a feature of the studio recording. From a compositional perspective, 'Return to Tahiti' also serves as a textural and tonal change from the previous piece, which features the full ensemble. Divided into two distinct phases – an initial drumming section followed by a fusion between the drumming and the hornpipe melody – 'Return to Tahiti' creates a narrative event through musical symbolism. The piece stages the meeting between two vastly different rhythmic and harmonic sound-worlds, and the overlaying of the hornpipe melody and the percussion serves as a microcosm for the broader fusion of the Pacific Island and British Isles into the joint Pitcairn–Norfolk culture.

'Return to Tahiti' is unusual in the context of the whole work because the clear difference between the two sound-worlds does not require extra-musical information for the listener to be able to 'make sense' of what is occurring. The basic tonal, rhythmic and harmonic distinctions between the drumming and hornpipe melody – contrasting the rhythmic energy of the drums with the lilting movement of the sax/trumpet – make it clear that two cultures are literally making an encounter. This intersection could be called a 'clash' if it were not for the relative consonance of the combination of rhythmic and melodic materials, and the acknowledged importance of Tahitian culture to Norfolk Islanders.

The presence of the Cook Island tradition of drumming in *Mutiny Music* reflects the position of Pitcairn and Norfolk Islands within the larger Polynesian archipelago. On a practical level the use of this drumming is also a compositional move made out of necessity. Cook Island drumming has been embraced throughout Polynesia in the wake of Christian missionary activities, and its ubiquity is similar to the use of the didgeridoo in contemporary Indigenous Australian music making. Tahitian drumming practices have been lost, and the use of elements of the Cook Island musical tradition enfolds and overlaps, spatially and sonically, the Cook Islands, Tahiti and Pitcairn/Norfolk Island. Cook Island drumming 'stands in' for the Tahitian music practices that would have constituted the sonic presence of Tahiti and been heard by the mutineers in 1789. Like a musical form of synecdoche, one sonic practice now refers to the sound of a whole region. Similarly, the use of the hornpipe melody also stands-in for the original sound of the hornpipe. The combination of melodic hornpipe and rhythmic drumming material binds the space and time of the island of Tahiti and the mutineers. Taking into consideration the original mission of the *Bounty*, and subsequent contact with whaling vessels, 'Return to Tahiti' also gestures towards the presence of imperial and commercial forces in the Pacific. Although the mutinous overthrow of Captain Bligh subverted the trade mission of the *Bounty*, 'Return to Tahiti' makes audible these oceanscapes and islands as spaces of imperial conquest, a significant historical reorientation of the background to the main story told in *Mutiny Music*.

The three hymn pieces in the work provide another set of textural, structural and spatial relations, although the spatio-temporalities sounded by the hymns create less anarchonstic turbulence with the narrative in comparison to 'Return to Tahiti' and 'Gut Everything'. Hymns were integral to the development of musical life on Pitcairn and Norfolk and in bolstering the historical authenticity of *Mutiny Music* they also make a powerful connection between real and imaginary space. 'Come Ye Blessed' is the first hymn piece in the work, and in terms of the surface layer of narrative it represents the arrival of the *Bounty* at Pitcairn Island. Composed by George Hunn Nobbs and Driver Christian, the lyrics are taken from Matthew 25:34-46, a text that talks about inheritance – 'Inherit the kingdom prepared for you' – and figures Christian mercy and generosity in a series of affirmative statements, such as 'I was a stranger and ye took me in.' The arrival of the mutineers and the development of the community on the island can therefore be cast in biblical terms that resonate with familiar island tropes. Through this hymn Pitcairn is the Edenic place of salvation. The arrival of the mutineers becomes the mythic and fated entrance of one of God's flocks of pious followers.

The importance of hymns to the tradition and development of music, identity and culture on Pitcairn and Norfolk Islands cannot be overstated. Tracing the history of singing for the fledgling post-religious-conversion community Hayward suggests that 'by the 1850s hymn singing had been a staple of island life for over fifty years' (30). Such a cultural expression was widespread in connection to the activities of Christian missionaries throughout the Pacific Islands, but hymn singing on Pitcairn and later Norfolk seems particularly integral to the cultural and musical lives of the islanders. 'As several visitors to the island [Norfolk] observed, the existence of original Pitcairn hymns was as surprising as the vocal competence of the choir' (Hayward, 33). Similarly, Fortescue Moresby, a visitor to Pitcairn Island in 1855, noted,'I have never heard any church singing that could equal theirs, except in Cathedrals' (quoted in Hayward, 32). The development of hymn singing and composition continued through the first half of the nineteenth century, with the arrival of key figures such as John Buffett in 1823 and George Hunn Nobbs in 1828. Nobbs is credited, along with Driver Christian (the son of Fletcher, the original leader of the mutineers), with composing, among several other hymns, the 'Pitcairn Anthem' and 'Gethsemane'. Figured as a central pillar within the developmental stages of Pitcairn and Norfolk cultural, religious and musical practice, the use of solo saxophone in the introductions to the live performance of the hymns in *Mutiny Music* seems to be a gesture towards the unaccompanied choirs that characterize historical hymn singing on the islands.

Hayward discusses the 'core repertoire' of hymns, often originally composed on Pitcairn and Norfolk Island. Four major collections of hymns have emerged in recent years, with eight recurring titles: 'Ahava', 'Bethlehem', 'Gethsemane', 'Oakleigh', 'The Pitcairn Anthem'/'Come Ye Blessed', 'The Beautiful Stream' and 'Unto Us a Child is Born'. Three of these titles are used in Mutiny Music, and a fourth hymn, 'Oakleigh', has also been featured in past performances. Hayward argues the genesis of 'Gethsemane' and 'The Ship of Fame' can be attributed to 'the close association between visiting US whalers (and particularly captains' wives) and the island community [...] and the introduction of Methodism', suggesting 'it is perhaps unsurprising that [the hymns] originated from the United States' (120). Robertson has indicated that, in terms of lyrics and melodic/harmonic content, there was no specific rationale behind which of the core Pitcairn/Norfolk hymns were used in *Mutiny Music*. But as Hayward has relayed in *Bounty Chords*, there are many profound expressions of island life and identity contained in the lyrics of the hymns, and they do enrich the telling of the story in *Mutiny Music*.

Listening to 'Come Ye Blessed' with the spatio-temporal thematics of *Mutiny Music* in mind, the overall atmospheric quality – the floating, static mood – of Baecastuff's performance is highly evocative of the 'mismapped' or 'unmapped' status of Pitcairn Island between the first arrival of the mutineers and Pacific Islanders and the discovery of the community in 1790. It is as if Pitcairn Island is lost and sits somewhere outside of time and (Imperial) space. The movement of the ensemble between the simple chord structure of the hymn and the relatively 'free' improvisation of the middle part of the piece further intensifies this feeling of cartographic freedom. Offering another perspective on the 'nervous duality' (Baldacchino 2005, 248) of the island as both a paradise and a hell, the harmonious and peaceful quality of the performance elides the turmoil that characterized most of the early years of the community on Pitcairn Island.

'Gut Everything You Want Deya'

The first speech sample piece in *Mutiny Music*, 'Gut Everything You Want Deya' emerges out of the tranquil detachment of 'Come Ye Blessed'. The spatial discourse surrounding the work is clearly apparent in the texts of the four songs based on speech samples, and I have selected 'Gut Everything' as a case study because it is the most profuse in terms of language content, melodic material and harmonic imitation, in a sense covering the most island and archipelagic territory of the four compositions. Following the turmoil of the mutiny and the rejection from Tahiti narrated in the opening pieces, 'Gut Everything' also acts as an introduction to the vocal world of the island.

The origin of the speech samples used throughout this piece and the rest of the work is a double LP record obtained by Robertson from a Norfolk Island contact (Les Quintal – descendent of one of the original Pitcairn Island families). I have been unable to access this original LP recording, although Robertson did give me several tracks of the voices he sampled, which he had digitized. The LP contains conversations recorded in 1956, on the Centenary of the arrival of the original Pitcairn Islanders to Norfolk Island (what is celebrated annually as Anniversary Day, or Bounty Day).

Robertson was clear to state that the musical appeal of the voice, rather than any particular semantic meaning, was the most important factor in deciding on which samples to use in the four speech sample pieces. Although he emphasized the importance of musicality over semantic meaning several times during our conversation, Robertson also commented that 'it's definitely about what they were saying [...] the most profound things they were saying were the ones that worked the best' (Robertson). These remarks bind the semantic aspects of the samples to their musical characteristics, but musicality is clearly intended to be the controlling factor both in terms of composition (the choices of the composer) and performance (the audience focuses on melody rather than semantic meaning). Robertson used musical terms to describe his engagement with the melodious rise and fall of the voices speaking the Pitcairn-Norfolk Island language, with some voices 'speaking in certain keys'. He described choosing certain phrases from the LP because they were 'typical phrases on the island'. These phrases were also most attractive in terms of melodic and rhythmic interest. On the language spoken, he says [the language samples came from] 'Old Norfolk, [they are] unadulterated'. These statements draw attention to the way that time and place are enfolded, even within short phrases of spoken language.

The historical significance of the LP marks a three-part archipelagic spatio-temporal constellation, between the arrival of the Pitcairners on Norfolk in 1856, the centenary of that arrival in 1956, and the retelling of the Pitcairn/Norfolk story in the present. These relations are complicated by the tension between the narrative position of the speech sample pieces and the original time and place of their recording. Using voices recorded almost exactly 100 years after the arrival of the Pitcairners on Norfolk in a narrative position before the Pitcairners get to Norfolk Island could be termed anachronism. A composition that represents the development of language and culture on Pitcairn after the first arrival of the mutineers in 1789, in 'Gut Everything' the homesickness of the Pitcairners who were visiting Norfolk and the picnic celebrating Anniversary Day on Norfolk Island are both mentioned. Phrases and sounds that refer to anachronistic temporalities within the historical time narrated in the work are mobilized in ways that lend a unique spatial and sonic authenticity. These spatio-temporal resonances amplify the resistance of *Mutiny Music* to restriction within the confines of a linear narrative. At the same time, the complex looping and contradictory impulses activated by the speech samples harmonize with the concepts of tidalectics and relation. *Mutiny Music* as mythic narrative is more concerned with the relations between islands than it is with embedding sound artefacts in a temporal chronology.

While the historical context and musical formation of the speech samples used in 'Gut Everything' underscores their relevance to concepts of relation between islands, the samples also simply illustrate the experience of living on an island. The sampled voice is that of Granny Quintal, a Norfolk identity who at the time of recording was matriarch of a foundational island family. The composition also features an unidentified male speaker. The phrase *gut everything you want deya* explicitly relates to the annual Anniversary or Bounty Day picnic, a day of festivities commemorating the arrival of the Pitcairn Islanders on Norfolk Island on 8 June 1856. Even more specifically, the phrase refers to the abundance of food at the picnic. The complete text that is used in 'Gut Everything' is comprised of six separate phrases that are mostly delivered individually, although at times phrases are delivered in contrapuntal patterns, with Granny Quintal's phrase 'answered' by the male speaker.

Considering the speech samples are in the Norfolk-Pitcairn language, much of the semantic meaning is veiled to non-Pitcairn/Norfolk Island listeners, although several of the phrases, such as the important title phrase 'gut everything you want deya', are easily intelligible to an English speaking audience. This barrier elevates the musical characteristics of the phrases above their semantic meaning, a listening perspective that aligns with Robertson's stated intentions in favour of music over language. Once the speech samples have been translated in their entirety, they do create a distinct representation of islands and archipelagos. The following translations and contextual explanations were provided by Robertson; my additional commentary relates them to the spatial discourse mapped by the work as a whole.

1. *Gut everything you want deya.* The title phrase describes the profusion of food available at the annual Anniversary Day picnic. The implicit location is Norfolk Island. This phrase can also be viewed within the tradition of the Edenic 'island paradise'.
2. *Got the yams, tia ti, that's true.* Yams and tia ti are two forms of vegetable eaten on Pitcairn and Norfolk Islands. The 'everyday-ness' of listing food sources is emphasized by tone of the speaker. At the same time, this phrase also gives specificity and detail to the island location.
3. *All them that sick for pitcairn they donnay what to do.* To celebrate the anniversary of 100 years of the Norfolk Island community, members of the Pitcairn Island community visited Norfolk Island. In one way this phrase describes how these Pitcairners missed their home. The phrase also contains an underlying reference to the Norfolk Islanders who may still miss their former home on Pitcairn Island, one hundred years later.
4. *Cry, laugh or what? Well they looka sight.* Related to the previous phrase, this expresses the melancholy wish for a return to home.
5. *das dem a tulla me too* (that's what they told me too). This phrase is delivered by a male voice and refers to the two previous phrases concerning homesickness.
6. *I won the prize – and as for ugly.* Another reference to the Anniversary Day picnic, this time to the tradition of fancy dress competitions that took place on Norfolk Island. With the '*as for ugly*' Granny Quintal is making a self-deprecating joke.

The subject matter of these phrases range between the everyday, such as the title phrase, through to expressions that locate the speakers as inhabitants of specific islands, such as the references to types of food, or the fancy dress contest. The third and fourth phrases are perhaps the most interesting in terms of the space of the archipelago. Drawing a concrete relation between the two islands, Granny Quintal comments on the emotional ties that existed for Norfolk Islanders in relation to their previous home[is]land. Voicing this link to Pitcairn Island, Granny Quintal also refers to the island space opened in the narrative by the previous piece 'Come Ye Blessed'. The homesickness of the Pitcairn Islanders on the occasion of the Anniversary Day picnic is foregrounded in the counterpoint initiated by the interaction of Granny Quintal's voice and the male voice. He says *'das dem a tulla me too'* – that's what they told me too – which extends the scope of Granny Quintal's observation beyond the individual and into the wider community.

In melodic and harmonic terms, 'Gut Everything' traces a movement between C minor and F, or a minor dominant to the tonic chord. Accordingly the harmony of the piece is based around this progression. Breaking up the phrase, the first three syllables – *got eve-ry* – are sounded on the C, and the next four syllables – *thing you want deya* – are sounded on the F. The electric bass and the left hand of the electric piano outline this harmony using a rising and falling pentatonic pattern primarily using C, Eb and F. See Figure 1 for a notation of the first two phrases. This harmony does not develop beyond the two-chord structure, but it does unfold in terms of melodic complexity and speech melody activity. As the piece progresses more speech samples are introduced, creating a counterpoint pattern, as can be seen in 'speech motif two' of Figure 1. An arpeggiated soprano saxophone and trumpet melody – a setting of the Irish jig 'The Three Sea Captains', performed in a minor tonality – is layered over the top of the basic harmony supplied by the foundational speech sample. This melody acts as a musical symbol, similar to the Cook Island drumming heard elsewhere. Weaving a melodic structure highlighting the British foundations of the Pitcairn–Norfolk community into the 'authentic' texture of the Pitcairn–Norfolk language mines another strata of the cultural bedrock of the two islands.

Samples and Space

The sonic presence of the samples and the singularity of the musical texture that they embody reroutes the historical narrative of *Mutiny Music* away from the geoimaginary of Australian convictism or island isolation, emphasizing the tidalectic link between Pitcairn and Norfolk. Listened to as imagined sound, the voice sample pieces create the most complex spatio-temporal relations in

Figure 1 Speech motif one and two.

Mutiny Music, both through their explicit voicing of the texture of island life and in the anachronistic tension they generate with the time and space of the narrative. Voice samples literally embody the archipelagic links between the islands. This geoimaginary function of sampled voice has links to Maurice Merleau-Ponty's work in *The Phenomenology of Perception*, where he discusses the work of the voice in 'worlding', suggesting the 'phonetic 'gesture' brings about, both for the speaking subject and for his hearers, a certain structural coordination of experience, a certain modulation of existence' (2012, 84). For Merleau-Ponty, the voice opens 'a world' (84). The sampled voices in *Mutiny Music* utter phrases that convey the everyday experience of island life: they are, after Merleau-Ponty, a 'modulation of experience'. But in the context of *Mutiny Music*'s retelling of a mythic history, the labour of the voices is increased by their sampled form and place in the narrative. They now not only project the experience of their time of recording (1956) but also serve as one of the many threads in the fabric of spatio-temporal relation between Pitcairn and Norfolk.

Steven Connor's concept of 'vocalic space' is a useful articulation and extension of Merleau-Ponty's discussion of the voice. Opening 'vocalic space', Connor argues, 'The voice may be grasped as the mediation between the phenomenological body and its social and cultural contexts' (12). Similar to the operation of the soundscape – which amplifies the relation between the sonic environment and the individual or society – Connor argues, 'The voice is held both to operate in, and itself to articulate, different conceptions of space, as well as to enact the different relations between the body, community, time, and divinity' (12). Placing the body of the anachronistically located speaker of Pitcairn-Norfolk language into the work strengthens the *relation* between the distant places and times that are performed by *Mutiny Music*. Vocalic space is not just a vocal soundscape, it also emphasizes the bodily presence of sampled voices. At the same time, this space is also occupied or filled by the bodies of the performers in the present. The friction created by the different registers of sonic presence, between the recorded voice and the live performers, is productive of both a beautifully textural music assemblage and a unique listening experience.

Greg Dening's scholarship on the *Bounty* offers another more historically specific perspective on these discussions of the symbolic and geoimaginary space activated by the speech sample. Underscoring the nascent emergence of the language that would become the *lingua franca* of the Pitcairn and later Norfolk Islanders, Dening suggests that 'what stuck in the memory of those who tried to describe Christian on the morning of the mutiny was the sort of Tahitian-English pidgin he was using. "Mammoo" (mamu), "Silence", they remember him shouting' (1992: 57). Dening suspects that 'the crew of the Bounty had been marked by something more than tattoos at Tahiti. They had begun to intersperse Tahitian words in their speech with one another' (57). The mutineers were becoming island people of the Pacific, and their pidgin language set them apart. 'It bred familiarity. It lessened distinction between them and increased distance between their present and their former selves' (57–58). Dening's discussion of the use of Tahitian words by Christian and the other mutineers in the period leading up to the mutiny highlights the importance of language and linguistic transgression to the foundations of the Pitcairn/Norfolk Island community. The new creole language, a fusion of various forms of English (as spoken by the assortment of English, Irish, Scottish and West Indian sailors on board the *Bounty*) and Tahitian, is a pivotal aspect of the Pitcairn–Norfolk myth, but the narrative anachronism and complex spatio-temporality wrapped up in *Mutiny Music*'s use of the speech sample amplify the tidalectic tensions at the historical and linguistic foundations of Pitcairn and Norfolk. Dening's discussion of the distinction created by the new language used by the mutineers also underscores the symbolic potency of Robertson's re-use of this sound in his four speech sample compositions.

While the use of language is central to the representation of unique space in much music produced by island people, only a small number of works use speech samples in this way. A pertinent antecedent from the jazz tradition is the first part of John Coltrane's suite *A Love Supreme* (1965): 'Acknowledgment' features a four-note motif that copies the speech melody of Coltrane's mantra 'a love supreme'. Steve Reich's Grammy award-winning composition *Different Trains* (1988), for string quartet with prerecorded string parts and speech samples on tape, was the first work to use speech samples in a similar mode to Robertson's arrangement of Pitcairn-Norfolk phrases in *Mutiny Music*. *Different Trains* performs a complex exploration of memory and loss, interweaving Reich's childhood travels between divorced parents in Los Angeles and New York with the roughly contemporary events of World War II and the Holocaust. A striking similarity between *Different Trains* and *Mutiny Music* is the theme of movement and travel, although Robertson and Baecastuff's work is explicitly concerned with relation while dispersal is central to Reich. Perhaps this resonance offers an insight into why sampling was chosen by both composers above other compositional strategies.

The fusion of melody/rhythm and speech refuses to position either element as more important than the other. Discussing the differences between the use of speech samples and the conventional delivery of text in *The Cave*, another work by Reich that also deploys speech samples, Eric Prieto argues, 'One of Reich's major accomplishments is to encourage us to meditate on the meaning of the words spoken without simply subordinating the music to the text' (n.p.). Prieto goes on to suggest Reich's use of speech samples, and his various techniques of orchestration, such as doubling the speech sample with an instrument, enables the exploration of the intricate content of *The Cave* 'in dialogic terms without sacrificing the strictly musical values that make the piece compelling as an aesthetic object' (n.p.). The use of speech samples in *Mutiny Music* enacts a similar fusion of conceptual and narrative forces. The specific and idiosyncratic character of the Pitcairn-Norfolk Island language is exposed through the transposition of the language into the melodic, harmonic and narrative fabric of the piece, a move that also heightens the semantic relevance of the phrases to the larger archipelagic framework.

Extending Prieto's discussion of speech sampling beyond the direct technological similarities shared by *Mutiny Music* and Reich, one of the most important operatic composers concerned with speech melody was Leos Janacek (1854–1928). Expressing the profound role of speech to his compositional practice, Janacek stated 'pitches, the intonation of human speech, of any creature's speech, contained the deepest truth for me' (Janacek quoted in Christiansen 2004, 242). Discussing Janacek's treatment of the spoken word, Paul Wingfield says 'the nature and mood of the person' and 'environmental factors such as place, time, state of the light and prevailing temperature' (1992, 282) all contributed to how the 'components' of speech melody – speed of delivery, register, rhythm and intonation, through to the spatio-temporal factors – function as a seed of space/place buried in the structures of music. 'In short, speech embodies both external and internal "realities" or "truths"' (282). Paul Christiansen suggests Janacek's use of speech melody was 'an attempt to seize the moment and retain it in all its immediacy and tangibility; he was seeking the poetry of the present' (243). Both Wingfield and Christiansen stress that for Janacek the use of speech melody was a search for the authentic and contemporary Czech or Moravian voice. In *Mutiny Music* the use of speech is modified beyond Janacek's transcription/notation/setting methodology. Instead, the speech melody becomes the speech *sample*, an audio recording of speech operating in a different order of technological mediation. This shift – in a sense from 'analogue' to 'digital' – is reflected in the move away from the search for national authenticity, in Janacek, to a concern with the exploration of the past and its subjective reconstruction.

As a mythology fundamentally concerned with movement, *Mutiny Music* relies on the semantic, harmonic and textural 'sound' of a language that, through speech sampling, literally performs this mobility and relation between islands. This sampled voice, which is also the musical materiality of the work, configures the melodic with the geographic and the textural with the semantic. The same impulse towards relation is also sounded by the pieces constructed from Pitcairn and Norfolk Island-composed hymns, and the pieces using pan-Polynesian Cook Island drumming rhythms and textures alongside hornpipe melodies. The fusion of the sonic materiality and semiotic presence from the Norfolk Island language with these other musical elements produce the Pacific archipelago of *Mutiny Music*.

As a contemporary musical work that charts figurations of oceanic movement, transgression and cultural fusion, *Mutiny Music* is a musical map that moves (Kun). Following Kun's discussion of popular music and postnational space, the suite contests and consolidates the mythic and historical foundations of Pitcairn and Norfolk. And following Glissant and Brathwaite, Robertson and Baecastuff locate the shared cultural origins as much in *relation* – historical, cultural and spatial relationships between islands – as the traditions of language and song that the suite both commemorates and reenergizes. The journey between islands, the memory and longing for the home[is]land, the sounds and forms of origin and identity, the movements and meetings of different cultures and the intersections and folds of time – these are the tidalectic links of *Mutiny Music*. Built from both imagined and real sounds the suite ventures far out into the Pacific and reaches from the present back to the late eighteenth century. Decentering Australia, the 'mainland' territory on which the composer and performers now stand, *Mutiny Music* sounds a dynamic archipelago that reaches across the globe. As Godfrey Baldacchino proclaims, island 'songs thrive as sites and sounds of resistance' (2011, xxvi).

Part Three

LISTENING TO THE CONTINENTAL ARCHIPELAGO

Chapter Seven
NOISY SONGLINES IN THE TOP END

Mapping the transformation of the colonial continental landmass into a recycled, postcolonial archipelago, Alexis Wright's acclaimed novel *Carpentaria* (2006) refigures the Top End of Australia as a space defined by circular weather patterns, charted by sonorous songlines and shrouded in both colonial and Indigenous noise. This chapter will examine how the constellation of landscapes and events depicted in *Carpentaria* create a *novelistic songline*, a contemporary reimagining of the novel. Recording the creative movements of ancestral figures, songlines have been commonly performed through a combination of singing and dancing (Stubington 2007). Although this original form has transformed significantly in *Carpentaria*, I argue that Wright's novel performs this songline function.

But not only is *Carpentaria* a novelistic songline, it is a *noisy* novelistic songline. Noise, the transgressive power of which is often associated with meaninglessness, distraction and excess, makes sense of the precise character of the sonically saturated fabric of Wright's work. Theorists of noise also describe how it is able to reform a structure or system. I extend these insights to see how the revisionist mythopoeics of Wright's novel couple the often-ungainly vibrations of noise to the heroic, geographic, animistic and synoptic characteristics of the songline, creating a map of political resistance, spiritual vitality and continental regeneration. Listening to the noise that inhabits several pivotal soundscapes of the novel – extra-resonant sites along its songline – complicates *Carpentaria*'s place inside the borders and official histories of the nation. I divide these soundscapes into 'neocolonial' – the soundscapes of Desperance and the Gurfurrit mine – and 'Indigenous' – the storm and the island of rubbish. Like a kind of Deleuzian noise machine, in *Carpentaria* the sonic waste of the colonial is transformed into a refreshed location on the noisy Indigenous songline.

Reading *Carpentaria* with an ear for imagined sound is reliant on the web of ecological, historical, sociological and cosmological resonances shared by both the novel and the singing tradition. By providing a larger historical and narrative context to the mapping of specific places and times, this reading and listening approach gives an almost sacred or ceremonial function to the text. In other words, through imagined sound we hear *Carpentaria* as a contemporary iteration of Indigenous Dreaming. Deborah Bird Rose discusses this complex and multifaceted concept, referring to 'Dreamings' as 'the great creative beings who came out of the Earth and travelled across the land and sea'. Bird Rose explains how Australia is

> criss-crossed with the tracks of the Dreamings: walking, slithering, crawling, flying, chasing, hunting, weeping, dying, giving birth. They were performing rituals, distributing the plants, making the landforms and water, and making the relationships between one place and another, on–e species and another. (2008, 111)

These 'great creative beings' are manifest throughout *Carpentaria*, most importantly as the Ancestral Serpent described in the opening and the storm spirits that dominate the end of the novel. Bird Rose's description of Dreamings is complemented by Max Charlesworth, who states, 'the Dreaming may refer to the personal "way" or vocation that an individual Aboriginal might have by virtue of his membership of a clan, or by virtue of his spirit-conception relating him to particular sites' (1984, 10). The constellation of creation, spirituality, Law and localized duty discussed by Bird Rose and Charlesworth is highly visible in *Carpentaria*. Aileen Morton-Robinson has also highlighted how the 'knowledge and beliefs tied to the Dreaming inform the present and future. Within this system of beliefs, there is scope for interpretation and change by individuals through dreams and their lived experiences' (2015, 11–12). With its cyclical evocation of Indigenous and colonial histories and present/future movements, Wright as contemporary novelist is also clearly working within this conception of Dreaming.

Placing *Carpentaria* in this eco-mythic nexus casts it as explicitly concerned with the past and the future, colonial and Indigenous, the spiritual and the material, the local and global. Asking Benedict Anderson's question – what sounds the nation? – Wright's novel answers with a mass of noisy soundscapes. At the same time, as a novel, an art form intimately linked to the foundations of Western modernity, *Carpentaria* performs a contemporary Dreaming in a non-traditional mode – scholars of Indigenous performance history such as Mary Rose Casey (2012) and Anna Haebich (2018) have also highlighted the similar malleability of multiple other Indigenous performance traditions. The time-space continuum of the novel, and its productive difference from the spatio-temporality of the nation under globalized industrial modernity, overturns the racist binaries that have historically emphasized European concepts of space, religion and industry over and against Indigenous knowledge and spirituality.

The Indigenous noise of this contemporary Dreaming enfolds the colonial, sounding a reconciliatory undertone beneath the harsher critique that sits centre stage in the work. The literary and imaginative breadth of the novel easily supports the merging of songlines and noise, two traditions of sonic thought and practice. Explicating the rich soundscapes of the Gulf country region setting of the novel, I hope that my analysis in this chapter will prick the ears of Indigenous readers (and listeners) who are familiar with the area, as well as readers without such direct access to the sound-world and landscape of Wright's Waanyi nation homeland.

An interconnected series of family and community disagreements are woven into the epic sonic complexity of *Carpentaria*, and it is no surprise that Wright's two protagonists – Normal Phantom and his son Will – are adept at listening to this noisy landscape. Norm Phantom – a name that echoes the central character of Xavier Herbert's 1938 novel *Capricornia* – is leader of the Pricklebush mob. Norm and his son Will have had a falling out as a result of Will's involvement in guerilla sabotage of a nearby mine – and because of his relationship with Hope (whose father is Norm's nemesis Joseph Midnight, the leader of the Eastside mob). Both sides of the Indigenous community of Desperance reside on the outskirts of the town and are despised by its hysterical non-Indigenous inhabitants. A brief chronology of events depicted in the novel includes the battle and fire started by Norm's wife Angel Day, the death of the mysterious amnesiac fisherman Elias Smith (who Norm buries at the sacred ground of the gropers), Will's rescue by religious zealot Mozzie Fisherman, the deaths in custody of three Indigenous children, the explosive destruction of the Gurfurrit mine by Mozzie's followers, Norm's search for his grandchild Bala, and the final storm that destroys Desperance and creates an island of rubbish. Enfolded within the larger cyclical patterns of weather, destruction and renewal, these events mark the different locations on *Carpentaria*'s noisy songline map.

Wright's description of the political, cultural and imaginative footings of her novel also connects the songline to *Carpentaria*. Wright states how the novel 'started to be written like a long song, following ancient tradition, reaching back as much as it reached forward, to tell a contemporary story on our ground' (2007, 7). In a statement echoing Anderson, Wright later asks, 'What songs should be sung in recognition of our national collectivity?' (14). Taking up Anderson's imperative, Wright is asking the singer and listener of the national song – in other words, the writer and the reader of *Carpentaria* – to be historically and politically aware. Wright also highlights the need for the song to be contemporary, a requirement that harmonizes with the overall reconstructive statement of the novel. Contemporaneity also means political urgency, a major concern in both Wright's fiction and non-fiction writing.

ARMAGEDDON BEGINS HERE

Wright's efforts to 'tell a contemporary story on our ground' are crystallized in the opening paragraph of *Carpentaria*. Titled 'From Time Immemorial', the prologue to chapter one is a fanfare introducing the profuse and furious sounds and noises projected throughout the rest of the novel.

> A NATION CHANTS, *BUT WE KNOW YOUR STORY ALREADY.*
> THE CHURCH BELLS PEAL EVERYWHERE.
> CHURCH BELLS CALLING THE FAITHFUL TO THE TABERNACLE WHERE THE GATES OF HEAVEN WILL OPEN, BUT NOT FOR THE WICKED. CALLING INNOCENT LITTLE BLACK GIRLS FROM A DISTANT COMMUNITY WHERE THE WHITE DOVE BEARING AN OLIVE BRANCH NEVER LANDS. LITTLE GIRLS WHO COME BACK HOME AFTER CHURCH ON SUNDAY, WHO LOOK AROUND THEMSELVES AT THE HUMAN FALLOUT AND ANNOUNCE MATTER-OF-FACTLY, *ARMAGEDDON BEGINS HERE*. (Capitalization in the original, 1)

The paragraph is a forceful beginning, shrill and menacing in its layering of satire and mockery. Every word is capitalized – by typographic standards, the narrative voice here is shouting – lending an urgency and volume to the tone of the soundscape. The first sonic element here is the collective intonation of a phrase – '*BUT WE KNOW YOUR STORY ALREADY*' that seeks to erase the forward momentum of the 'story' that is only just unfolding. The nation is chanting this passive-aggressive mantra, orchestrated by Wright as a monophonic embodiment of the attitudes of the majority of non-Indigenous Australians towards Indigenous 'complaints' over colonial history and present discrimination. The phrase acts as a buffer against negative silence, a regressive and boringly unmusical refrain.

The opening is highly compressed in its symbolic and sonic function, proleptic in its foreshadowing of later noisescapes, and microcosmic in its spatial implications – perhaps a 'radio edit mix' to the symphony of the whole. The movement of the Ancestral Serpent and the chanting of the nation etch a continental topography. European and Indigenous forces are described in the act of creating a landscape that is simultaneously regional, spiritual and sonic (although the sound of Indigenous creation is not heard until the storms at the conclusion of the novel). The soundscape signals the incredible vibrancy and tension at the heart of one of the most sonically profuse novels in Australian literature. At the same time, this first page is also a forewarning to the reader that *listening* will be of central importance to the experience of the novel.

The uninterested echo of the chant '*BUT WE KNOW YOUR STORY ALREADY*' resonates with the church bells that 'PEAL EVERYWHERE', although the warning of the bells eventually overpowers the chanting chorus. Church bells are sonic signs associated with the marking of time, locality, and in many Western cultures, religious observance, and Wright's use of bells plays upon all of these functions. The bells are 'CALLING' the faithful, interpolating them into both the national space and a certain version of Australian history. But bells are not only conservative tolls of regulation, of what already is – they can also be signs of warning, of what is approaching, and the final line of the paragraph shows this: '*ARMAGEDDON BEGINS HERE*'. It is ironic that the next section of text in *Carpentaria* describes the movements of the Ancestral Serpent, the spiritual being responsible for the creation of the whole ecosystem of the novel. The serpent embodies not the end of the world, but its constant recreation. The apocalypse announced by the prophet-like 'LITTLE BLACK GIRLS' refers to the destruction of the colonialist paradigm. *Carpentaria* performs this 'end' with a literal deconstruction of Australian capitalist and colonialist space through the annihilation of the Gurfurrit mine and the township of Desperance. Despite the intimately local and regional space of *Carpentaria*'s setting, the space filled by the opening chant and the church bells reaches beyond, projecting the cultural, ecological and historical tensions of the novel onto a national stage.

The ringing bells of the opening scene also demarcate and stratify an inside and an outside. The bells call 'THE FAITHFUL', those insiders hailed by the sounds of institutional power, most directly the church. At the same moment that a divide is created through the call to the faithful, the mockery and drama of Wright's characteristic satire is in full effect – the church bells are calling the faithful to 'THE TABERNACLE WHERE THE GATES OF HEAVEN WILL OPEN'. This image explicitly creates a delineation of space equal parts religio-carceral fire and brimstone and absurdist comedy – Wright's comical fetishization of the miniature architecture of the Christian sacrament contrasts with the proceeding section of the novel, dealing with the Ancestral Serpent, which is itself described in relation to a mythical architecture of rivers and limestone caves.

Moving from 'THE FAITHFUL' to 'THE WICKED' outsiders, Wright again illustrates her point using broad strokes. The 'LITTLE BLACK GIRLS FROM A DISTANT COMMUNITY WHERE THE WHITE DOVE BEARING AN OLIVE BRANCH NEVER LANDS' is an allusion to the flooding that takes place at several points in the novel. If the biblical character Noah was to release a dove into the world of *Carpentaria*, the bird would be unable to alight because the land is still (and constantly) being washed clean by floodwaters. It could also be heard as a reference to the Christian metaphorics of colour in William Blake's *Songs of Innocence and Experience* (1789). Alternatively, the white dove cannot land because the Gulf of Carpentaria is not its natural habitat: it is symbolically and literally out of place. The 'LITTLE BLACK GIRLS' are also a link back to Wright's first work of fiction, *Plains of Promise* (1997), a novel that follows three generations of Indigenous women through the horrific experiences of institutionalized colonialism. The presence of triple generations is a temporal structure shared by the two novels, reflecting the importance of filial relationships to Indigenous culture as much as it literally figures the passing down of knowledge and story in an oral tradition.

Highlighting the non-linearity of Indigenous eco-mythology, the final phrase of the opening paragraph – *ARMAGEDDON BEGINS HERE* – is another stormy foreshadowing of the cyclonic weather that precedes the end of the novel. The biblical register of this opening – a preview of the language used in a number of religio-musical soundscapes and sections of the novel focused on characters like Mozzie Fisherman and Father Danny – is neutralized by the proceeding descriptions of the Ancestral Serpent, 'A creature larger than storm clouds [...] laden with its own creative enormity' (1). The jarring dissonance of this transformation between sacred registers sits within the traditions of Aboriginal literature in English, particularly the first letters written to newspapers by Aboriginal people in the 1800s. Anita Heiss and Peter Minter state in their introduction to the *Macquarie Pen Anthology of Aboriginal Literature* that 'one of the persistent and now characteristic elements of Aboriginal literature [is] the nexus between the literary and the political' (2009, 20).

Songlines 'Round Midnight'

Bundling together the spatial, sacred and geographic within sound, songlines offer a texturally and contextually apt mode of thinking about *Carpentaria*. Largely introduced to non-Indigenous audiences by Bruce Chatwin in his comparative travelogue-ethnography *The Songlines* (1986), the insights provided by Aboriginal elders, ethnomusicologists and anthropologists contextualize the significance of the songline as an Indigenous practice and concept with scant equivalent in Western societies. Murrandoo Yanner, from the Ganggalida nation in North Queensland – the basis for Wright's fictional character Will Phantom – explains the interconnection of travel, trade and the landscape within the concept of the songline: 'Travel was made possible by songlines and the rivers are connected to the songlines and naturally trade routes followed the rivers [...] Most of the rivers are in song [...] and trade routes are the physical evidence of the songlines' (quoted in Kerwin 2012, 47). Yanner's statement speaks to the pragmatic use of the songline as a map for trade and movement, but the spiritual underpinning of the concept is always integral. Indigenous leader, politician and anthropologist Kado Muir underscores Yanner's sentiment: 'My mob traded in songs, intellectual property, we traded in information technologies. If you know the songs, water and food resources are easily found' (quoted in Kerwin 2012, 40). Muir's assertion of the ceremonial, intellectual and practical importance of songlines is a through-running refrain across the various related disciplinary fields that engage with the concept. Muir's comment on trading and songs as 'information technologies' also shows the parity of these ancient traditions with contemporary forms of knowledge sharing, commerce and cartography.

Anthropologist Paul Tacon's description of the songline resonates between Muir and Yanner's ideas: 'Before the recent era of European-induced change, creation and destruction, these tracks were maintained through ceremony, song, visual art, the transmission of oral history, trade and other forms of exchange' (2005, 72). Tacon suggests that in contemporary times the tracks 'illustrate ways of conceptualising land other than through the printed maps, roads and hard political boundaries so typical of the modern world' (72–73). Tacon's description of songline 'tracks', which he says have immense 'social, historical, geological, biological, ecological and archaeological' value (72), aligns with the major labour of *Carpentaria* to present a complex portrait of 'country', its Aboriginal and colonial past and present, and the organic and cultural plasticity of its future. Judy Atkinson's scholarship draws out the value of songlines as narratives 'about relationships between people and relationships with country' (2002, 26). In *Trauma Trails, Recreating Song Lines: The Transgenerational Effects of Trauma in Indigenous Australia* (2002) Atkinson emphasizes the ceremonial importance of the songline.

> Relationships with the natural world, and in particular the distressed feelings that accompany a natural disaster such as drought or flood, were ritualised and ceremonised so that healing, or a restoration of good relationships, could occur in the land with other living species, and between the land and the people. (2002, 26)

The way Atkinson underlines the restorative function of songline as ceremony, which she also says 'were used to re-establish the sense of creative power after being made to feel powerless, and to help to heal the distress that accompanies natural disasters and as a consequence of human conflict' (32), harmonizes with the distress caused by mining, the stormy renewal that brings the novel to its conclusion, and the domestic and community dramas that run parallel to these events.

Reading and listening to *Carpentaria* as a novelistic songline must take into account the myriad of formal, cultural and contextual differences that define a traditional songline – sung in language, with a specific 'placed' cultural and spiritual purpose – from a contemporary novel written in a poly-vocal English. Despite the seeming disparity of the forms, and beyond their shared sonic articulation, there is a strong sympathy *within* the songline tradition for this kind of critical reading engagement with the novel. Ethnomusicologist Jill Stubington discusses the many regional and situational variations that the songline can encompass, describing it as 'anything but fixed' (49). Variations in time, place and ceremony can effect 'the nature of a songline', but Stubington suggests the 'broad themes remain constant: the journey, the interrelationship between people, land and myth, the expression of these relationships in ceremonies, the explanatory power of dreaming stories' (49). These various cultural practices, contexts and themes have an immense history in comparison to the recent emergence of the novelistic songline in *Carpentaria*, despite the strong thematic resonances.

The diverse set of cultural practices of Aboriginal music also links the songline tradition to Wright's novel. Discussing performance in Aboriginal culture, Stubington suggests that, in contrast with most Western societies, 'music in traditional Aboriginal society has always held a central place. In health, education, political power and displays of social and cultural resources, music is the first thing to be considered' (25). Music is 'highly valued for its ability to integrate: it can hold the balance; promote good health in both individuals and groups' (25). On an individual level, people with the 'combination of musical talent, ritual knowledge and the authority and ability to reveal the true nature of things confer a power and status impossible to acquire by any other means' (25). Emphasizing the functional and geopolitical similarities between the novel and songline in terms of musical performance, in *Carpentaria* Wright attends to the multiple strands of knowledge mentioned by Stubington: environmental, historical and mythical themes are fundamental to the fabric of the novel.

Despite being relatively unheralded in the narrative of the novel there are several explicit references to songlines that contain information of exactly the type discussed by Stubington, Yanner, Muir, Tacon and Atkinson. One performance takes place when Joseph Midnight, leader of the Eastside mob, gives Will Phantom instructions on how to find his partner Hope and child Bala. The scene literally stages (but does not transcribe) the singing of a songline, and I quote it at length because of its significance to *Carpentaria* as a novelistic songline:

> The old man gave him directions to the safe place in his far-off country – a blow-by-blow description sung in song, unraveling a map to a dreamtime

place he had never seen [...] old man Midnight remembered a ceremony he had never performed in his life before, and now, to his utter astonishment, he passed it on to Will. He went on and on, fully believing he was singing in the right sequence hundreds of places in a journey to a place at least a thousand kilometers away. 'Sing this time. Only that place called such and such. This way, remember. Don't mix it up. Then next place, sing, such and such. Listen to me sing it now and only when the moon is above, like there, a bit lower, go on, practice. Remember, don't make mistakes [...]' The song was so long and complicated and had to be remembered in the right sequence where the sea was alive, waves were alive, currents alive, even the clouds. (360)

Placed within the swirling momentum leading into the final storm sequence of the novel, the scene is pivotal to the narrative because it maps out Will's pathway as he searches for his partner and daughter. Joseph's songline signals a moment of ceremonial importance while also demonstrating knowledge transmission between generations. But possessing the knowledge of the songline does not lead Will to his family. At the conclusion of the novel he is still searching for Hope and Bala, and he does not return home. Will's individual journey is only one strand in the larger fabric of the novel, but, as one of two heroes (the other being Norm), his movements are important events on the larger songline of *Carpentaria*. The travels of Mozzie Fisherman and his band of disciples are another direct expression of a songline, although in that instance it is not explicitly sonic in its realization. Just as Will Phantom uses song in his attempts to find his family, the Fisherman's convoy of cars literally follows the tracks of a songline or Dreaming track in their own secret business.

The materiality of Joseph Midnight's songline is presented in such a way that its specific form and content remains hidden from the ears and eyes of the reader, putting even more emphasis on the imagination. Unlike when Wright uses figurative language to describe sounds, here none of the textural or tonal information regarding the actual 'sound' of the songline is provided. There is very little indication of the tone of Joseph's voice – although his surprise at being able to remember and perform the songline is noted – and none of the exact places and directions contained in the songline are named. All that is mentioned is that the map leads to a 'dreamtime place'. Perhaps this elision is a mark of respect for a ceremonial practice whose expressive breadth lies outside the range of the novel? And maybe by not signposting this important event Wright is writing for readers with knowledge or familiarity of the practice? As scholars suggest, a songline is a detailed geographic description, a specific sequence of places, names, plants, totemic animals and weather conditions. Joseph Midnight shows that it is also a challenging feat of memory: 'Remember, don't make mistakes [...] Listen to me sing now and only when the moon is above, like there, a bit lower, go on, practice.' Considering the lack of specific detail given about the songline, Joseph's commentary on its correct usage perhaps indicates the structural and methodological utility of the practice over its aesthetic value. That much Aboriginal music is secret – only to be performed by/for the initiated – is an important context for Wright's depiction here.

A Noisy Song

The sound of contested territory and reformation, noise infiltrates many of the soundscapes of *Carpentaria*. Rather than obscurity and interruption, noise provides renewal and reorientation: as noisy songline the novel reaches forward to the projected future and back to (and beyond) the foundations of colonial Australia. Defined in the Oxford English Dictionary as 'a sound, especially one that is loud or unpleasant or that causes disturbance', the use of 'unpleasant' and 'loud' is superficially related to some of the noise that resounds in the novel. Although this definition is almost unhelpful in its generality, it does gesture towards the useful discussions of noise to emerge from cybernetic theory, where noise denotes nonsignifying matter or meaninglessness.

Foregrounding the aesthetic utility of noise in making audible and complicating the *border* between sound and sense (and nonsense), or self and other, Bruce Buchan and David Ellison define noise as a 'vexatious fault line between nuisance and purpose, labour and rest, pleasure and pain' (2012, 7). Buchan and Ellison's definition provides a set of binary terms that introduce the conceptual and affective territory of noise, underscoring the illusive and Janus-like character of this order of sound. Douglas Kahn's definition moves closer to the noise I argue resonates throughout *Carpentaria*. For Kahn, 'Noise can be understood in one sense to be that constant grating sound generated by the movement between the abstract and empirical. It need not be loud, for it can go on unheard in the most intense communication' (1999, 25). Within the context of *Carpentaria*, Kahn's 'grating sound', produced by the meeting of the 'abstract and empirical', is a particularly apposite explication of noise. Weather events like the major storm at the end of the novel embody the clash of the abstract and the empirical, but as a whole Wright's work stages the dissonant encounter between colonial and Indigenous, history and Dreamtime temporalities, and traditional and scientific epistemologies.

Examining the role of noise and music in the various stages of European social history, George Revill locates the place of noise 'outside understanding and beyond culture, [in] the nonsignifying province of value-free science and the primordial wilderness of raw nature' (2000, 599). The demarcation between music and non-music mirrors the spatial and communicational divide foundational to more general discussions of noise. Michel Serres, who has theorized noise in several influential books, most notably in *The Parasite* (1982), extends Revill's gesture towards the space of noise. Serres links the origin of the word noise with a tempestuous sea: 'Noise, intermittence and turbulence, quarrel and sound; this marine noise is the original one but the original hatred as well. We hear it on the high seas' (51). Riffing on the etymology of noise, for Serres the sea is a space in wild excess of the land-locked continent. Similarly, Wright's storm literally performs the aquatic invasion of the terrestrial, the crossing over and mixing of continent and border.

If noise can be the sound of the abstract and the empirical, the inside and the outside, *Carpentaria*'s noise is the sound of continental regeneration and archipelagic reorientation. As economist and cultural theorist Jacques Attali states in *Noise: The Political Economy of Music*, 'The presence of noise makes sense, makes meaning. It makes possible the creation of a new order on another level of organization, of a new code in another network' (1985, 33). Similarly, art theorist Joseph Nechvatal discusses how the 'art of noise' can 'take the meaninglessness of noise and convert it into the meaningful' (2011, 17). Extending this idea of transformation, for Nechvatal noise 'is what awakes us from our silent dream and leads us to the excesses of ecstatic encounters [...] It suggests an outside other and points us elsewhere by sabotaging our sense of harmonious balance' (35). In *Carpentaria*, noise carries this doubleness and utility. Initially Wright uses it to embody the destructive productivity of neocolonial activities, but later it marks the victory of the Ancestral Serpent and the storm that levels Desperance. The conversion of the meaningless noise of the Gurfurrit mine into the 'ecstatic encounter' with the storm and the island of rubbish, or the final coda scene where Norm and Bala are 'singing the country afresh' (499) after the complete annihilation of Desperance are key moments of *Carpentaria*'s 'art of noise'. The two tonalities of noise – neocolonial and Indigenous – are overlapping strata upon which the action of the novel takes place. The Desperance noise-scape fortifies the neocolonial space of the town and underscores the racial segregation that has forced the Indigenous population onto its outskirts. In turn, the Indigenous noise of the storm reclaims and utterly transforms the landscape.

The neocolonial points on *Carpentaria*'s noisy songline have their foundations in one of the earliest descriptions of Australian colonial space, published in 1804 by David Collins, first judge advocate for New South Wales. The account is the historical footings of the colonial noise heard in *Carpentaria*, but listening Collins's soundscape also reveals the extent of Wright's reharmonization of noise into a productive, non-racist force. Although early colonial Australia was a different kind of frontier space from the contemporary one depicted in Wright's novel, there are important resemblances, including the fraught sense of otherness surrounding the violent and paranoid residents of Desperance. Collins hears a braided harmony of noise and silence linked with the introduction of imperial ways of seeing and hearing signaled by the arrival of Captain Arthur Philip and the First Fleet in 1788. Describing the landing of the First Fleet, Collins states,

> The spot chosen [...] was at the head of a Cove near a run of fresh water, which stole silently through a very thick wood, the stillness of which had then, for the first time since the creation, been interrupted by the rude sound of the labourer's axe, and the downfall of its ancient inhabitants: – a stillness and tranquility which, from that day, were to give place to the noise of labour, the confusion of camps and towns, and the busy hum of its new possessors. (1804, 10)

Constructing an idealized scene of Edenic natural bounty and unfulfilled potential, Collins listens as movement and noise emerge from stillness and silence. Initially he describes the soundscape of the 'spot chosen' – a phrase that evokes a kind of predestined fate – as silent. It is as if the land had been captured in suspended animation since its creation. Tellingly, Collins is unsure about the new noise of the 'labourer's axe', later suggesting 'the spot which had so lately been the abode of silence and tranquility was now changed to that of noise, clamour, and confusion' (10). As historian Peter Denney notes, Collins also appreciates this scene of colonial origin for its aesthetic beauty, and perhaps this, or his distaste for the derogatory vigour of the labouring class, is the reason for his uncertainty. Essential to the power structure being outlined by Collins is the lack of any sound from Indigenous Australians – his thoughts here can be placed within the context of *terra nullius* (2012).

Collins explicitly yokes noise to labour, a sonic relation played out in *Carpentaria* in descriptions of Desperance and the Gurfurrit mine. Commenting on the noisy soundscapes of colonial Australia, Denney suggests that 'standards of politeness were used in novel ways to justify racial hierarchies and to bring order to confused social arrangements', although he maintains 'there remained a taste, however muted and compromised, for a countryside pulsating with noise, especially the noise of empire' (95). Addressing this racial demarcation, Denney says, 'There was thus a hierarchy established in the colonial imagination with the noise of industrious European labour ranked well above the noise of Aboriginal activity' (98). This hierarchy of noise is overturned in Wright's novel, although, as is hinted at in the prologue and confirmed later, such a transformation is already underway in the time before the direct scope of the narrative. European labour and the noise of its productivity has already been subverted by more powerful and local forces: Desperance once sat on the banks of the river, but the Ancestral Serpent years ago caused the river to bypass the town, rendering the once profitable colonial outpost an absurdly dry port.

Despite how the colonial project is profoundly undermined throughout *Carpentaria*, 'noises of empire' still resound throughout the first half of the novel. Anticipating the stormy conclusion, the noise created by wind and music defines the soundscape of Desperance:

> Noise was everywhere, and if there was an original God who had come along with all the white people, who created everything for them, then this place was where he made his music. There could not be a more windy town anywhere in the world of tin flapping, like an orchestra growing louder with age. And they never know it, or realised, but that music drove those town people half mad. You should watch the wind music for it is the undoer of a man's soul. (54)

Wright's characterization of Desperance as the place where an 'original God' would make music is ironic – the noise driving the townspeople half mad is actually created by the flapping tin roofs of their own houses. Noise here signifies the instability of the colonial project, and the tinny, annoying frequency is contrasted with the immense rumble of the storms that come later. Wright also expands the scope of the sounds produced by the noise-machine of Desperance to a national scale. Referring to the noise produced by the town, the narrator comments,

> This indescribable concoction of rhythms escaped into the atmosphere, and was spirited away across the continent to somewhere else more fraught with modernity than Desperance. There, wafting into the minds of modern day composers like lights of stardust, inspiring them to create weird, unfathomable orchestral music which the old people heard on the radio and recognised as the uncontrollable airs of Desperance. What a fright! They turned the radio off. (55)

Irony is pushed almost into the territory of travesty, with the narrator speculating that the noise of Desperance could influence contemporary composition. The noise-infused art music created by these urban composers is retransmitted, via the radio, to the 'old people' of Desperance. Acting as a kind of Greek chorus of voices throughout *Carpentaria*, the old people reject this reconfigured noise – 'What a fright' they exclaim. Paul Sharrad argues that 'the old people (and we readers) appear to be haunted by a cacophony of voices past and dreaming voices as well as present waking ones, voices of black and white, all threatening madness and confounding purpose: Sonic nets of confusion' (2009, 62). These 'sonic nets of confusion' also feature prominently in Wright's novel *The Swan Book* (2013). In *Carpentaria*, the old people are, through the nationwide media networks that reach even to the outskirts of Desperance, doubly subjected to the noise that has already banished them to the outskirts of town. Here Wright pokes fun at the popular fetishization of 'exotic' Australian soundscapes, bringing to mind the bird cries of Peter Sculthorpe's lauded composition *Kakadu* (1988).

The Gurfurrit mine sits alongside Desperance at the neocolonial end of *Carpentaria*'s noise continuum. In comparison to the mobile, shrill noise of the town, the noise that emanates from the mine is a powerful bass synthesizer. Instead of the noises of production – recall the underground rumblings in Alex Miller's *Landscape of Farewell* – Wright's mine is an explosive soundscape, the first reverberation in a series of destructive events that finally manifest the island of rubbish.

> The soundwaves coming off the explosion in the aeroplane hangers at the biggest mine of its type in the world, Gurfurritt, were just about as tremendous a sound you could ever expect to hear on this earth. Like guyfork night. Booom! Booom! Over and over. But one hundred times more louder than that. Ripped the lot. We were thinking, those of us lying on the ground up in the hills smelling ash – what if our ears exploded? What would deafness sound like? We should have thought of that first. (393)

The explosion is perceived from a group perspective in a similar way to the chorus of the old people. The extreme noise of the explosion makes the young activists (whose sabotage causes the explosion) question the limits of sound and hearing: 'The sound of his young voice being the first sound was a relief for the others who had been thinking they were listening to the sound of their own deafness' (395). The sound of deafness is an abject inversion of normal sense perception, perhaps referring to the noise of tinnitus as much as the absence of meaningful resonance in the aftermath of annihilation. These fears reflect the magnitude of the explosion – after all, Gurfurrit is 'the biggest mine of its type in the world' – and the damage to the entire ecosystem created by the mine and its demise is immense.

Singing the Country Afresh: Two Sound Heroes

Counterbalancing the violence of the explosion and the few moments of existential silence that echo after it, a second soundscape offers some solace to the activists:

> However relieved and pacified they were to hear speech, everyone kept listening, listening, for what else remained missing – Ah! It was the

noise of the bush breathing, the wind whispering through the trees and flowing through rustling grasses. We needed to hear the birds chirping, the eaglehawk crying out something from the thermals high above, but the eery silence lingered on. The birds were nowhere to be seen or heard, not even a willy-wagtail lightly fluttering from rock to rock wherever anyone walked, or a mynah bird haggling at your feet. (395)

The sonic interest generated here is increased by Wright's use of the phrase 'the noise of the bush'. While perhaps curious in light of definitions of noise as the non-signifying data of the outside, here it holds with Wright's productive and reparative use of noise in key moments of *Carpentaria*. Characterizing the sound of the bush as noise aligns the natural, non-human soundscape with the restoration of ecological balance. While the bush is once more allowed to breathe, what is not heard in this soundscape – but which nevertheless haunts it – are birds, the sonic signs of a healthy and balanced sonic ecology. This inaudible spectre is brought back to life later in the novel, particularly in the last scene.

The destruction of the Gurfurrit mine is a salient point of noise along the songline of *Carpentaria*, but the major storm that destroys Desperance and creates the island of rubbish is the defining event of the novel, the climax of its noisy synoptic structure. The survival and renewal of *Carpentaria*'s natural and spiritual ecosystem realized in the storm sequence is in part reliant on two heroic characters, Norm and Will Phantom. The ability of Norm and Will (and to a lesser extent, Mozzie Fisherman and Joseph Midnight) to be careful and skilled *listeners* is essential to their status as heroes, the keepers of the songlines of *Carpentaria*. Their adventures along a noisy songline literally map *Carpentaria* as a contemporary Dreaming story. The fractured relationship between father and son (caused by Will's connection with Hope) provides the forward momentum for the human drama of the work: centred on Norm and Will, the contemporary events in the novel are couched within and constantly relate back to a huge historical span, beginning with the creative movements of the Ancestral Serpent described in the prologue.

Norm is the most spiritually and ecologically knowledgeable character portrayed by Wright. His legendary fishing trips, and the journey to the dreaming place of the Gropers for Elias Smith's sea burial, are almost superhuman in the distances and times involved. As Mozzie Fisherman relates to Will, Norm may in fact be superhuman in his abilities. Sharing his knowledge of Norm's 'synoptic powers', Mozzie Fisherman tells Will how 'Norm was in a storm-making place [...] singing up the spirits in the water, boy, to make storms for his enemy' (467). Mozzie actually recounts a songline to Will – 'Even though the Fisherman never went to sea, he mentioned an itinerary of site places along the coast for making storms and counter storms powerful enough to wipe out the entire enemy' (467) – but, 'after naming several hundred sites in a geography he had never traveled', he makes it clear that Norm's knowledge of the songline is greater. 'I don't know all of these places. But some do. Your father knows, because he can fly through storms like an angel' (467–68). The 'storm-making place' is another location on the noisy songline of *Carpentaria*, although its exact position is not mentioned.

Norm's singing abilities are again at the fore in the final paragraph of the novel, as he explores post-storm Desperance with his grandchild Bala. Wright's choice of the name Bala is perhaps an allusion to the search for ecological *bala*nce that underpins the whole project of *Carpentaria*:

> 'I reckon we will go home then,' he [Norm] said. So, they walked in mud away from the town left to the dogs that tried to howl for their owners. Neither spoke, because neither would have heard the other. It was much better to listen to the mass choir of frogs – green, grey, speckled, striped, big and small, dozens of species all assembled around the two seafarers, as they walked.
>
> It was a mystery, but there was so much song wafting off the watery land, singing the country afresh as they walked hand in hand out of town, down the road, Westside, to home. (499)

Carpentaria's explicitly sonic conclusion offers hope for the future. The contrast between the clamour of the homeless dogs and the ecstatic 'mass choir' of frogs – a rainbow of colour as much as a croaking eco-symphony – is extreme. Frogs, thought to indicate a healthy aqua environment, are here an answering call to the interpolating bells of the opening of the novel.

'Singing the country afresh' is another clear reference to songline singing. Norm and Bala are performing a songline, creating the land through the act of singing. The intergenerational symbolism of Norm and Bala suggests some future unity in the midst of the feud between Eastside and Westside, a point of shared hope for the process of rebuilding amidst the *tabula rasa* of post-storm Desperance. The phrase 'there was so much song wafting off the watery land' also implies that the song is being produced by more than just Norm and Bala. But like her evocation of songlines by Joseph Midnight and Mozzie Fisherman, Wright does not describe the exact nature of this soundscape. Apart from the frogs, the open character of this final scene reflects the newness of the landscape as much as it sounds an unsure note for the future – the precise shape of tomorrow is in a state of becoming.

Between Norm and Bala, the two figures of age and renewal, is Will Phantom. Like his father, Will is highly attuned to sound, although he does not exhibit the same mystical weather-related powers. But as the novel progresses an aptitude for listening, to soundscapes and the advice of his elders, is revealed. Traveling with Mozzie Fisherman to a sacred burial ground, Will is able to hear:

> The song cycles' arias of devotion that had droned on in this place for days and days like locusts before rain [...] Only Will heard it, while leading the Fisherman away, when he looked back over his shoulder. 'Hear it? Listen!' He heard a droning sound, and imagined the sound was converging from many different directions. (420–23)

The song cycle is performed in commemoration of three boys murdered by the police. Composed of a combination of human and landscape elements, this soundscape is another sonic node on the larger songline of *Carpentaria*. That Will is the sole person to hear this somber resonance points to his skill in reading and listening to a landscape crowded with significant spiritual and natural data. The multidirectionality of this harmony of lament doubles Will's fierce sense of ownership and responsibility to his country, a commitment evident in his fight against the Gurfurrit mine.

Will's ultimate test as a listener is the storm. Leading into the night where he is forced to take shelter in the local pub, Will encounters Joseph Midnight among the stream of Desperance residents fleeing the weather. Joseph, who had earlier given Will songline instructions to help in his search for Hope and Bala, again offers advice to his son-in-law. This time Joseph's wisdom focuses on listening to the fast-approaching weather:

> 'What are you doing here?' he asked Will with a flick of his hand.
> 'Going home', Will replied with sign language.
> 'But! Big cyclone coming, boy, everybody *barrba, jayi, yurrngijbangka* – you better come with us', old Joseph again indicated with his hands.
> 'Can't. I am going to find Bala and Hope', Will replied.
> 'Better hurry – it won't be long.'
> 'How long?' Will was starting to judge the distance he still had to get to the town and find shelter.
> '*Ngamiri*. Nobody told me. Everyone *kayi*. Big fella coming this time – I heard them, *barraku* talking. Cover the town. Everything will go. Listen to the ocean. Soon. *Warawarayanjingawa ninja lajibi*.'
> 'Alright, old malbu – until next time', Will replied. [...]
> Will followed the road into Desperance. He became conscious of what the sea ahead was doing once more, and although he knew it was kilometres away, he heard the spirit waves being rolled in by the

ancestral sea water creatures of the currents, and conspiring with the spirits of the sky and wind to crash into the land as though it was exploding. The earth murmured, the underground serpent, living in the underground river that was kilometres wide, responded with hostile growls. This was the old war of the ancestors making cyclones grow to use against one another. (452–53)

'Listen to the ocean.' Joseph's advice is an ominous environmental warning for the current era of climate change – 'Everything will go' – but it also sets up the concluding events of the novel, with Will marooned on the noisy island of rubbish. The creation of the storm soundscape is here attributed to several interconnected spiritual identities – ancestral seawater, spirits of the sky and wind, and the underground serpent are all active. The spiritual and environmental are integrated into a highly resonant harmony that generates the storm.

The inclusion of Wright's Waanyi language in the encounter between Will and Joseph augments the polyglossia that characterizes the whole work. Indigenous language is sprinkled throughout *Carpentaria*, but the above excerpt features the most concentrated collection of words, a presence that accentuates the opening of Indigenous space in the storm and amplifies the importance of this scene in the sonic cartography of the novel. Indigenous language is also a call to Indigenous readers; considering the worldwide acclaim of *Carpentaria*, this readership would be a tiny minority. Nevertheless, in hailing her local Gulf country community Wright not only highlights a specificity of place, she emphasizes the living sonic *difference* of this landscape.

As Will moves away from Joseph and the rest of the Desperance locals, 'the noise of the town faded away in the clouds, and the sound of the wind blowing the mist became more prominent' (448). This is the final fanfare of the neo-colonial in the novel. The storm soundscape that overshadows the end of *Carpentaria* is produced by the 'old war of the ancestors', and is distinctly noisy:

The roar of the sea showed no mercy. There would be no letting up. No respite for quietness. There was noise in the movement of water flooding back to the sea carting the wreckage with it. All passed over the flooded land groaning with remains of buildings, boats, cars, trees, rocks, electricity poles, fences, cargo from fallen ships, plastic consignments scrambled like licorice allsorts and dead animals. (469)

The storm performs the role of sonic accompaniment to the 'war of the ancestors' – the sound produced by their battle – while also signaling the destruction and renewal of Desperance. The clue to this second capacity is in the description of the 'noise in the movement of water flooding back to the sea'. The noise created by the listed items from Desperance is matched by another raucous description – 'The flooded land groaning with the remains [of the town].' The blank-slate in which Norm and Bala later 'sing the country afresh' is a landscape purged of neocolonial resonance, and this sonic purification is the result of an Indigenous soundscape that is itself characteristically noisy.

Perhaps contrary to the storm as noise machine, on two separate occasions the final storm is described as music: 'All day and all night the wind played ancestor music' (441) which later transforms into a 'catastrophic requiem' (474). References to non-Indigenous musical forms including 'Italian opera' (370), 'classical Japanese song' (420) and the 'aria' of the song cycle sung by Mozzie Fisherman for the three murdered children (420) extend the structural range of sound in the novel. Deploying musical terminology to describe sound creates a radically different tonality, one that, in the case of the 'catastrophic requiem', forges a sonic connection between Christian and Indigenous spirituality and contrasts with the noise heard throughout the other soundscapes. Listening to this requiem – a compositional form drawn from the Roman Catholic tradition, composed for the repose of the souls of the dead – Will hears 'hundreds of God's angels singing: *Gloria in excelsis Deo, Et in terra pax hominibus bonae voluntatis*' [*Translation*: Glory to God in the Highest, and on Earth Peace to People of Good Will] (474). The inclusion of Latin here, and in several other places throughout *Carpentaria*, also accentuates the polyglossia that permeates the whole work. Transitioning from the typical register of the novel into biblical Latin expands and textures the verticality of space. The multileveled strata of the storm is teeming with spiritual figures, all of which contribute to the ruckus of the soundscape.

Remixing the noise created by the passing of the wreckage of Desperance in the floodwaters of the storm, the island of rubbish – a real-life occurrence as a result of oceanic currents – is a complex soundscape:

> The clouds broke, the new moon shone its halo of peace. Relieved for such an absolution of light, [Will] looked down to find he had been dumped onto an extraordinary floating island of rubbish.
>
> While the serpentine floatation rocked in the waves, the sum total of its parts rubbed, grated and clanked together, as it became more tightly enmeshed into a solid mass that squashed every inch of oil and stench out of the dead marine life it had trapped in its guts. Will listened to the embryonic structure's strange whines echoing off into the darkness, then, he realised the enormity of those sounds was familiar to him. He was astonished and then weakened by the feeling of helplessness, that a man feels, hearing the sounds of labour. He felt like he was an intruder to be

clinging to a foetus inside the birth canal, listening to it, witnessing the birth of creation in the throes of a watery birth. (475)

The rubbing, grating and clanking of the island, its 'strange whines', are sounds familiar to Will as sonic source materials gathered from the cacophony of Desperance and its surrounding ecology. The neocolonial noise of the town, passing through the destructive and transformative conditions of the stormy 'ancestor music', emerges on the other side in an island-sized sonic and material precipitation. Will's feeling that he is in the birth canal – an experience of listening surreal in its sensation of interiority – figures the island as a baby, newborn and developing. 'Hearing the sounds of labour' is at once a reference to childbirth, but at the same time it captures the grinding movement and sound that is continuing to form the island.

For Will, swept away by the storm while embarking on a search for Hope and Bala, the island is both a lifeboat and a search vessel, an Edenic garden and a prison. Addressing the formation of the island and the permeability of continental borders, Laura Joseph argues,

> The materiality deployed by [*Carpentaria*] to resist coercive forms of nationhood arises from the substance of region as both natural elements and artificial or waste matter. In *Carpentaria* the dynamic, disobedient, alchemical and archipelagic material elements of the gulf country are harnessed to challenge juridical, discursive and economic claims to the region made by both the nation and international corporations. (2009, 2)

In Joseph's lexicon, the island of rubbish is 'dynamic' and 'alchemical' in its violent material reconstruction, 'disobedient' of continental unity and 'archipelagic' in its relation to the mainland of Australia and the surrounding expanse of sea. The literal unmooring of the island from continental confines, as well as the sounds Will hears while 'onboard', position the island within the familiar discourse associated with noise – beyond, outside, in excess. Drifting away from the mainland and the bounds of the nation, the island is the locus of *Carpentaria*'s regenerative achievement, a new space formed through the prism of Indigenous noise, a symbol loaded with resonance and meaning.

The Australian mainland recedes into the distance. Like a miniaturized *Carpentaria*, the island is a microcosmic formation of space, a local cartography moving away from the nation. Alongside the final scene of Norm and Bala singing the croaking mudflats of Desperance, the island of rubbish explicitly manifests *Carpentaria*'s statement of postcolonial renewal through noise. Listening closely to these soundscapes has revealed the spatial and temporal complexity of *Carpentaria*, and its contemporary ecological relevance. Wright's joyfully cacophonous novel is a novelistic songline that, in reimagining a traditional form of Indigenous performance, knowledge and cartography, reorients Australian continental space.

Following such a diversity of imagined sounds across the previous six chapters, it is significant that I have concluded with the noisy imagined sound in *Carpentaria*. Redefining the continent as a songline encompassing island *and* archipelago, in Wright's novel we listen to a Northern coastal landscape that offers an alternative to ideas about Australian landscape, a profound shift away from the images and experiences created in the axis of the urban/metropolitan and the bush/centre. Listening to noise is a practice that moves us forward, into new sonic territories outside conventional maps, beyond received forms of space and time. This is the territory of the future as much as it is, in *Carpentaria*, a part of a cycle of renewal.

CODA

Imagined Sound maps a diversity of spaces, historical timeframes, conceptual approaches and creative reimaginings. From the centre of the continent to the coastal fringe, from the 'island continent' to tiny landmasses far out in the Pacific, from the 1960s, 1970s, 1980s, 1990s, 2000s and 2010s, the range of spaces and times that emerged from the works of literature and music assembled in this book cohered around two pivotal geoimaginaries: the continent, and the island and archipelago. The multiplicity of responses to these two spatial configurations, and the related-but-distinct nature of listening to novels, songs, jazz suites, poems, video clips, and song lyrics, echoes the potential for these forms to be reimagined by writers and composers, to be transformed by personal artistic aims and historical contexts. Soundscapes of terror, refrains of transcendence, verses and choruses sung to raise political awareness or remind us of the unburied past, sampled voices from the past bourn on oceanic tides, screams echoing across haunted landscapes, the visceral abjection of the colonial island, the chains of a global archipelago. The situations and environments resounding through the last seven chapters are a unique kind of catalogue of Australian space and time. Listening to 'imagined sound' enables us to hear this diversity of sonic situation.

The continent, the island, the archipelago: each has its own harmony of imagined sounds. The soundscapes and refrains of the continent – the replaced desert centre walk walked by the mytho-Modernists Webb and Lumsdaine, the iconic images of Uluru, sorry suits and lyrical refrains of recognition sung by Midnight Oil, or the subtle bush soundscapes of Miller's postcolonial novels – sound out the 'geo-becoming' that has taken hold of Australian artistic production since World War II. In these works, the continent – sometimes the 'island continent' – is both insular and vast, a series of landscapes teaming with sounds sometimes haunting, sometimes refreshing. Building and rebuilding what the continental landmass *is* in our ears and minds, Webb and Lumsdaine made discoveries – sites of isolation, paranoia and transcendence. Later, around the turn into the post-*Mabo* era, Midnight Oil and Miller revisited these continental myth-scapes, but progressed further by working to recognize Indigenous Australia. The sonic cartography of islands and archipelagos opened by the abject lyrics of the Drones and Liddiard, the spectral scream-scapes of Flanagan and Bird's Tasmanian novels, and the archipelagic jazz suite of Baecastuff, *Mutiny Music*, were each characterized by different types of relation – historical, mythic, personal, musical, linguistic, cultural, colonial, and postcolonial. These experiences, and the time and space they unlocked, were realized through abject, haunted, sung, sampled and screamed configurations of imagined sound.

Sounding a new and simultaneously ancient reformation of the Australian landmass, in many ways the analysis of Wright's *Carpentaria* synthesized the soundscapes and refrains of the continent and the island or archipelago of the previous six chapters. The noisy soundscapes of Wright's *Carpentaria* placed it both in dialogue with the colonial paradigm and in excess of it. Its 'time immemorial' scope, references to the creative role of the Ancestral Serpent, and the heroic abilities of central characters Norm and Will Phantom – in other words, the complete reorganization of the continent that is performed by the novel – make *Carpentaria* unique among the literature and music collected in *Imagined Sound*. Braiding cartographic knowledge and sonic transmission, *Carpentaria* as noisy novelistic songline is a singular constellation of space, time and sound.

Listening to this sonic corpus uncovers difference: difference in perspective and approach, in the orientation of landscape, in the merging of history and myth and in the relationship between the past and the present. *Imagined Sound* draws together a diversity of resonant experience, narrative, and multimedia texture. Each work has been repositioned in a way that was only possible through listening – and only through listening to *both* literature and music can we hear this new cartography. In other words, this particular combination of works creates a unique soundscape, a unique refrain. This is a sonography of new imagined pathways around Australia. Listened to as a whole, imagined sound reveals both resonances and dissonances, between the distinct times of production, landscapes and histories of each work. The noise of *Carpentaria* recalls the disorienting cacophonies of Lumsdaine's *Aria*, Webb's psychospiritual crisis in 'Eyre All Alone', and the disturbing spectrality of the screams that echo across the Tasmania of both Flanagan and Bird; the refrains of Flanagan's Tasmanian pub rock evokes the carceral archipelago of the vocal abjection in Liddiard and the Drones; the texture of renewal in *Carpentaria*'s noisy songline suggests that peace can follow the distress voiced by the screams in Flanagan and Bird; the soundscapes of connection that resound within Miller's novels – webs of sound linking characters and histories – perform a similar function to the archipelagic links sounded by voice and song forms in *Mutiny Music*. Heard both between unique Australian histories and landscapes and in different 'takes' of the same territory, each of these resonances – and this is not exhaustive list of possible intertextual harmonies – mark new routes into and away from these works, into and away from the geoimaginaries of the continent and the island and archipelago.

While the consonance of these imagined sounds is striking, intricacies within the same history or landscape are also amplified by listening. Such dissonances underscore the multiplicity of approaches each geoimaginary can support. The dissimilarity between the carceral abjection we hear in the Drones and Gareth Liddiard's convict and outsider songs and the distant-but-homely vocal soundings of the archipelago in *Mutiny Music* is profound. Within the continent, the subtle sounds and silences in Miller's novelistic soundscapes, or the transcendence and confusion that characterize Webb and Lumsdaine's incursions into the centre, are a far cry from the political urgency of the song refrains and imagery we see and hear in the work of Midnight Oil. These divergences reflect personal artistic projects, but again, they also gesture towards the massive expanse of possibility available within each geoimaginary. At the same time, the unique necessity of each historical moment is a vital factor in the range of sound forms employed by writers and composers. For example, while both mark the shift into the post-*Mabo* period, Midnight Oil's need to project a message to an international audience of millions during their Olympic Games closing ceremony is vastly different to the intercontinental histories of massacre activated by Miller's soundscapes. Following the same logic, the unique noisiness of Wright's novel-as-songline echoes both her Indigenous identity, her political convictions and the radicality of the spatio-temporal reformation performed by that work.

In this book the ways of relating to Australian history and its landscapes that listening emphasize – the links between past and present created by the refrain, the intense isolation, confusion or connection evoked by the soundscape, or the sacred refreshment of noisy songlines – are, to return to Georg Lukacs, a certain kind of 'poetic awakening' through sound. Why listen to imagined sound? How can one ignore it! This series of sounds call us to recognize the violence of the past, to hear what has been silenced, to imagine different manifestations of the past, present and future, and to anticipate what can be remade anew.

Many of the works I listened to in *Imagined Sound* have previously received little or no scholarly attention. Baecastuff's *Mutiny Music* and the songs by the Drones and Liddiard are powerful and relevant explorations of the interconnection between Australian and Pacific space. Both redefine Australian mythic landscapes and locate the Australian continent in relation to its Pacific neighbours and global heritage. It is essential to place these contemporary works, as well as the genres they represent, into relation with other more well-known and critiqued works and genres, like the novel. Simply to place Webb's 'Eyre All Alone' and Lumsdaine's *Aria* into dialogue is of critical and conceptual worth. But to augment this with an analysis of Midnight Oil's multimedia rock music vision of the centre creates a valuable account of the history and evolution of a pivotal Australian geoimaginary, one that amplifies the expressive and imaginative value of both high and popular art forms.

Listening to imagined sound, what I called 'an experiment in method', took a small part of Benedict Anderson's theorization of nationalism and, via a harmony of sonorous concepts, created a new approach to literature and music, and a new shared critical territory between these mediums. While listening to music 'with an ear to sound matter as the herald of society' (Attali, 5) is an expected approach, this book has shown that the first counter-intuitive practice of listening to literature also exposes the rich and complex work of sound in that medium. Moving across divides of media, register and context, the set of listenings or readings produced by imagined sound addresses and undermines the ocularcentricism rooted in colonial modes of control. Listening to literature and music *together* creates resonant lines of discussion, not only between each work, landscape and history, but also between intersecting disciplines of literary studies, musicology, Australian history, philosophy and sound studies. The past seven chapters have extended groundbreaking scholarship on the formation of Australian geoimaginaries by Paul Carter, Roslyn Haynes and Elizabeth McMahon. *Imagined Sound* also builds on work in the field of sound studies, particularly by Steven Connor and Josh Kun, who take up issues of nation, voice and sound without engaging with Australian colonial and postcolonial history. At the same time, the interaction of these works of music and literature with various theorizations of sound – principally the soundscape and the refrain, but also the sound in-between, the scream, the sampled voice, the songline and noise – created different senses of how sound operates in music and literature, how it places, how it recalls, how it evokes. In this application of sound theory to Australian literature and music, its landscapes and its histories, I pushed forward these theories, often rerouting their North American or European aligned coordinates and generating new and productive work/theory combinations.

I hope that *Imagined Sound* also shows a way forward for other multimedium studies. The conceptual, historical and textual fabric created by the network of scholarly fields I synthesize contributes a valuable critical dimension that was, for the most part, lacking from each. In particular, nationally focused studies that interweave literature and music, as well as the range of genres from these two mediums, are presently non-existent. Listening to imagined sound could also be applied to works from other periods, such as before World War II, just as productively as it could be used to engage with literature and music being published and performed today, or material that depicts other geoimaginary spaces, such as the urban or the war zone. What are the landscapes mapped by the imagined sounds of 'Five Bells' (Kenneth Slessor's 1939 poem, or Gail Jones's 2011 novel of the same name) – the littoral harbour of Modernist/postmodernist mourning? – what of Xavier Herbert's novel *Capricornia* (1938) – an auditory precursor to Wright's *Carpentaria*? – Henry Lawson and Barbara Baynton's short stories – the depressive and silent bush? – Tim Winton's *Dirt Music* (2001) – a postcolonial symphonic poem on the West Australian coastline? Listening to the imagined sound of works being produced today, or to works that fell outside the bounds of the present study, will surely also provide unique mappings of Australian space and time. And with contextual recalibration, imagined sound and critical close listening could also be used to map other national landscapes beyond my Australian focus.

NOTES

Chapter One: Reimagining 'The Centre': Francis Webb's 'Eyre All Alone' and David Lumsdaine's *Aria for Edward John Eyre*

1 The Gemini recording, which is of higher audio quality, was used in my analysis in this chapter. Track numbers refer to this recording.
2 A matrix is a representation of the 48 permutations of a 'tone row' – a tone row is 12 pitch classes in an equal tempered chromatic scale. A 'Gemini matrix' is a specific matrix devised by Lumsdaine. This compositional practice has its foundations in Lumsdaine's study of serialism.

Chapter Two: Midnight Oil: Sounding Australian Rock around the Bicentenary

1 Midnight Oil, *Diesel and Dust* (1987).
2 Midnight Oil, *Diesel and Dust*.

Chapter Three: Sound and Silence: Listening and Relation in the Novels of Alex Miller

1 Miller on 'The Book Show', *ABC Radio National* (2007).

Chapter Four: An Archipelago of Convicts and Outsiders: The Songs of the Drones and Gareth Liddiard

1 All lyric quotations are my own transcriptions and therefore are without pagination.

Chapter Six: A Sonic Passage between Islands: *Mutiny Music* by Baecastuff

1 http://www.mutinymusic.org/. Accessed 6 February 2014.
2 All quotes from Robertson are from an informal interview I conducted on 2 May 2013.

WORKS CITED

Albright, Daniel. 2004. *Modernism and Music: An Anthology of Sources*. Chicago, IL: University of Chicago Press.
Alessio, Dom. 'Gareth Liddiard – The Sound of Australia'. Accessed 2 March 2012. http://www.abc.net.au/triplej/homeandhosed/blog/s3048576.htm.
Alexander, Caroline. 2003. *The Bounty: The True Story of the Mutiny on the Bounty*. London: HarperCollins.
Amoamo, Maria. 2013. '(De)Constructing Place-Myth: Pitcairn Island and the "Bounty" Story'. *Tourism Geographies: An International Journal of Tourism Space, Place and Environment* 15.1: 107–24.
Anderson, Benedict. 1991. *Imagined Communities: Reflections on the Origin and Spread of Nationalism*. London: Verso.
Anderson, Jessica. 1975. *The Commandant*. London: MacMillan.
'Aria'. 2019. *Oxford Music Online*. Accessed 2 March 2013. https://www.oxfordmusiconline.com/grovemusic/view/10.1093/gmo/9781561592630.001.0001/omo-9781561592630-e-0000043315.
Arnold, David. 2006. *The Tropics and the Travelling Gaze: India, Landscape, and Science, 1800–1856*. Seattle: University of Washington Press.
Ashcroft, Bill. 1996. *The Gimbals of Unease: The Poetry of Francis Webb*. Nedlands: Centre for Studies in Australian Literature, University of Western Australia.
——. 2011. 'Australian Transnation'. *Southerly* 71.1: 18–40.
Ashcroft, Bill, Lyn McCredden and Francis Devlin-Glass. 2009. *Intimate Horizons: The Post-Colonial Sacred in Australian Literature*. Hindmarsh: AFT Press.
Atkinson, Judy. 2002. *Trauma Trails, Recreating Song Lines: The Transgenerational Effects of Trauma in Indigenous Australia*. North Melbourne: Spinifex.
Attali, Jacques. 1985. *Noise: The Political Economy of Music*. Manchester: Manchester University Press.
Attwood, Bain. 2005. *Telling the Truth about Aboriginal History*. Sydney: Allen & Unwin.
Baldacchino, Godfrey. 2005. 'Islands: Objects of Representation'. *Geografiska Annaler: Series B, Human Geography* 87.4: 247–51.
——. ed. 2011. *Island Songs: A Global Repertoire*. Lanham, MD: Scarecrow Press.
Barthes, Roland. 1977. 'The Grain of the Voice'. *Image Music Text*. London: Fontana.
——. 1985. *The Responsibility of Forms: Critical Essays on Music, Art, and Representation*. Trans. L'obvie et l'obtus. Oxford: Basil Blackwell.
Beckett, Samuel. 2009. *Endgame*. London: Faber & Faber.
Belfrage, Jane. 2001. 'The Great Australian Silence: Inside Acoustic Space'. *The Australian Sound Design Project*. University of Melbourne. Accessed 28 April 2011. http://www.sounddesign.unimelb.edu.au/site/papers/AusSilence.html.

Bennett, Roger, ed. 1995. *Voices from the Heart: Contemporary Aboriginal Poetry from Central Australia*. Alice Springs: IAD Press.
Bird, Carmel. 1996. *The White Garden*. St. Lucia: University of Queensland Press.
———. 1998. *The Red Shoes*. Milsons Point: Vintage.
———. 2004. *Cape Grimm*. Sydney: HarperCollins.
———. 2010. *Child of the Twilight*. Pymble: Fourth Estate.
Bird Rose, Deborah. 2008. 'Dreaming Ecology: Beyond and Between'. *Religion and Literature* 40.1: 109–12.
Birns, Nicholas. 2013. '1982: Pre-*Mabo* Popular Song: Icehouse Releases "Great Southern Land"'. *Telling Stories*, edited by Paul Genoni and Tanya Dalziell, 392–97. Melbourne: Monash University Press.
Blake, William. 1967. *Songs of Innocence and Experience*. London: Hart-Davis in association with Trianon Press.
Bongie. Chris. 1999. 'Reading the Archipelago'. *New West Indian Guide* 73.1: 89–95.
Born, Georgina, ed. 2013. *Music, Sound and Space: Transformations of Public and Private Experience*. Cambridge: Cambridge University Press.
Botstein, Leon. 1980. 'Modernism'. *The New Grove Dictionary of Music and Musicians*, edited by Stanley Sadie. London: Macmillan.
Brathwaite, Edward Kamau. 1999. *ConVERSations with Nathaniel Mackey*. New York: WePress.
Brennan, Bernadette. 2005. 'Recognizing the "Face of Love" in Francis Webb's "The Canticle"'. *Antipodes* 19.1: 31–38.
Brewster, Anne. November 2010. 'Indigenous Sovereignty and the Crisis of Whiteness in Alexis Wright's Carpentaria'. *Australian Literary Studies* 25.4: 85–101.
Brumby, Colin. 1999. *The Vision and the Gap*. Grosvenor Place: Australian Music Centre.
Buchan, Bruce, and David Ellison. 2012. 'Introduction: Speaking to the Eye'. *Cultural Studies Review* 18.3: 4–12.
Bucknell, Brad. 2000. 'T.S Eliot's Impossible Music'. *T. S Eliot's Orchestra: Critical Essays on Poetry and Music*, edited by John Xiros Cooper, 111–28. New York: Garland Publishing.
———. 2001. *Literary Modernism and Musical Aesthetics: Pater, Pound, Joyce and Stein*. Cambridge: Cambridge University Press.
Bunn, David. 1994. '"Out Wattled Cot": Mercantile and Domestic Space in Thomas Pringles' African Landscape'. *Landscape and Power*, edited by W. J. T. Mitchell, 127–74. London: University of Chicago Press.
Byron, George Gordon, Lord. 1823. *The Island, or, Christian and His Comrades*. London: John Hunt.
Cage, John. 1961. 'Experimental Music Doctrine'. *Silence: Lectures and Writings*. Middletown, CT: Wesleyan University Press.
Carter, Paul. 1988. *The Road to Botany Bay: An Essay in Spatial History*. London: Faber & Faber.
———. 1992. *The Sound In Between: Voice, Space, Performance*. Kensington: University of New South Wales Press.
Casey, Maryrose. 2012. *Telling Stories: Aboriginal Australian and Torres Straight Islander Performance*. North Melbourne: Australian Scholarly Publishing.
Chambers, Iain. 1996. 'Signs of Silence, Lines of Listening'. *The Post-Colonial Question: Common Skies, Divided Horizons*, edited by Chambers, Iain and Lidia Curti, 47–64. London: Routledge.
Charlesworth, Max. 1984. *Religion in Aboriginal Australia: An Anthology*. St. Lucia: University of Queensland Press.

Chatwin, Bruce. 1986. *The Songlines*. London: Jonathan Cape.
Christiansan, Paul. 2004. 'The Meaning of Speech Melody for Leos Janacek'. *Journal of Musicological Research* 23: 241–63.
Clarke, Marcus. 1884. 'Preface'. *Poems of the Late Adam Lindsay Gordon*. Melbourne: Massina.
———. 1970. *For the Term of his Natural Life*. Hawthorne: Lloyd O'Neil.
Collins, David. 1804. *An Account of the English Colony of New South Wales*. T. London: Cadell & W. Davies.
Columpar, Corinn. 2002. 'The Gaze as Theoretical Touchstone: The Intersection of Film Studies, Feminist Theory, and Postcolonial Theory'. *Women's Studies Quarterly* 30.1/2: 25–44.
Connell, John, and Chris Gibson. 2003. *Sound Tracks: Popular Music, Identity and Place*. London, New York: Routledge.
Connor, Steven. 1997. 'The Modern Auditory I'. *Rewriting the Self: Histories from the Renaissance to the Present*, edited by Roy Porter, 203–23. London: Routledge.
———. 2001. *Dumbstruck: A History of Ventriloquism*. Oxford: Oxford University Press.
Conyngham, Barry. 1973. *Edward John Eyre*. London: Universal Edition.
Creswell, Toby, Craig Mathieson and John O'Donnell. 2010. *100 Best Australian Albums*. Prahran: Hardie Grant Books.
Creswell, Toby. 1990. 'Bullet the Blue Sky'. *Rolling Stone Australia* issue 442, 44–9.
Dahlhaus, Carl. 1989. *Nineteenth-Century Music*, translated by Bradford Robinson. Berkeley: University of California Press.
Damousi, Joy, and Desley Deacon, eds. *Talking and Listening: The Age of Modernity*. Canberra: ANU Press, 2007.
Davidson, Jim. 1989. 'Tasmanian Gothic'. *Meanjin* 48.2: 307–24.
Davidson, Toby. 2013. *Christian Mysticism and Australian Poetry*. Amherst, New York: Cambria Press.
Deleuze, Gilles. 2002. *Desert Islands and Other Texts 1953–1974*, translated by Mike Taormina. Cambridge: MIT Press.
Deleuze, Gilles, and Felix Guattari. 1987. *A Thousand Plateaus: Capitalism and Schizophrenia*, translated by Brian Massumi. London: Continuum.
DeLoughrey, Elizabeth. 2001. '"The Litany of Islands, the Rosary of Archipelagoes": Caribbean and Pacific Archipelagraphy'. *Ariel: Review of International English Literature* 32.1: 21–51.
———. 2007. *Routes and Roots: Navagating Caribbean and Pacific Island Literatures*. Honolulu: University of Hawai'i Press.
Delrez, Marc. 2007. 'Nationalism, Reconciliation, and the Cultural Genealogy of Magic in Richard Flanagan's Death of a River Guide'. *Journal of Commonwealth Literature* 42.1: 117–30.
Dening, Greg. 1992. *Mr. Bligh's Bad Language: Passion, Power and Theatre on the Bounty*. Cambridge: Cambridge University Press.
Denney, Peter. 2012. 'Picturesque Farming: the Sound of "Happy Britannia" in Colonial Australia'. *Cultural Studies Review* 18.3: 85–108.
Derrida, Jacques. 2008. *Writing and Difference*, translated by Alan Bass. London: Routledge.
———. 1994. *The Specters of Marx: The State of Debt, the Work of Mourning, and the New International*. New York: Routledge.
———. 1998. *Of Grammatology*, translated by Gayatri Chakravorty Spivak. Baltimore, MD: John Hopkins University Press.

———. 2011. *The Beast and the Sovereign, Volume II*, translated by Geoffrey Bennington. Chicago, IL: University of Chicago Press.
Devlin-Glass, Frances. 2008. 'A Politics of the Dreamtime: Destructive and Regenerative Rainbows in Alexis Wright's *Carpentaria*'. *Australian Literary Studies* 23.4: 392–407.
Dixon, Robert. 2014. *Alex Miller: The Ruin of Time*. Sydney: Sydney University Press.
———. ed. 2012. *The Novels of Alex Miller: An Introduction*. Sydney: Allen & Unwin.
Dodshon, Mark. 2004. *Beds Are Burning. Midnight Oil: The Journey*. Camberwell: Penguin Group Australia.
Dunmore, J. 1987. *Utopias and Imaginary Voyages to Australasia*. Canberra: National Library of Australia.
Dutton, Geoffrey. 1967. *The Hero as Murderer: The Life of Edward John Eyre Australian Explorer and Governor of Jamaica 1815–1910*. London: Collins Cheshire.
———. 1982. *In Search of Edward John Eyre*. Melbourne: Macmillan.
Edmond, Rod, and Vanessa Smith, eds. 2003. *Islands in History and Representation*. London: Routledge.
Eliot, T. S. 1950. *The Sacred Wood: Essays on Poetry and Criticism*. London: Methuen.
Emison, Patricia. 1995. 'The *Paysage Moralise*'. *Artibus et Historiae* 16.31: 125–37.
Evans, Julie. 2005. *Edward Eyre, Race and Colonial Governance*. Dunedin: University of Otago Press.
Excell, Patricia. 1989. *Dancings of the Sound: A Study of Francis Webb's* Eyre All Alone. Duntroon: English Department, University College, Australian Defence Force Academy.
Eyre, Edward John. 1964. *Journals of Expeditions of Discovery into Central Australia, and Overland from Adelaide to King George's Sound, in the Years 1840–1*. Adelaide: Libraries Board of South Australia.
Fitzmaurice, Andrew. 2007. 'The Genealogy of *Terra Nullius*'. *Australian Historical Studies* 38.129: 1–15.
Flanagan, Richard. 1994. *Death of a River Guide*. Ringwood: McPhee Gribble.
———. 1997. *The Sound of One Hand Clapping*. Sydney: MacMillan.
———. 2007. *The Unknown Terrorist*. Sydney: Pan MacMillan.
———. 2015. *Gould's Book of Fish: A Novel in Twelve Fish*. North Sydney: Random House Australia.
Frith, Simon. 2007. *Taking Popular Music Seriously: Selected Essays*. Aldershot: Ashgate.
Gelder, Ken. 'Australian Gothic'. *The Routledge Companion to Gothic*, edited by Catherine Spooner and Emma McEvoy. London: Routledge, 2007.
Gelder, Ken, and Rachel Weaver, eds. 2007. *The Anthology of Colonial Australian Gothic Fiction*. Carlton: Melbourne University Press.
Gibson, Ross. 1992. *South of the West: Postcolonialism and the Narrative Construction of Australia*. Bloomington: Indiana University Press.
Gillis, John. 2004. *Islands of the Mind: How the Human Imagination Created the Atlantic World*. New York: Palgrave Macmillan.
Glissant, Edouard. 1990, 1997. *The Poetics of Relation*, translated by Betsy Wing. Ann Arbor: University of Michigan Press.
———. 2003. 'The French Language in the Face of Creolization', translated by Georges Van Den Abbeele. *French Civilization and Its Discontents: Nationalism, Colonialism, Race*, edited by Tyler Stovall and Georges Van Den Abbeele, 103–13. Lanham, MD: Lexington Books.
Goehr, Lydia. 1998. *The Quest for Voice: Music, Politics and the Limits of Philosophy*. Oxford: Oxford University Press.

Gordon, Avery. 1997. *Ghostly Matters: Haunting and the Sociological Imagination*. Minneapolis: University of Minnesota Press.

———. 2011. 'Some Thoughts on Haunting and Futurity'. *Borderlands* 10.2: 1–21.

Grosz, Elizabeth. 2008. *Chaos, Territory, Art: Deleuze and the Framing of the Earth*. New York: Columbia University Press.

Haebich, Anna. 2018. *Dancing in Shadows: Histories of Nyungar Performance*. Crawley: University of Western Australia.

Hall, Michael. 2003. *Between Two Worlds: The Music of David Lumsdaine*. Todmorden: Arc Publications.

Hassall, Anthony J. 1988. 'Quests'. *The Penguin New Literary History of Australia*, edited by Laurie Hergenhan and Bruce Bennett. Ringwood: Penguin.

Haynes, Roslynn. 1998. *Seeking the Centre: The Australian Desert in Literature, Art and Film*. Cambridge: Cambridge University Press.

Hayward, Philip, ed. 1992. *From Pop to Punk to Postmodernism: Popular Music and Australian Culture from the 1960s to the 1990s*. North Sydney: Allen & Unwin.

———. 2006. *Bounty Chords: Music, Dance and Cultural Heritage on Norfolk and Pitcairn Islands*. London: John Libbey.

Heiss, Anita, and Peter Minter, eds. 2009. *Macquarie Pen Anthology of Aboriginal Literature*. Crows Nest: Allen & Unwin.

Henderson, Ian. 2000. 'Eyeing the Lady's Hand: The Concealed Politics of Mary Morton Allport's Colonial Vision'. *Journal of Australian Studies* 24.66: 103–15.

———. 2002. 'Young Colonists on the Stage: Adaptations of Paul et Virginie by James Cobb and Marcus Clarke'. *Australasian Drama Studies* 40: 90–105.

Homan, Shane. 2000 (January). 'Losing the Local: Sydney and the Oz Rock Tradition'. *Popular Music* 19.1: 31–49.

———. 2003. *The Mayor's Square: Live Music and Law and Order in Sydney*. Newtown: Local Consumption Publications.

Homan, Shane, and Tony Mitchell, eds. 2008. *Sounds of Then, Sounds of Now: Popular Music in Australia*. Hobart: Australian Clearinghouse for Youth Studies.

Hooper, Michael. 2012. *The Music of David Lumsdaine: Kelly Ground to Cambewarra*. Burlington, NJ: Ashgate.

Human Rights and Equal Opportunity Commission Report. 1997. *Bringing Them Home: Report on the National Inquiry into the Separation of Aboriginal and Torres Strait Islander Children from Their Families*.

Ihde, Don. 2007. *Listening and Voice: Phenomenologies of Sound*. Albany: State University of New York Press.

James, Ian. 2006. *The Fragmentary Demand: An Introduction to the Philosophy of Jean-Luc Nancy*. Stanford, CA: Stanford University Press.

Jameson, Fredrick. 1999. 'Postmodernism, or, the Logic of Late Capitalism'. *Modernity: Critical Concepts. Volume IV after Modernity*, edited by Malcolm Waters, 119–60. London: Routledge.

Jay, Martin. 1993. *Downcast Eyes: The Denigration of Vision in 20th Century French Thought*. Berkeley: University of California Press.

Johnston, J., and Anderson, M, eds. 2005. *Australia Imagined: Views from the British Periodical Press 1800–1900*. Crawley: University of Western Australia Press.

Joseph, Laura. 2009. 'Dreaming Phantoms and Golems: Elements of the Place beyond the Nation in Carpentaria and Dreamhunter'. *Journal of the Association for the Study of Australian Literature* 9.2: 1–10.

———. *Brimstone Flowers: Towards an Antipodean Poetics of Space*. PhD Thesis, University of New South Wales, 2010.
Kahn, Douglas. 1999. *Noise, Water, Meat: A History of Sound in the Arts*. Cambridge: MIT Press.
Kaplan, Amy. 2005. 'Where is Guantanamo?' *American Quarterly* 57.3: 831–60.
Kerwin, Dale. 2012. *Aboriginal Dreaming Paths and Trading Routes: The Colonisation of the Australian Economic Landscape*.
Kreutzfeld, Jacob. 2012. 'Street Cries and the Urban Refrain: A Methodological Investigation of Street Cries'. *Sound Effects* 2.1: 62–80.
Kristeva, Julia. 1982. *The Powers of Horror: An Essay on Abjection*. New York: Columbia University Press.
Kun, Josh. *Audiotopia: Music, Race, and America*. Berkley: University of California Press, 2005.
LaBelle, Brendan. 2006. *Background Noise: Perspectives on Sound Art*. New York: Continuum.
Lawson, Tom. 2014. *The Last Man: The British Genocide in Tasmania*. London: I. B. Tauris.
LeFanu, Nicola. 2004. 'Modalities of Metaphor in the Music of David Lumsdaine'. *Modernism in Australian Music 1950—2000: Eight Case Studies*, edited by Graham Hair. Amaroo: Southern Voices.
———. 2012. 'David Lumsdaine: A Biographical Appreciation'. Accessed 9 May 2013. http://www.davidlumsdaine.org.uk/biog.php.
Lefebvre, Henri. 2004. *Rhythmanalysis: Space, Time and Everyday Life*. London: Continuum.
Leichhardt, Ludwig Van. 1964. *Journal of an Overland Expedition in Australia from Moreton Bay to Port Essington, a Distance of Upwards of 3000 Miles, during the Years, 1844–1845*. London: T & W Boone.
Livett, Kate. 2007. 'Thieves and Fascists: The Politics of Abjection in Radiohead's "Hail to the Thief (The Gloaming)"'. *Australian Humanities Review* 41. Accessed 3 March 2013. http://australianhumanitiesreview.org/2007/02/01/thieves-and-fascists-the-politics-of-abjection-in-radioheads-hail-to-the-thief-the-gloaming/.
Longley, Edna. 2013. *Yeats and Modern Poetry*. New York: Cambridge University Press.
Lukacs, Georg. 1962. *The Historical Novel*. London: Merlin Press.
Lumsdaine, David. 1967. *Kelly Ground* London: Universal Edition.
———. 1975. *Flights* London: Universal Edition.
———. 1989. *Mandala 5*. York: University of York Press.
———. 1990. *This is My Myth for the Making of Aria*. Unpublished lecture.
———. 1997. *Mandala 3*. York: University of York Press.
———. 1997. *Aria for Edward John Eyre*. Heslington: University of York Press.
———. 1997. *Hagoromo*. York: University of York Press.
Lynch, Tom. 2007. 'Literature in the Arid Zone'. *The Littoral Zone: Australian Contexts and Their Writers*, edited by C. A. Cranston and Robert Zeller. Amsterdam: Rodopi.
Mahood, Kim. 2000. *Craft for a Dry Lake*. Sydney: Anchor.
Manne, Robert. 2003. *Whitewash: On Keith Windschuttle's Fabrication of Aboriginal History*. Melbourne: Black Inc.
McAuley, James. 1964. *Captain Quiros: A Poem*. Sydney: Angus & Robertson.
McMahon, Elizabeth. 2010. 'Australia, the Island Continent: How Contradictory Geography Shapes the National Imaginary'. *Space and Culture* 13.2: 178–87.
———. 2005. 'Encapsulated Space: The Paradise Prison of Australia's Island Imaginary'. *Southerly* 65.1: 20–30.
———. 2012. 'Continental Heartlands and Alex Miller's Geosophical Imaginary'. *The Novels of Alex Miller: An Introduction*, edited by Robert Dixon, 125–38. Sydney: Allen & Unwin.

———. 2016. *Islands, Identity and the Literary Imagination*. London: Anthem Press.
McMillan, Andrew. 1988. *Strict Rules*. Rydalmere: Sceptre.
Meale, Richard. 1985. *Voss*. Sydney: Australian Music Centre.
Merleau-Ponty, Maurice. 2012. *The Phenomenology of Perception*, translated by Donald A. Landes. New York: Routledge.
Middleton, Richard. 2006. *Voicing the Popular: On the Subjects of Popular Music*. New York: Routledge.
Miller, Alex. 1989. *The Tivington Nott*. London: Hale.
———. 1995. *The Sitters*. Ringwood: Viking.
———. 2002. *Journey to the Stone Country*. Crows Nest: Allen & Unwin.
———. 2007. *Landscape of Farewell*. Crows Nest: Allen & Unwin.
———. 2011. *Autumn Laing*. Crows Nest: Allen & Unwin.
———. 2012. *Watching the Climbers on the Mountain*. Sydney: Allen & Unwin.
———. 2013. *Coal Creek*. Sydney: Allen & Unwin.
Mitchell, Tony. 2009. 'Sonic Psychogeography: A Poetics of Place in Popular Music in Aotearoa/New Zealand'. *Perfect Beat* 10.2: 145–75.
Mitford, Mary Russell. 1811. *Christina, the Maid of the South Seas: A Poem*. London: F.C. and J. Rivington,.
Moses, A. 2004. *Genocide and Settler Society: Frontier Violence and Stolen Indigenous Children in Australian History*. New York: Berghahn Books.
Mountz, Alison. 2011. 'The Enforcement Archipelago: Detention, Haunting, and Asylum on Islands'. *Political Geography* 30.3: 118–28.
Mulvey, Laura. 1999. 'Visual Pleasure and Narrative Cinema'. *Screen* 16.3: 44–53.
Mutiny Music. 2014. Accessed 6 February 2014. http://www.mutinymusic.org.
Nancy, Jean-Luc. 2007. *Listening*, translated by Charlotte Mendel. New York: Fordham University Press.
Nechvatal, Joseph. 2011. *Immersion into Noise*. Ann Arbor: Open Humanities Press.
Negus, Keith. 1992. *Producing Pop: Culture and Conflict in the Popular Music Industry*. London: Edward Arnold.
Newman, Judy. 1994 (Spring). 'Postcolonial Gothic: Ruth Prawer Jhabvala and the Sobhraj Case'. *Modern Fiction Studies* 40.1: 85–100.
Ng, Lynda. 2013. 'Translocal Temporalities in Alexis Wright's *Carpentaria*', edited by Mark Stein, Markus Schmitz, Silke Stroh, Marga Munkeit, 109–26. Amsterdam: Rodopi.
Ng, Martin. 2007. 'The Wider Shores of Gothic'. *Meanjin* 66.2: 149–56.
Niles, Daniel, and Godfrey Baldacchino. 2011. 'Introduction: On Island Futures'. *Island Futures: Conservation and Development across the Asia-Pacific Region*, edited by Godfrey Baldacchino and Daniel Niles, 1–9. Tokyo: Springer.
'Noise'. 2014. *Oxford Dictionaries Online*. Accessed 17 April 2014. http://www.oxford dictionaries.com/definition/english/noise.
O'Donnell, John. 'Band of the Eighties'. Accessed 2 April 2013. http://www.dead heart.org.uk/opinion/articles/.
Olubas, Brigitta, and Lisa Greenwall. 1999. 'Re-membering and Taking Up an Ethics of Listening: A Response to Loss and the Maternal in "the Stolen Children"'. *Australian Humanities Review* 15. Accessed 14 July 2015. http://www.australianhumanitiesreview.org/archive/Issue-July-1999/olubas.html.
Ong, Walter. 1982. *Orality and Literacy: Technologizing of the Word*. London: Routledge.
Palmer, Vance. 1954. *The Legend of the Nineties*. Melbourne: Melbourne University Press.

Pater, Walter. 1986, 1893. *The Renaissance: Studies in Art and Poetry*. Oxford, Oxford University Press.
Pratt, Mary Louise. 1992. *Imperial Eyes: Travel Writing and Transculturation*. London: Routledge.
Prieto, Eric. 2002. 'Caves: Technology and the Total Artwork in Reich's *The Cave* and Beckett's *Ghost Trio*'. *Mosaic: A Journal for the Interdisciplinary Study of Literature* 35.1: 197–214.
Proust, Marcel. 2002. *In Search of Lost Time Part 1: The Way by Swann's*, translated by Lydia Davis. London: Penguin Books.
Reed, Liz. 2002. '"Awakening", the Politics of Indigenous Control and Authenticity at Sydney 2000'. *Australiasian Music Research* 7: 95–101.
Revill, George. 2000. 'Music and the Politics of Sound: Nationalism, Citizenship, and Auditory Space'. *Environment and Planning D: Society and Space* 18: 597–613.
Reynolds, Henry. 1982. *The Other Side of the Frontier: Aboriginal Resistance to the European Invasion of Australia*. Ringwood: Viking.
———. 2001. *The Questions of Genocide in Australia's History: An Indelible Stain?* Ringwood: Viking.
———. 2013. *Forgotten War*. Sydney: New South Publishing.
Richards, Fiona. 2007. *The Soundscapes of Australia: Music, Place and Spirituality*. Aldershot: Ashgate.
Robin, Libby. 2007. *How a Continent Created a Nation*. Sydney: UNSW Press.
Ruskin, John. 1907. *Modern Painters*. London: Dent.
Ryan, Simon. 1996. *The Cartographic Eye: How Explorers Saw Australia*. Melbourne: Cambridge University Press.
Saint-Pierre, Bernardin de. 1982. *Paul and Virginia*. London: Peter Owen.
Salas, Gerado Rodriquez. 2005. 'The Tide That Riffles Back: Spiral Femininity in Carmel Bird's *Cape Grimm*'. *Antipodes* 19.1: 85–90.
———. 2006. '"Time and Tide": An Interview with Carmel Bird'. *Atlantis* 28.2: 125–32.
Schafer, R. Murrey. 1993. *The Soundscape: Our Sonic Environment and the Tuning of the World*. Rochester: Destiny Books.
Schultz, Andrew. 1991. 'Identity and Memory: Temporality in the Music of David Lumsdaine'. *Studies in Music* 25: 95–101.
———. 2003. *Journey to Horseshoe Bend*. Grosvenor Place: Australian Music Centre.
Scott, Kim. 1999. *Benang: From the Heart*. South Fremantle: Fremantle Arts Centre.
Sculthorpe, Peter. 1982. *Quiros*. Grosvenor Place: Australian Music Centre.
———. 1988. *Kakadu*. London: Faber Music.
Serres, Michel. 1982. *The Parasite*. Baltimore, MD: John Hopkins University Press.
———. 1983. 'Noise'. *SubStance* 12.3: 48–60.
Sharrad, Paul. 1998. 'Pathways in the Sea: A Pelagic Post-colonialism?' *Literary Archipelagoes*, edited by Jean-Paul Durix, 95–107. Dijon: University of Dijon.
———. 2009. 'Beyond Capricornia: Ambiguous Promise in Alexis Wright'. *Australian Literary Studies* 24.1: 52–65.
Short, John Rennie. 1991. *Imagined Country: Environment, Culture and Society*. Syracuse, NY: Syracuse University Press.
Slessor, Kenneth. 1957. *Poems*. Sydney: Sirius Books.
Smith, Bernard. 1985. *European Vision and the South Pacific*. Sydney: Harper & Row.
Smith, Geoffrey, Sidney Nolan and Damian Smith. 2003. *Sidney Nolan: Desert and Drought*. Melbourne: National Gallery of Victoria.
Smith, Vanessa. 1998. *Literary Culture and the Pacific: Nineteenth-Century Textual Encounters*. Cambridge: Cambridge University Press.

———. 2010. *Intimate Strangers: Friendship, Exchange and Pacific Encounters*. Cambridge: Cambridge University Press.

Stanner, W. E. H. 1969. *After the Dreaming*. Sydney: Australian Broadcasting Commission.

Steggels, Simon. 1992. 'Nothing Ventured, Nothing Gained: Midnight Oil and the Politics of Rock'. *From Pop to Punk to Postmodernism: Popular Music and Australian Culture from the 1960s to the 1990s*, edited by Philip Hayward. North Sydney: Allen & Unwin.

Sterne, Jonathan. 2003. *The Audible Past: Cultural Origins of Sound Reproduction*. Durham: Duke University Press.

Stewart, Douglas. 1960. *Voyager Poems*. Brisbane: Jacaranda Press.

Stewart, Garrett. 1990. *Reading Voices: Literature and the Phonotext*. Berkeley: University of California Press.

Stowe, Randolph. 1958. *To the Islands*. Harmondsworth: Penguin Books.

———. 1963. *Tourmaline*. London: Macdonald.

Stratford, Elaine, Godfrey Baldacchino, Elizabeth McMahon, Carol Farbotko and Andrew Harwood. 2011. 'Envisioning the Archipelago'. *Island Studies Journal* 6.2: 113–30.

Stratton, Jon. 2006. 'Nation Building and Australian Popular Music'. *Continuum: Journal of Media and Cultural Studies* 20.2: 243–52.

———. 2007. *Australian Rock: Essays on Popular Music*. Perth: Network Books.

Stubington, Jill. 2007. *Singing the Land: The Power of Performance in Aboriginal Life*. Strawberry Hills: Currency House.

Tacon, Paul. 2005. 'Chains of Connection'. *Griffith Review* 9: 1–7.

Thomas, Bruce, ed. 2003. *Jumangkarni Wimi: Dreaming Stories from the Desert*. South Headland: Wangka Maya Pilbara Aboriginal Language Centre.

Thompson, Emily. 2002. *The Soundscape of Modernity: Architectural Acoustics and the Culture of Listening in America, 1900–1933*. Cambridge: MIT Press.

Toop, David. 2010. *Sinister Resonance: The Mediumship of the Listener*. New York: Continuum.

Truax, Barry. D., ed. 1978. *Handbook for Acoustic Ecology*. Vancouver: A.R.C.

Turcotte, Gerry. 1998. 'Australian Gothic'. *The Handbook to Gothic Literature*, edited by Marie Mulvey-Roberts. Basingstoke: Macmillan.

Turner, Graeme. 1993. *National Fictions: Literature, Film and the Construction of Australian Narrative*. St Leonards: Allen & Unwin.

———. 1994. *Making It National: Nationalism and Australian Popular Culture*. St Leonards: Allen & Unwin,.

Vellutini, Laetitia. 2003. 'Finding a Voice on Indigenous Issues: Midnight Oil's Inappropriate Appropriation'. *Journal of Australian Studies* 27.79: 129–33.

Voegelin, Salome. 2010. *Listening to Noise and Silence: Towards a Philosophy of Sound Art*. New York: Continuum.

Ward, Russell. 1958. *The Australian Legend*. Melbourne: Melbourne University Press.

Watson, Irene. 2007. 'Aboriginal Sovereignties: Past, Present, Future (Im)Possibilities'. *Our Patch: Enacting Australian Sovereignty Post 2001*, edited by Suvendrini Perera. Perth: Network Books.

Webb, Francis. 2011. 'Eyre All Alone'. *Collected Poems: Francis Webb*, edited by Toby Davidson. Crawley: University of Western Australia.

White, Laura A. 2012. 'Submerging the Imperial Eye: Affective Narration as Environmental Intervention in Richard Flanagan's Death of a River Guide'. *Commonwealth Journal of Literature* 47: 265–79.

White, Patrick. 1960. *Voss*. Harmondsworth: Penguin.

———. 1990. 'The Prodigal Son'. *Critical Essays on Patrick White*, edited by Peter Wolfe. Boston: G. K. Hall.
———. 1966. *The Solid Mandala: A Novel*. London: Eyre & Spottiswoode.
Whiteley, Sheila, ed. 1997. *Sexing the Groove: Popular Music and Gender*. London: Routledge.
Williams, George. 1962. *Wilderness and Paradise in Christian Thought*. New York: Harper.
Windschuttle, Keith. 2005. *The Fabrication of Aboriginal History*. Sydney: Macleay Press.
Wingfield, Paul. 1992. 'Janacek's Speech Melody Theory in Concept and Practice'. *Cambridge Opera Journal* 4.3: 281–301.
Wiseman, Beth. 1983. *The Music of David Lumsdaine 1964–80: Structure and Aesthetic*. MMus thesis, University of Manchester.
Worby, Gus, and Ali Gumillya Baker. 2007. 'Aboriginality since Mabo: Writing, Politics, and Art', *A Companion to Australian Literature since 1900*, edited by Nicholas Birns and Rebecca McNeer, 17–40. Rochester, NY: Camden House.
Wright, Alexis. 1997. *Grog War*. Broome: Magabala Books.
———. 1997. *Plains of Promise*. St Lucia: University of Queensland Press.
———. ed. 1998. *Take Power, Like This Old Man Here: An Anthology of Writings Celebrating Twenty Years of Land Rights in Central Australia, 1977–1997*. Alice Springs: IAD Press.
———. 2000. *Croire en L'incroyable* [*Believing the Unbelievable*]. Arles: Actes Sud.
———. 2007. *Carpentaria*. Artarmon: Giramondo.
———. 2007. 'On Writing *Carpentaria*'. *Heat* 13: 79–95.
———. 2013. *The Swan Book*. Artarmon: Giramondo.
Wright, Judith. 1965. *Preoccupations in Australian Poetry*. Melbourne: Oxford University Press.
Yeats, W. B. 1992. *Collected Poems*. London: Vintage Books.

Film Clips

'Beds Are Burning'. Andrew De Groot (director) 1987. Viewed at: http://www.youtube.com/watch?v=ejorQVy3m8E.
'The Dead Heart'. Ray Argall (director) 1986. Viewed at: http://www.youtube.com/watch?v=16bFBzx7I_0.

Discography

Australian Youth Orchestra/ Diego Masson. 1997. *A Garden of Earthly Delights*. Tall Poppies.
Baecastuff. 2016. *Mutiny Music*. Self Released.
Bandt, Ros. 1999. *Mungo*. Ars Acoustica.
Callahan, Mark. 1985. 'Sounds of Then'. *GANGgajang*. True Tone Records and Mercury Records.
David Lumsdaine, Gemini, 1991. *Aria for Edward John Eyre; What Shall I Sing* NMC Recordings.
Davies, Iva. 1982. 'Great Southern Land'. *Primitive Man*. Chrysalis Records.
The Drones. 2006. *Gala Mill*. ATP Recordings.
Hay, Colin, and Ron Stryker. 1982. 'Land Down Under'. *Business as Usual*. Columbia Records.
Howard, Shane. 1982. 'Solid Rock'. *Spirit of Place*. WEA Australia.
Liddiard, Gareth. 2010. *Strange Tourist*. Frenchkiss Label Group/ATP Recordings.
Lumsdaine, David. 1990. *Cambewarra Mountain*. Tall Poppies.
———. 1990. *Lake Emu*. Tall Poppies.

Midnight Oil. 1978. *Midnight Oil*. Powderworks, Sprint Music.
———. 1979. *Head Injuries*. Powderworks, Sprint Music.
———. 1981. *Place without a Postcard*. CBS.
———. 1982. *10, 9, 8, 7, 6, 5, 4, 3, 2, 1*. CBS.
———. 1987. *Diesel and Dust*. CBS.
———. 1990. *Blue Sky Mining*. CBS.
———. 2012. *Essential Oils: The Best of Midnight Oil*. Sony Music.
Murrey, Neil. 1987. 'My Island Home'. Parole.
Sculthorpe, Peter. 1996. *Sun Music*. ABC Classics.
Warumpi Band. 1983. 'Jailanguru Pakarnu' (Out from Jail). Hot Records.
Warumpi Band. 1985. 'Blackfella/Whitefella'. *Big Name, No Blankets*. Powderworks Records, RCA.

Radio Programmes

Alex Miller's Landscape of Farewell. *The Book Show*. ABC Radio National. Broadcast Date: Monday, 19 November 2007, 10.07 am.

INDEX

abject, the 7, 12, 85–98, 152, 161
Aboriginal Australians 9, 24, 28, 37, 47, 49, 53–63
activism 46–63
Afghanistan 97
Akhrif, Aykho 116, 125
Albany 19, 28, 34, 38
Alessio, Dom 85
Alice Springs 54
American War of Independence 119
Amoamo, Maria 121
Ancestral Serpent 140–56
Anderson, Benedict
　Imagined Communities 2, 140, 164
Anderson, Jessica
　The Commandant 92
anechoic chamber 67, 73
Anniversary Day 128–131
antipodes 7
Antler Hotel 48–50
Anu, Christine 54, 62
archipelago
　carceral 12, 85–89, 97–98, 123, 162
　Caribbean 88, 96, 120–121
　global 12, 48, 85
　Irish 87
　Pacific 7, 115–116, 125, 135
archipelography 87, 115, 123
Argall, Roy 48, 60
aria 36
Arnhem Land 54
artist 72–73, 81
Ashcroft, Bill 22, 26, 31, 56, 79
Atkinson, Judy
　Trauma Tails 145
Attali, Jacques 4, 52, 149

Attword, Bain 9
audience response 86, 98
Australian
　desert 17–27, 30–43, 54–57, 85, 161
　Gothic sound 13
　Gothic literature 81, 100–103, 111
　Labor Party 48, 67
　mainland 8, 14, 23, 89, 120, 135, 158
　mythopoeics 17, 19, 24, 26, 35
authenticity 9, 45–53, 126, 129, 135
avant-garde 11, 41

Baker, Ali Gumillya 66
Ballad 86, 89, 92
Bandt, Ross
　Mungo 105
Barker, Simon 116, 123–125
Baxter 18–19, 28–39, 43
Baecastuff 8–13, 115
　Big Swell 116
　Mutiny Music 115–135
　One Hand Clapping 116
　Out of this World 116
Baldacchino, Godfrey 90, 92, 104, 120, 128
Beasts of Bourbon, the 89
being with 6, 65, 76
Barthes, Roland 4
Baynton, Barbara 165
Beckett, Samuel
　Endgame 74
Belfrage, Jane 67–68
Berio, Luciano 22
Bible, Judeo-Christian 25
Bicentenary 11, 45–47, 55
bildungsroman 87

bird call 3, 68, 71–80, 152–153
Bird, Carmel
   Cape Grimm 99–113
   Child of the Twilight 100
   Red Shoes, The 100
   White Garden, The 100
Bird-Rose, Deborah 140
Birns, Nicholas 52
Blackfella/Whitefella tour, the 11, 45, 51–56, 61–63
Blake, William
   Songs of Innocence and Experience 144
Bligh, Captain 121, 126
Bongie, Chris 120
borders 10, 17, 22, 26, 28, 30–34, 44, 89, 148
Boulez, Pierre 22
Bounty, the 115, 119–133
Boyd, Arthur 23
Braithwaite, Edward 135
Bringing Them Home report 9, 67
Brisbane 87
British
   Empire 91
   Isles 14, 85–89, 98, 104, 119, 122, 125
Brooklyn 94, 97–98
Brumby, Colin 23
Buchan, Bruce 148
Bucknell, Brad 20
Buffett, John 127
Bunn, David 103
Burarrwanga, George 54
bush 29, 32, 65, 68, 77, 80, 87, 102, 153, 159, 161, 165
Butcher, Gordon and Sammy 54
Byron, Lord
   'The Island, or, Christian and his Comrades' 121

Cage, John 22, 67–68, 73
cannibal 87, 90–92
Carey, Peter
   True History of the Kelly Gang 105
carillons 32
Carter, Paul 6, 19, 81, 101, 108
   The Road to Botany Bay 4, 24, 31
Casey, Mary Rose 140
Cave, Nick 89

Central Queensland 12, 65, 74–75, 77–78, 81
centre, the
   fragmented 34, 37, 40, 42
   seeking 17, 24
Chambers, Iain 68
Charlesworth, Max 140
Chatwin, Bruce
   The Songlines 144
Chauvel, Charles
   In the Wake of the Bounty 121
Chorus 59, 63, 80, 98
Christian, Driver 124, 126–127
Christian missionaries 127
Christiansen, Paul 134
church bells 142
Clarke, Marcus
   For the Term of His Natural Life 102
   Preface to the Poems of Adam Lindsey Gordon 81, 102
Clash, The 50
Cold Chisel 49, 63
Coleman, Ornette
Collins, David 116
Coltrain, John
   A Love Supreme 134
colonial
   noises 149, 151, 158
   settlers 6, 8, 13, 24, 80, 99
   society 21, 90
   violence 9, 14, 67, 82, 92, 96, 101–103, 107, 111
'Come Ye Blessed' 123–131
Connell, John 4
Connor, Steven 4, 7, 132, 164
Conyngham, Barry 23
continent 3, 7–8, 11–14, 19, 23, 26, 30, 37, 43, 46, 51–53, 57, 59, 75, 79, 85, 87, 97, 115, 120
continuum of sound 3, 13, 37, 99, 103, 105, 113
convict
   bodies 94, 96
   Irish Catholic 86, 92
   myth 12, 85, 88, 93
Creswell, Toby 55, 87

Dahlhaus, Carl 22
Damousi, Joy 4

INDEX

Davidson, Jim 102, 104
Davis, Miles 116
Deacon, Desley 4
deject, the 88, 97
Deleuze, Gilles 120
Deleuze, Gilles and Felix Guattari 6, 11, 18, 23, 34, 36, 101
Dening, Greg 133
Denny, Peter 150
DeLoughrey, Elizabeth 120
Derrida, Jacques 31, 35, 104
desert continuum 25, 43
Devlin-Glass, Francis 26, 56
didgeridoo 126
discovery 19, 23, 28, 31, 37, 41, 81
Dixon, Robert 70, 73, 78
Dreamings 24, 67 120, 140, 146, 151, 153
Drones, The 85–98, 162
   Gala Mill 86
   'Sixteen Straws' 86–98
   'Words from the Executioner to Alexander Pearce' 85, 90–92, 98
Drum'n'Bass 116
Drysdale, Russell 23
Dylan, Bob 50, 89

Easy Beats, the
   'Friday on My Mind' 85
echoes 13, 52, 99–101, 106, 111, 141, 161
Edmond, Rod 90
electro-acoustic 8, 10, 22, 35
Eliot, T. S 21, 73
Ellison, David 148
England 22, 27, 65, 70, 122
Excell, Patricia 22, 27, 31–33
exile, the 89–94
Exmoor 70
extinction 13, 90, 99, 105, 112
Eyre, Edward John 10, 17–44
   Journals of Expeditions of Discovery into Central Australia, and Overland from Adelaide to King George's Sound, in the Years 1840–1 19, 25, 28–31, 37, 81

family 96, 99, 113, 129, 141, 147
   history 100, 107, 109, 111
First Fleet, the 150

Flanagan, Richard 80, 90, 99–113, 162
   Death of a River Guide 99–113
   Sound of One Hand Clapping, The 100, 116
folk songs 3, 85
foreigner 91
Frank McNamara, poor old.
   'Moreton Bay' 86
Franklin River 100, 105, 110
French Revolution 119
friendship 68, 75, 78
frogs 154
frontier 4, 6, 81, 98, 101, 103, 108, 113, 149
   wars 92, 103

Galiwinki 54
GANGgajang 51
Ganggalida nation, the 144
Garbarek, Jan 116
Garrett, Peter 47–48, 57, 61, 63
Gelder, Ken 102
Gemini 35
genealogical narratives 13, 99, 107, 113
genocide 9, 101
geo-becoming 45, 161
geoimaginary 4, 8, 10, 12, 17, 23, 31, 46, 59, 63, 65, 99, 104, 120, 131
'Gethsemane' 124, 127
Gifford, Peter 'Giffo' 47
Gillis, John 90, 104, 120
Glissant, Edouard 89, 120
global mobility 87, 91, 135
Goanna
   'Solid Rock' 51
Gordon, Avery 103
Gothic novel 111
Great Australian Bight, The 30
Great Australian Silence, The 4, 24, 67, 79, 113
Greenwell, Lisa 67
Grenville, Kate
   The Secret River 105
Guantanamo Bay 85–89, 96
guitar 4, 49, 54, 86, 94, 97
Gulf country 141, 144, 156
Guthrie, Woody 89
Guy, Barry 35

Haebich, Anna 140
Hassall, Anthony 24, 35

haunting 103, 161
  sonic 6, 9, 13, 28, 42, 99–103
Haynes, Roslyn 57
  Seeking the Centre 17, 24, 164
Hayward, Philip
  Bounty Chords 119–122, 127
hearing 5, 66–69, 80, 101, 150, 157
Heiss, Anita 144
Henderson, Ian 101
Herbert, Xavier
  Capricornia 141, 165
heroes 147, 152
Hicks, David 87, 96
hip-hop 4, 76
Hillman, Bones 47
Hirst, Rob 47, 50
historical fiction 8, 13, 79, 99, 102, 105
History Wars, The 9, 13, 47, 61, 65, 105
Hobart pub 100, 113
Holland, Dave 116
Homan, Shane 4, 49, 51
home 6, 19, 24, 36, 54, 60, 67, 75, 78, 88, 91, 94, 105
Howard, John 9, 47, 61
hymns 13, 119, 124–128, 135

Icehouse
  'Great Southern Land' 51
Ihde, Don 66, 82
improvisation 6, 22, 35, 123, 128
Indigenous Australian
  culture 99, 107, 144
  noise 14, 139, 149, 158
  rights 9, 49
  song 4
inland sea 17, 19, 30, 34, 57
innocence 95, 100, 144
interiority 10–12, 17–19, 21, 26, 29, 36, 43, 73, 158
INXS 48, 62
Iraq 97
Isiaiah 37
island
  carceral 88, 98
  Cook 119, 123–126, 131, 135
  community 127, 130, 133
  continent 7, 87, 94, 96, 161
  Cuba 88, 96

Elcho 54
geoimaginary 13, 104
of incarceration 85, 96
Ireland 87, 89–91, 98
Manhattan 85, 89, 97
Mauritius 100
Norfolk 13, 85, 88, 92, 119–135
Pitcairn 13, 119–135
of rubbish 139, 141, 149, 152, 156–158
Sarah 88, 90, 94
songs 54, 135
Tahiti 119, 122–128, 133
Tubuai 122

James, Andrew 47
James, Ian 69
Jameson, Frederick 112
Janacek, Leos 134
Jay, Martin 5
jazz 115–117, 119, 121, 123, 134
Jones, Gail
  Five Bells 165
Joseph, Laura 158
journey 1, 8–12, 17–19, 23, 26–28, 31, 34, 36, 41–43, 45, 48, 65, 74, 79, 98, 115, 135, 146, 153
Jungle 116

Kahn, Douglas 148
kangaroo 95
Kaplan, Amy 88
Kelly, Ned 61, 85, 105
Kelly, Paul 89
Kerwin, Dale 144
King George's Sound 28, 34, 43
Kristeva, Julia 10, 12, 88, 91, 93
  Powers of Horror, The 7
Kun, Josh 2, 52, 118–119, 135, 164
kunstlerroman 81

LaBelle, Brendan 66
labyrinth 18, 41
Lake Torrens 18, 30
language
  Latin 157
  Luritja 54
  of Norfolk-Pitcairn Island 117, 130

Tahitian-English pidgin 133
Waanyi 141, 156
Lawson, Henry 165
Leichhardt, Ludwig van 19, 80
Liddiard, Gareth
  Radicalisation of D, The 85–98
  Strange Tourist 85–98
line of flight 46, 52, 61, 63
listening
  ethics of 1, 67, 82
  method 1, 5
  perspective 4, 101, 108, 111, 130
Lloyd, Frank
  The Mutiny on the Bounty 121
log drums 125
Logan, Commandant 86, 92–94
London Sinfonietta 35
Longley, Edna 20
Long March for Justice rally 48
loss 68, 71, 78, 104, 109, 122, 134
Lukacs, Georg 163
  The Historical Novel 105
Lumsdaine, David
  A Garden of Earthly Delights 22
  Annotations of Auschwitz 22
  Aria for Edward John Eyre 17–26, 34–44, 65, 81, 161
  Cambewarra Mountain 22
  Flights 22
  Hagoromo 22
  Kelly Ground 22
  Lake Emu 22
  Mandala 5 22

Mabo
  decision, the 9, 46, 55, 61–63
  era 9–11, 45, 52, 65–67, 74, 80, 161, 163
Macquarie Harbour 90
Malouf, David 23
Manning, Jane 35
maps 115, 145, 159
massacre 79, 108, 163
McAuley, James 23
McCubbin, Frederick 85
McCredden, Lyn 26, 56
McMahon, Elizabeth 7, 26, 62, 65, 79, 90, 164

McMahon, Matt 116
McMillan, Andrew
  Strict Rules 49, 53, 54
Meale, Richard 23
memory 7, 9, 66, 70–74, 79, 109, 133–135, 148
Men at Work 49
  'Land Down Under' 51
Meningrida Literature Production Centre 24
Merleau-Pony, Maurice 132
Metro Theatre, the 85, 88, 94, 98
Middle East, t-he 97
Midnight Oil
  'Beds Are Burning' 47, 52, 56, 61–63
  Blue Sky Mining 47, 56
  Diesel and Dust 45, 47, 51, 53, 55, 61
  'Dead Heart, The' 45–47, 52, 55–61
  Place Without a Postcard 47, 56
  Red Sails in the Sunset 56
Miller, Alex
  Autumn Laing 66, 68, 80–82
  Journey to the Stone Country 65, 68, 70, 74, 78, 80
  Landscape of Farewell 65, 68, 74, 78, 80
  Sitters, The 66, 69, 71, 73, 79
  Tivington Nott, The 66, 69–71, 76, 80
mining 54, 59, 78, 139, 141, 143, 145, 149, 152, 155
Minter, Peter 144
Mitchell, Tony 4, 118
Mitford, Mary Russell
  'Christina, The Maid of the South Seas' 121
Modernist 8–12, 17, 20–23, 31, 34, 41, 44–46, 63, 82, 112
Moginie, Jim 47
Morayshire, HMS 122
Moreseby, Fortescue 127
Moreton Bay 85–89, 92–94, 98
Morton-Robinson, Aileen 140
Muir, Kado 145
Multimedia 12, 45, 63
Munch, Edvard
  The Scream 112
Murray, Neil
  'My Island Home' 54, 62
mutiny 115, 117, 119, 121, 124, 128, 133

musical symbolism 13, 115, 123, 125
Mutitjulu community 54, 56
mythology 33, 48, 58, 89, 93, 116, 121, 135, 144

Nancy, Jean-Luc 6, 12, 68, 75
Narrabeen 48
nation 2, 6, 9, 17, 23, 49, 51–53, 55, 61–63, 79, 89, 98, 115, 119, 139–142, 144, 158, 164
    myth 12, 32
Nechvatal, Joseph 149
New York City 94, 96, 134
Newman, Judy 103
nightmare 9, 40, 94, 97
Niles, Daniel 120
nineteenth century 9, 20, 23, 25, 87–89, 92–94, 106, 127
Nobbs, George Hunn 124, 126
noise 4, 7, 14, 102, 109, 112, 139, 141, 148–153, 156–159, 162, 164
    hierarchy of 150
    neo-colonial 139, 149, 152, 156–158
Nolan, Sidney 81
non-Indigenous 2, 11, 17, 23, 49, 54, 56, 59–61, 66, 80 98, 141, 144, 157
Northern Beaches 46
Northern Territory 45, 53, 56, 65
Nuclear Disarmament Party 48

objective correlative 21, 73
'old world' of Europe 100
Olubas, Brigitta 67
origins 7, 43, 47, 45 50, 53, 90, 99, 120, 135
outback 23, 55, 81, 85
outsider 11, 69, 74, 76, 87–89, 92–96, 105, 163
Oz rock 11, 45, 48–51, 53, 62

Pacific Ocean 13, 115, 120–122, 124–128, 133, 135, 161, 163
Palmer, Vance 24
Paterson, Banjo 85
paradise 90, 121, 128, 130
paranoia 4, 18, 34, 41, 44, 97, 161
Patar, Walter 20, 34, 37, 110
paysage moralise 21

performance 4, 11, 14, 35, 42, 47–51, 54, 58, 60–63, 85, 88, 98, 110, 116–118, 120, 123, 125, 127–129, 140, 146, 159
penal settlement 87, 94, 122
Pennemukeer 108
phantasmagoria 40
Philip, Arthur 150
'Pitcairn Anthem' 123, 127
places of condemnation 92–94
Polynesians 119, 122, 124–126, 135
popular music 4, 45, 48, 51–53, 61, 63, 85, 115, 118, 135
Porter, Peter 22
postcolonial 1, 4, 8, 12, 14, 21, 45–47, 61, 63, 65, 68, 74, 96, 103, 112
postnation 52
post-war period 2, 8, 10–12, 17, 19–24, 26, 45, 48, 79
Prieto, Eric 134
Proust, Marcel
    In Search of Time Lost 74
pub rock 4, 49, 162

Quamby Bluff 116
Quintal, Granny 129–131

reader 5, 70, 73, 89, 101, 141, 147
refrain 5, 11, 13, 17, 20, 23, 26, 30, 32–34, 43, 90, 94, 97, 101, 107, 110–112, 142, 162–164
regionality 113, 126, 141, 158
Reed, Liz 62
Reed, Sunday 81
Reich, Steve
    Cave 134
    Different Trains 134
requiem 157
retelling 7, 13, 90, 99, 105, 117, 129, 132
Revill, George 148
Reynolds, Henry 103
Richards, Fiona 4
Roach, Archie 89
Robertson, Rick 115–119, 123, 127–130, 134
Robin, Libby 9
    How a Continent Created a Nation 23
Robinson, George Augustus 108

rock music 1, 3, 8, 10–12, 45, 48, 51, 54, 85, 89, 110, 164
Rolling Stone magazine 55
Romanticism 17, 20, 25, 32, 103
Rotsey, Martin 47
Rudd, Kevin 9, 67
Ruskin, John 21
Ryan, Simon 7, 24

Saint-Pierre, Bernardin de
    Paul et Virginie 100
Saints, the
    'I'm Stranded' 85
sealers 105
serialism 22
Serres, Michel 149
Seymour Group 35
Schafer, R Murray 2, 5
Schultz, Andrew 22, 41
Scientists, the 89
Scott, Kim 24
Sculthorpe, Peter
    Sun Music 8
    Quamby 105
screams 99, 109, 112, 162, 164
September 11 terrorist attack 12, 87, 94
Short, John Rennie 25
silence 5–7, 11, 20, 28, 30, 34, 37, 65–82, 133, 142, 150, 152
silenced histories 24, 104–106
singing 2, 4, 6, 41, 109, 127, 139, 146, 149, 152–154, 157
Slater, Phil 116
Slessor, Kenneth 23
    'Five Bells' 165
Slovenia 100
Smith, Alexander 122
Smith, Vanessa 90
Somerset 90
songline 7, 14, 139, 141, 144–146
    novelistic 8, 139–149, 153–155, 159, 162–164
song cycle 155, 157
song structures 6, 10, 13, 103, 110
sonorous body 69
soprano 18, 22, 34–37, 41–44, 76
sound environment 5, 14, 21, 66–70, 107, 133

sound in between, the 4, 6, 13, 81, 101, 164
soundscape 4–7, 9–14, 18, 22, 26, 28, 31, 34, 41, 44, 65, 68–81, 99–101, 103–106, 108–113, 133, 139–142, 148–158, 161–164
South America 104
speakers 22, 35
spectral 101, 104, 162
speech melody 131, 134
speech samples 7, 13, 115–117, 123–125, 128–131, 133–135
Splinter Orchestra, The 1
Stanner, W. E. H
    After the Dreaming 24
Sterne, Jonathan 5
Stewart, Douglas 23
Stolen Generations, the 9, 47, 59
Stravinsky, Igor 22
Stockhausen, Karlheinz 22
storm 4, 14, 139–142, 144–149, 151–158
Stowe, Randolph 23
Steggels, Simon 46, 49, 53
Stratford, Elaine 120
Stratton, Jon 50
Stubington, Jill 139, 146
suicide 86, 96, 111
Surry Hills 117
Sydney 1, 11, 22, 45–48, 50, 54, 56, 60, 85, 117, 119
Sydney Cove 86
Sydney Opera House 57
Sydney 2000 Olympics 11, 45–48, 61, 163
    closing ceremony
synecdoche 60, 126

Tacon, Paul 145
Tasmania 85, 87, 90, 99–102, 104, 108, 111, 113, 162
    North Western Coast 106
television 1, 51, 55, 95, 97
Ten Point Plan, the 47
terra nullius 9, 62, 150
terror 10, 19, 97, 161
tidalectics 115, 118, 120, 125, 129, 131, 133, 135
Toop, David 5, 66
Top End, the 2, 14, 54, 139

tour 11, 45, 47, 49, 51, 53–57, 60, 63, 116
transcendence 17, 25, 28, 30, 32, 34, 37, 43
transgression 102, 117, 119, 133, 135
transhistorical continuum 88, 94, 103, 105, 110
transnation 52
Truax, Barry 5, 110
Truganini 108
trauma 19, 66, 99, 110–113

Uluru 45, 56–61
United States 12, 14, 50, 52, 55, 77, 87, 94, 96, 119, 122, 127
uncanny 101
utopian 6, 12, 38, 77, 79

Van Diemen's Land 12, 87, 89–91, 94, 98–101, 104, 110
Vellutini, Laetitia 63
Victoria, Queen 122
Vietnam War 49
visionary 10, 25, 28, 33, 43
visual dominance 68, 104
vocalic space 7, 132
vocals 49, 54, 89, 94
voice 4, 7, 29, 36, 42, 49, 58, 75–77, 79, 97, 124, 128–133, 135, 142, 152, 163, 164

Wagner, Richard 20
War on Terror, the 97
Ward, Russell 24
Warumpi Band, the 53, 62
wasteland 25, 94, 96
weather 14, 27, 29, 40, 111, 122, 139, 141, 144, 147, 155

Weaver, Rachel 102
Webb, Francis 17–34, 41, 44–46, 65, 71, 80, 161–164
  'A Drum for Ben Boyd' 21
  'April 29th' 26, 28, 34, 38, 41
  'Eyre All Alone' 17–22, 26–28, 32–34, 44
  'From the Centre' 30, 34
  'Leichhardt in Theatre' 21
  'The Sea' 26, 30–34, 38
  'South Australian Settler' 26
White, Patrick
  Solid Mandala, The 26
  Voss 8, 19, 23, 81
Whitlam government 49
Wik decision 9, 46
wilderness 10, 19, 23, 25–30, 34–39, 41–43, 57, 87, 89, 94, 102, 148
Williams, George 25
Wingfield, Paul 134
Winton, Tim
  Dirt Music 165
Worby, Gus 66
World War II 1, 8, 17, 74
Wright, Alexis 71, 139–159, 162, 165
  Carpentaria 45
  Plains of Promise 144
  Swan Book, The 151
Wright, Judith 10, 21, 26, 73
Wylie 29, 34, 38, 43

Yanner, Murrandoo 144
Yeats, W. B 20

2PAC 75–77
505 Jazz Club 117